Digital Divide

There is widespread concern that the explosive growth of the Internet is exacerbating existing inequalities between the information rich and poor. *Digital Divide* sets out to examine the evidence for access and use of the Internet in 179 nations across the world. A global divide is evident between industrialized and developing societies. A social divide is apparent between rich and poor within each nation. And within the online community, evidence for a democratic divide is emerging between those who do and those who do not use Internet resources to engage, mobilize, and participate in public life.

Part I of the book outlines the theoretical debate between cyber-optimists who see the Internet as the great leveler and cyber-pessimists who envisage greater inequality emerging. Part II examines the virtual political system and the way that representative institutions around the globe have responded to the new opportunities available on the Internet. Part III analyzes how the public has reacted to these developments in Europe and the United States and develops the civic engagement model to explain patterns of participation via the Internet.

Pippa Norris is Associate Director (Research) of the Joan Shorenstein Center on the Press, Politics and Public Policy at Harvard University, and she lectures at the John F. Kennedy School of Government. A political scientist, she focuses on comparing political communications, elections, and gender politics. She has published two dozen books including *A Virtuous Circle: Political Communications in Post-Industrial Societies,* a companion volume also published by Cambridge University Press. The author of more than 100 articles and chapters on comparative political behavior, she also co-edits *The Harvard International Journal of Press-Politics.*

Politics and relations among individuals in societies across the world are being transformed by new technologies for targeting individuals and sophisticated methods for shaping personalized messages. The new technologies challenge boundaries of many kinds – between news, information, entertainment, and advertising; between media, with the arrival of the World Wide Web; and even between nations. *Communication, Society and Politics* probes the political and social impacts of these new communication systems in national, comparative, and global perspectives.

Digital Divide

CIVIC ENGAGEMENT, INFORMATION POVERTY, AND
THE INTERNET WORLDWIDE

Pippa Norris
Harvard University

CAMBRIDGE
UNIVERSITY PRESS

PUBLISHED BY THE PRESS SYNDICATE OF THE UNIVERSITY OF CAMBRIDGE
The Pitt Building, Trumpington Street, Cambridge, United Kingdom

CAMBRIDGE UNIVERSITY PRESS
The Edinburgh Building, Cambridge CB2 2RU, UK
40 West 20th Street, New York, NY 10011-4211, USA
10 Stamford Road, Oakleigh, VIC 3166, Australia
Ruiz de Alarcón 13, 28014 Madrid, Spain
Dock House, The Waterfront, Cape Town 8001, South Africa

http://www.cambridge.org

First published 2001

Printed in the United States of America

Typeface Minion 11/13 pt.   *System* QuarkXPress™   [HT]

A catalog record for this book is available from the British Library.

Library of Congress Cataloging in Publication Data
Norris, Pippa.
Digital divide? : civic engagement, information poverty, and the Internet worldwide/
Pippa Norris.
p.   cm. – (Communication, society, and politics)
Includes bibliographical references and index.
ISBN 0-521-80751-4 – ISBN 0-521-00223-0 (pb.)
1. Digital divide. 2. Internet – Political aspects. 3. Internet – Social aspects.
4. Political participation – Computer network resources. I. Title: Civic engagement,
informaiton poverty, and the Internet Worldwide. II. Title. III. Series
HN49.I56 N67 2001
320′.285′4678 – dc20   2001025407

ISBN 0 521 80751 4 hardback
ISBN 0 521 00223 0 paperback

Contents

CONTENTS

List of Tables

List of Figures

Preface

Two decades ago, when my computer odyssey started, I used a series of massive mainframes humming in a hushed, air-conditioned room in the basement of Newcastle University, a mysterious place, and glimpsed through locked doors where I collected inches of perforated printout or asked technician demigods to mount magnetic tapes. Data arrived through the mail, weeks after ordering, in metal cans the size of film reels. Inexplicable things like the appropriate blocking factor took days to sort out before the columns of numbers all fell into place. The room next door was dedicated to rows of women at data input machines who all day efficiently and accurately typed endless columns of figures, fueled by gossip and endless cigarettes to relieve the tedium. In the early 1980s a personal desktop computer came into my life, driven by MS-DOS commands and Wordstar, freeing me from the clattering mainframe and my Olivetti typewriter. A backbreaking Compaq "luggable" arrived next, at the time a marvelous object of technological envy although the size of a small suitcase and quite heavy to carry through customs. Email became ubiquitous by the mid-1980s although modems ran at 300 bauds per minute. Floppies were actually floppy. In 1993 at Edinburgh University, I persuaded a technician to purloin an early version of the Mosaic browser, although, as I recall, my initial reaction was one of disappointment. Yes, it was sort of interesting, I remarked, but what would I do with it, was there anything out there that I really wanted to browse beyond the library catalog? The Internet was still a world of dry lines of text. Macs came and went in my life. In the 1990s, I passed through an endless succession of laptops, each smaller, faster, and more powerful, but each inevitably died just when I hadn't backed up essential materials. Somewhere along the line the Internet became my "24/7" lifeline whether as a global network of friends and colleagues, a place to browse the news or download music, as a research assistant, library and data source, or classroom resource. My website was born late in 1997, grew like Topsy, then relaunched again as *www.pippanorris.com* two years later. Now the Internet streams through ever lighter digital devices – pocket computers, dedicated email units, and cellular phones – with microchips everywhere in toasters, CD players, automobiles, and answering machines. We live in a world of *All Internet, All the Time.*

This book is about this transformation. In particular, in the process of writing my previous study, *A Virtuous Circle,* I became aware that the growth of the Internet had generated a burgeoning literature on its social and political impact within the United States. Elsewhere there were many speculative theories about the democratic potential of new info-tech, and scattered case studies about its role in particular countries, but there was little systematic empirical work that compared the political impact of the Internet in a wide range of societies. Hence the origins of this study.

This book would not have been possible without the encouragement and stimulation provided at the Joan Shorenstein Center on Press, Politics and Public Policy, the John F. Kennedy School of Government, at Harvard University. Many colleagues helped by providing feedback and criticisms of earlier drafts. In particular, Bruce Bimber, Derek Bok, Nolan Bowie, Tami Buhr, Ivor Crewe, Richard Davis, Mark Franklin, Rachel Gibson, Doris Graber, Anna Greenberg, Edie Holway, Deborah Hurley, Alex Jones, Marion Just, Marvin Kalb, Jennie Mansbridge, Viktor Mayer-Schönberger, Russell Neuman, Nancy Palmer, Richard Parker, Tom Patterson, and Fred Schauer all deserve special mention in this regard, for providing feedback, criticisms, and encouragement at different stages as the book progressed. The book would not have been possible without help from many quarters. I would also like to thank Joseph Nye and Elaine Kamarck, who originally stimulated my interest by asking me to contribute to a Bretton Woods meeting of the Visions of Governance project at the Kennedy School, which eventually produced the book, *democracy.org.* I am also greatly indebted to Andy Kohut at the Pew Center for the People and the Press for access to a series of surveys. Also I am most grateful to DG X.A2 Public Opinion at the European Commission, and in particular to Anna Melich for the Eurobarometer surveys. Many students at the Kennedy School helped stimulate my interest in this area, especially my PPP-185 Fall 2000 class on Internet Design for Democracy. The content analysis of party websites for Chapter 8 was produced by a first-rate international team of Kennedy School students including Santiago Creuheras, Tatiana Khabarosa, Myriam Mendex-Montalro, Anil Padmanabhan, Maria Raga, Irene Ramos, and Sabine Schaffer. Chris Cassatelli played an invaluable role in the gathering of data for the content analysis of parliamentary websites used in Chapter 5. I am most grateful to Todd La Porte and the CyPRG group who provided the data analyzing government department websites included in Chapter 6.

Previous draft chapters from this study have been presented at a series of professional meetings, and I would like to thank all the discussants and participants who provided feedback and stimulus in shaping my ideas as the work progressed. This included the Midwest Political Science Association annual meeting in Chicago in March 2000, the Political Studies Association of the United Kingdom annual meeting at the London School of Economics and Political Science in March 2000, a National Academies meeting on Digital Democracy at the National Research Council in Washington, DC, in May 2000, the Internet and Society IS2K conference at Harvard in May 2000, the International Political Science Association World Congress in Quebec in August 2000, the American Political Science Association annual meeting in Washington, DC, in September 2000, and the Elections, Parties and Public Opinion (EPOP) meeting in Edinburgh in September 2000. Details about all related papers, datasets, and teaching resources can be found on my website.

Finally, I would like to acknowledge the comments of the anonymous reviewers for Cambridge University Press, the invaluable support and suggestions of Lew Bateman at Cambridge University Press, and W. Lance Bennett and Robert M. Entman, the editors of the special series on Communication, Society and Politics, for their faith in this project.

Harvard University
Cambridge, Massachusetts

PART I

Introductory Framework

It was the best of times, it was the worst of times, it was the age of wisdom, it was the age of foolishness, it was the epoch of belief, it was the epoch of incredulity, it was the season of Light, it was the season of Darkness, it was the spring of hope, it was the winter of despair, we had everything before us, we had nothing before us, we were all going direct to Heaven, we were all going direct the other way – in short the period was so far like the present period, that some of its noisiest authorities insisted on its being received, for good and for evil, in the superlative degree of comparison only.
Charles Dickens A Tale of Two Cities (1859)

CHAPTER 1

The Digital Divide

The year 1989 dawned like any other but, in retrospect, it witnessed two major developments of immense historical significance. One was highly visible and widely celebrated: the symbolic dismantling of the Berlin Wall sparking the brushfire of electoral democracy spreading throughout the post-Communist world and beyond. The other was less generally recognized at the time, beyond a few scientific and technical cognoscenti: the invention of the World Wide Web. Dispersed computers communicating via packet-switching networks, and hence a rudimentary version of the Internet, had linked scientific elites for two decades. It took the invention of the Web by Tim Berners-Lee in CERN and the launch of a graphical browser, Mosaic, four years later to popularize this technology. Like a stone dropping into a pellucid pond, the ripples from this invention are surging throughout industrialized societies at the core, as well as flowing more slowly among developing societies at the periphery. With the size of the online community doubling every year, few doubt the potential importance of the Internet for transforming the way people live, work, and play. But, beyond these spheres, what are the causes of stratification in the networked world? In particular – the core focus of this book – will the Internet serve to reinforce or erode the gap between information-rich and poor nations? Will it exacerbate or reduce social divisions within countries? And will it strengthen representative democracy, as many hope, or will it buttress the power of established interests, as others fear?

In exploring these issues, this book focuses on understanding the root causes and the major consequences of inequalities evident during the first decade of the Internet age. The term "digital divide" has quickly become so popular as an instant sound bite that it has entered everyday speech as shorthand for any and every disparity within the online community. In this study the concept of the digital divide is understood as a multidimensional phenomenon encompassing three distinct aspects. The *global divide* refers to the divergence of Internet access between industrialized and developing societies. The *social divide* concerns the gap between information rich and poor in each nation. And finally within the online community, the *democratic divide* signifies the difference between those who do, and do not, use the panoply of digital resources to engage, mobilize, and participate in public life. To consider these matters, this introduction summarizes the contemporary debate about these issues, and then outlines the book's central argument, framework, and organization.

THE GLOBAL DIVIDE AMONG COUNTRIES

Few doubt the potential impact of digital technologies for reshaping the flow of investment, goods, and services in the global marketplace. Like the Californian Gold Rush of the 1850s, dot.coms have scrambled to stake their claims in the virtual frontier. Productivity and efficiency gains from investments in ICTs remain difficult to gauge but the U.S. Department of Commerce estimates that industries producing computer and communications hardware, software, and services have had a major impact on the U.S. economy.[1] These developments fueled an intense flurry of heady speculation about the emergence of a "new" economy breaking the traditional business rules, although, mirroring the fluctuating fortunes of the Nasdaq index and the death of hundreds of dot.com start-ups, more cautious voices have subsequently warned that beyond a few isolated sectors, such as the travel or insurance industries, "bricks and mortar" assets still count for successful business-customer relations, along with old-fashioned notions such as profitability for investors, brand names, sales, and distribution systems.[2]

In the social sphere, few question the significance of cyberculture for transforming leisure hours, community networks, and personal lifestyles.[3] Thousands of Internet sites and over 2 billion web pages cater to every conceivable interest from acupuncture to zoology.[4] Within a decade of its launch, America has become all Internet, all the time. The public has also flooded online in comparable countries such as Canada, Sweden, and Australia.[5] The Internet population surged from about 3

4

million worldwide users in 1994 to more than 400 million in late-2000.[6] Yet the potential for this medium, currently reaching about 7 percent of the world's population, has only started to be exploited. Despite some indications of a possible slowdown in sales of personal computers in the saturated U.S. market, connectivity seems likely to gain momentum in the near future: Metcalf's law suggests that the value of a network is proportional to the square number of people using it: the more people link to the Internet, the greater its utility, the more it attracts.[7]

But what has been, and what will be, the impact of digital technologies on poorer countries? Surf at random, click on this, click on that, and whose voices do you hear around the globe? There are many plausible reasons why the emerging Internet age may reinforce disparities between postindustrial economies at the core of the network and developing societies at the periphery.[8] As many warn, the basic problem is "To them that hath shall be given". If investment in digital technologies has the capacity to boost productivity, advanced economies such as Sweden, Australia, and the United States at the forefront of the technological revolution may be well placed to pull even farther ahead, maintaining their edge in future decades. A few middle-level economies like Taiwan, Brazil, and South Korea may manage to leverage themselves profitably into niche markets within the global marketplace, servicing international corporations based elsewhere by providing software development or manufacturing silicon chips. But most poorer societies, lagging far behind, plagued by multiple burdens of debt, disease, and ignorance, may join the digital world decades later and, in the longterm, may ultimately fail to catch up.[9]

International organizations have sounded the alarm. The OECD warns that affluent states at the cutting edge of technological change have reinforced their lead in the new knowledge economy but so far the benefits of the Internet have not yet trickled down far to Southern, Central, and Eastern Europe, let alone to the poorest areas in Sub-Saharan Africa, Latin America, and Southeast Asia.[10] The UN Development Report argues that productivity gains from information technologies may widen the chasm between the most affluent nations and those that lack the skills, resources, and infrastructure to invest in the information society: "*The network society is creating parallel communications systems: one for those with income, education and literally connections, giving plentiful information at low cost and high speed; the other for those without connections, blocked by high barriers of time, cost and uncertainty and dependent upon outdated information."*[11] Echoing these concerns, UNESCO emphasizes that most of the world's population lack basic access to a telephone, let alone a computer, producing societies increasingly marginalized at the periphery of communication networks.[12] Leaders in the World Bank, European Union, United Nations, and G-8 have highlighted the problems of exclusion from the knowledge economy, where know-how replaces land and capital as the basic building blocks of growth.[13] Initiatives have been launched to address this problem but disparities in the distribution of information and communication technologies are deep seated, suggesting that they will not easily be eradicated or ameliorated. The global flow of such traditional media as news, books, or scholarly research has long displayed center-periphery inequalities, with information flowing primarily from north to south; an issue generating heated debate during the 1980s centered on UNESCO's controversial New World Information Order.[14] Technology has always held promise as an engine of economic growth for transforming developing nations – including machines for printing, textiles manufacture, and iron railways in the nineteenth century, and automobiles, oil production, and television in the twentieth – but critics argue that in practice this promise has often mainly served to benefit the industrialized world.[15]

Yet at the same time *if* technological diffusion can be achieved in poorer societies, and it is a big "if," then many observers hope that the Internet provides multiple opportunities for socioeconomic and democratic development. Digital networks have the potential to broaden and enhance access to information and communications for remote rural areas and poorer neighborhoods, to strengthen the process of democratization under transitional regimes, and to ameliorate the endemic problems of poverty in the developing world. With connectivity as the umbilical cord, enthusiasts hope that the Internet will eventually serve multiple functions as the world's favorite public library, school classroom and medical database, post office and telephone, marketplace and shopping mall, channel for entertainment, culture and music, daily news resource for headlines, stocks and weather, and heterogeneous global public sphere. In the heady words of the G-8 Okinawa Charter: *"Our vision of an information society is one that better enables people to fulfill their potential and realize their aspirations. To this end we must ensure that IT serves the mutually supportive goals of creating sustainable economic growth, enhancing the public welfare, and fostering social cohesion, and work to fully realize its potential to strengthen democracy, increase transparency and accountability in governance, promote human rights, enhance cultural diversity, and to foster international peace and stability.*"[16] The Internet may allow societies to leapfrog stages of technological and industrial development. On the production side, if Bangalore companies can write software code for IBM or Microsoft, and if Costa Rica can manufacture chips for Intel, then potentially entrepreneurs can offer similar services from Malaysia, Brazil, and South Africa. The Internet encourages market globalization: small craft industries and the tourism industry in Bali or the Maldives can deal directly with customers and vacationers in New York and London, irrespective of distance, the costs of advertising, and the intermediate distribution chains of travel agents and retail businesses.[17] The Internet also offers promise for the delivery of basic social services such as education and health information across the globe, a function that may be particularly important for middle-level professionals serving their broader community.[18] Local teachers or community officials connected to the digital world in Lagos, Beijing, or Calcutta can access the same electronic journals, books, and databases as students at the Sorbonne, Oxford, or Harvard. Distance learning can widen access to training and education, via open universities in India, Africa, and Thailand, and language websites for schools.[19] Networks of hospitals and health care professionals in the Ukraine, Mozambique, and Stockholm can pool expertise and knowledge about the latest research on AIDS. Peasant farmers using village community centers can learn about storm warnings and market prices for their crops, along with employment opportunities in local towns. Where peripheral regions lack access to the traditional media, the convergence of communication technologies means that the Internet has the potential to deliver virtual local newspapers, streaming radio and television video, as well as other services.

It is hoped that within a few years many of the existing barriers to access will be overcome with the combination of technological breakthroughs, market competition, and state initiatives. Internet has usually been delivered via bulky desktop personal computers tethered to telephone wires, but multiple less expensive devices are rapidly facilitating wireless access, including NTT's DoCoMo mobile phones using I-mode in Japan, Nokia's Communicator using WAP-enabled services in Europe, and handheld personal digital assistants such as

Handspring and Palm Pilots which are popular in the United States.[20] Prototype disposable prepaid cell phones and laptops are under development, along with speech-recognition software and voice-activated Internet services. The price of hardware, software, and services has been plummeting, owing to increased competition in telecommunications combined with computer technologies' falling costs, faster speeds, and smaller microprocessors.[21] In the 1960s Intel founder Gordon Moore predicted that, for the foreseeable future, chip density, and hence computing power, would double every eighteen months while costs would remain constant. During the last thirty years "Moore's law" has proved remarkably prescient. Every eighteen months, you can get twice as much power for the same cost. Telecommunications bandwidth, the speed at which data can be moved through the phone network, is experiencing similarly dramatic improvements owing to high-speed fiber-optic cable, satellites, and wireless communication technologies, all of which can be used on the same network. There have been parallel developments with computer memory and storage devices such as rewritable CD-ROMs. In 1980, a gigabyte of storage cost several hundred thousand dollars and occupied a room. It now fits on a credit-card device that can be carried in your pocket. As well as technological innovations, public-sector initiatives in developing countries as diverse as Estonia, Costa Rica, and Bangladesh have promoted the infrastructure, skills training, and knowledge necessary to widen use of digital technologies.

The implications of these developments promise to sweep well beyond the economic sphere. Observers hope that digital technologies will shift some of the global disparities in power as well as wealth, by fostering a worldwide civic society countering the role of international agencies, strengthening the voice of the developing world, dissolving some of the boundaries of the nation-state, and reinforcing the process of democratization.[22] By directly linking political activists in different countries, and reducing the costs of communication and networking, the Internet may foster new types of mobilization by transnational advocacy networks around the world.[23] By connecting disparate social movements, coalitions can be formed that mobilize a global civic society, such as protestors concerned about the World Trade Organization meetings in Seattle and Washington, D.C., the anti-landmine campaign, the anti-sweatshop manufacture of Nike shoes, and opposition movements in Burma, linking indigenous groups in developing societies with a diverse mélange of Norwegian environmentalists, Australian trade unionists, and European human rights organizations.[24] The Internet may facilitate the networking and mobilizing functions of NGOs working across national borders, as a countervailing force to the influence of technocratic elites and government leaders running traditional international organizations.[25] The role of the Internet may be even more important as a force for human rights, providing a global platform for opposition movements challenging autocratic regimes and military dictatorships, despite government attempts to restrict access in countries like China and Cuba.[26] Therefore many observers have emphasized that the emerging years of the Internet Age have generated substantial worldwide inequalities in access and use although, if this could be overcome, it is widely believed that digital technologies will provide multiple opportunities for development.

The role of technology has therefore fueled a debate among optimists envisaging the positive role of the Internet for transforming poverty in developing societies, skeptics who believe that new technologies alone will make little difference one way or another, and pessimists who emphasize that digital technologies will further exacerbate the existing North-South divide. This debate generates a series of questions that will be considered in this book. Today which nations around the globe are digital leaders and laggards? What explains variations across countries in Internet use, in particular is it levels of socioeconomic development, investments in human capital, the process of democratization, or something else? Does the Internet create new inequalities, or reinforce existing divisions evident for decades in the spread of old communication technologies? Attempts to move beyond speculative theorizing about these questions face major challenges. The World Wide Web remains in its adolescence; any examination of trends is limited to just a decade. Technology continues to evolve rapidly, along with its social uses, so that projected estimates are often rapidly overtaken by events. Yet, despite the need for considerable caution in weighing the available evidence, if we can establish the main drivers behind the diffusion of the Internet, and if these prove similar to the reasons behind the adoption of older forms of information technologies, then we are in a much better position to understand and predict the probable pattern of future developments, the potential consequences of the rise of the Internet age, and also the policy initiatives most likely to overcome the global divide.

SOCIAL STRATIFICATION WITHIN COUNTRIES

Equally important, many official agencies have expressed concern about the development of a widening digital divide *within* societies. Technological opportunities are often unevenly distributed, even in nations like Australia, the United States, and Sweden at the forefront of the information society. As the Internet has become increasingly central to life, work, and play – providing job opportunities, strengthening community networks and facilitating educational advancement – it becomes even more important if certain groups and areas are systematically excluded, such as poorer neighborhoods, working-class households, or peripheral rural communities. Governments in many countries have recognized this issue and developed initiatives designed to tackle this potential problem. The EU prioritized social inclusion as one of the three key objectives when launching the e-Europe Action Plan in Lisbon in March 1999.[27] In the United States, a series of studies by the Department of Commerce, *Falling Through the Net,* have emphasized lower rates of Internet penetration among the poor.[28] The 1998 survey found that affluent households (with income of $75,000 and above) were twenty times as likely to have Internet access as those at the lowest income levels, and more than nine times as likely to have computer access.[29] In February 2000, President Clinton expressed concern about this situation and proposed a new plan to help bridge the "digital divide," offering private companies a $2 billion tax break, new teacher training programs, and the development of Community Technology Centers in low-income neighborhoods to help close the gap so that the Internet eventually becomes as ubiquitous as the availability of the telephone or television.[30] The Department of Commerce has headed this initiative, emphasizing the role of programs to widen public access, promote digital skills, and encourage content that will empower underserved communities. The most common policy strategy has been to wire classrooms, although some warn that by itself this may be insufficient to close the digital divide.[31] The survey in August 2000 found that many groups that have traditionally lacked digital opportunities have been making substantial gains in connectivity and computer ownership, with the rising Internet tide carrying many boats. Nevertheless notable divides in Internet penetration still exist between Americans with different levels of income and education, different racial and ethnic groups, old and young, single and dual-parent families, and those with and without disabilities.[32] Many industry leaders in the corporate sector have expressed concern that too many people are being left behind in the Information Age, and multiple nonprofit organizations and foundations have highlighted this problem.[33] Governments in Finland, Germany, Canada, and Sweden have all announced programs to address access inequalities, often blending private and public resources. The British government, for example, has established a network of city learning centers, introduced a scheme to distribute reconditioned computers to homes in poor neighborhoods, and developed a national grid linking all public libraries to the Internet.[34]

Will digital inequalities prove a temporary problem that will gradually fade over time, as Internet connectivity spreads and "normalizes," or will this prove an enduring pattern generating a persistent division between info-haves and have-nots? Again the debate divides cyber-pessimists who emphasize deep-seated patterns of social stratification and the growth of an unskilled underclass in technological access, cyber-skeptics who believe that technologies adapt to society, not vice versa, and cyber-optimists who hope that in affluent postindustrial societies, at least, the digital divide will eventually succumb to the combined forces of technological innovations, markets, and the state. Positive scenarios suggest that inequalities in Internet access may prove a short-term phenomenon, similar to the type of households that could afford to buy television sets when services were first introduced in the early 1950s. In this perspective, the profile of the online community will probably come to reflect society as a whole given the wider availability of simpler and cheaper plug-and-play technologies and faster broadband services, facilitating delivery of popular mass entertainment including streaming video-on-demand. Some suggest that high-tech companies will compete to connect the public with a speed and efficiency that no government program can match, even in the neighborhoods of the urban poor, if there is mass demand for the services.[35] For those with personal computers, free Internet services, email and Web hosting services are already widely available, albeit with advertising strings attached.[36] The market may be insufficient to close the gap but the nonprofit sector has also been active. Major American corporations including Microsoft, Intel, Hewlett-Packard, and AT&T have foundations devoted to expanding access to local communities, most often through donating educational equipment and fostering training in deprived areas, complementing state initiatives designed to furnish the younger generation with keyboard skills and training in wired schools. Telecommunications policy may play an important role here if the Internet is treated as a public utility, so that access is made widely available through public libraries, community centers, and private homes, much as telephone services were regulated to produce low-cost services and universal access to rural areas.[37]

The interesting question is not whether there will be *absolute* social inequalities in Internet access; of course there will be, as in other dimensions of life. Although Alexander Graham Bell's commercial telephone service was launched in the United States in 1877, today in America, more than a century later, there remain pockets of racial inequality in access to household telephones. Cable TV started to become available in the mid-1960s but today, owing to choice or necessity, only two-thirds of American households are connected, along with about half of all households in industrialized nations.[38] Given substantial inequalities in the old mass media, it would be naive to expect that the Internet will magically transcend information poverty overnight. The more intriguing series of questions addressed by this book concern whether there are special barriers to digital technologies, such as their greater complexity or costs, and whether *relative* inequalities in Internet use will be similar to disparities in the penetration rates of older communication technologies.

THE DEMOCRATIC DIVIDE

The last challenge, and perhaps the most intractable, concerns the potential impact of the digital world on the distribution of power and influence in political systems. Even if we assume, for the sake of argument, that Internet penetration rates will gradually widen throughout society there is growing awareness that a substantial *democratic divide* may still exist between those who do and do not use the multiple political resources available on the Internet for civic engagement. What will be the impact of digital technologies in the public sphere?

The Internet has generated deeply contested alternative visions about the future. Cyber-optimists emphasize the Panglossian possibilities of the Internet for the involvement of ordinary citizens in direct democracy. Digital technologies hold promise as a mechanism facilitating alternative channels of civic engagement such as political chat rooms, electronic voting in general elections and for referenda issues, and the mobilization of virtual communities, revitalizing levels of mass participation in public affairs.[39] The use of the Internet by groups and social movements is often believed to exemplify digital politics. This view was popular in the mid-1990s and the revolutionary potential of digital technologies continues to be expressed by many enthusiasts such as George Gilder.[40] Yet as the Internet evolved, a darker vision has been articulated among cyber-pessimists who regard digital technology as a Pandora's box unleashing new inequalities of power and wealth, reinforcing deeper divisions between the information rich and poor, the tuned-in and the tuned-out, the activists and the disengaged. This account stresses that the global and social divides already discussed mean that Internet politics will disproportionately benefit the elite.[41] In this perspective, despite the potential for technological innovations, traditional interests and established authorities have the capacity to reassert their control in the virtual political sphere, just as traditional multinational corporations have the ability to reestablish their predominance in the world of e-commerce.[42] Finally, cyber-skeptics argue that both these visions are exaggerated, because so far the potential of the Internet has not had a dramatic impact on the practical reality of "politics as usual," for good or ill, even in countries at the forefront of digital technologies.[43] For example, during the 2000 American presidential campaign the major candidates used their Web pages essentially as glossy shop-windows, as fund-raising tools, and as campaign ads, rather than as interactive "bottom-up" formats for public comment and discussion.[44] Technology, in this view, is a plastic medium that flows into and adapts to preexisting social molds. The demise of many dot.coms in the business world has reinforced the skeptical view.

Each of these viewpoints reflects an element of truth depending, like a Rorschach test, on whether studies are focusing on different multifaceted components of digital technologies. As with the blind men of Indostan in Hindu legend, observers touch different parts of an elephant – the tusks, the tail, and the trunk – and report their experience with absolute conviction as though describing the whole of the digital world.[45] Yet it requires a considerable stretch to get our arms around this beast. Multiple warnings should be posted before entering this territory. Deep-rooted hopes and fears about the potential for technology often outweigh dispassionate analysis. Powerful myths and vivid anecdotes commonly appear as plausible as concrete observations. The best forecasts often seem little more than intelligent guesses. "Facts" commonly exhibit a shelf life of weeks or months. And hucksters in the guise of market research hype the industry's wares.

THE CORE ARGUMENT, CONCEPTUAL FRAMEWORK, AND STRUCTURE OF THE BOOK

How can we move beyond speculative theorizing toward more systematic evidence on these issues? The overall structure of the book can be summarized as follows. Chapter 2 considers approaches to understanding the causes and consequences of Internet access and use, and the major challenges that arise owing to the rapid pace of technological and social development, the limitations of cross-national comparative evidence, and the need for a multimethod research design. The chapter concludes that the most effective way to meet these challenges is to develop a comparative multilevel research design covering a wide range of political system.

In this study, the conceptual framework used to understand these issues distinguishes among three nested levels of analysis, as illustrated in Figure 1.1. The *national* context, including the macrolevel technological, socioeconomic, and political environment, determines the diffusion of the Internet within each country. The *institutional* context of the virtual political system provides the structure of opportunities mediating between citizens and the state, including the use of digital information and communication technologies by governments and civic society. Finally, the *individual* or microlevel of resources and motivation determines who participates within the virtual political system. Most studies are limited to only one level. In contrast the more holistic approach used in this book compares the national context of Internet access in 179 countries around the globe, as well as the virtual political system within these nations, and then explores patterns of online civic engagement among individual citizens in Western Europe and the United States. The nested framework assumes that the national context, such as the process of technological diffusion, influences the development of the virtual political system. In turn, the core institutions of the political system available in the digital world provide the

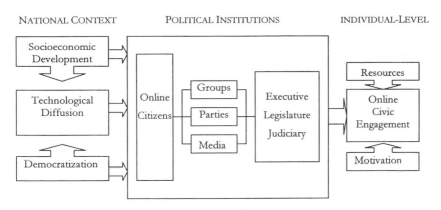

Figure 1.1. The Internet Engagement Model.

systematic context within which individual citizens have opportunities to participate online. Which particular citizens choose to take advantage of these opportunities is determined by their personal resources (like time, money, and skills) and their motivation (like interest, confidence, and efficacy).

Those preferring to go directly to the meat and potatoes of the evidence can turn directly to Chapter 3 which establishes what we know about the global divide in the networked world, drawing upon aggregate indicators to map the spread of digital technology around the globe, and then considers the causes of cross-national differences in Internet connectivity. The evidence indicates that some developing nations such as Malaysia, Brazil, and Taiwan have made substantial progress in the knowledge economy. But average rates of Internet penetration have grown sluggishly, at best, in most developing nations. Chapter 3 demonstrates that the global divide in Internet access is substantial and expanding: About 87 percent of people online live in postindustrial societies.[46] The contrasts worldwide are sharp: More than half of all Americans now surf the Internet compared with 0.1 percent of Nigerians. There are currently twice as many users in Sweden than across the vast continent of Sub-Saharan Africa.[47] In considering alternative explanations of this phenomenon, the evidence strongly suggests that economic development is the main factor driving access to digital technologies, so that the Internet reflects and reinforces traditional inequalities between rich and poor societies. Once we control for levels of economic development, then democratization plays an insignificant role in the process of technological diffusion. Far from a new pattern, the global spread of the Internet reflects existing patterns of access to the traditional mass media including television, newspapers, and radios, disparities that have existed for decades and that show no sign of gradually closing over time. Striking inequalities are evident worldwide: Half a billion people living in Sub-Saharan Africa share 14 million phone lines, fewer than in Manhattan or in Tokyo.[48] In Sub-Saharan Africa, for every 100 people there are only 17 radio sets, 5 televisions, and 0.5 percent mobile phones.[49] On this basis it seems likely that, despite initiatives by state and international agencies, and despite technological developments in the marketplace, the global digital divide will probably continue in the foreseeable future, driven by world poverty, even if new forms of Internet transmission eventually become inexpensive and as easy as pushing the power button on a radio.

Chapter 4 goes on to analyze the extent and the causes of social inequalities in digital opportunities within different countries, focusing on Internet penetration rates broken down by social class, education, gender, and generation. The composition of the online population is analyzed using representative surveys in Western Europe and the United States. The study concludes that unequal rates of Internet penetration are due to deep divisions of social stratification within postindustrial societies – such as patterns of household income, education, and occupational status – that shape not just digital opportunities but also access to other common forms of mass communications including cable and satellite television, VCRs, and fax machines. Far from narrowing as the information society expands, the income gap in Internet penetration is currently greatest in societies such as Sweden and the Netherlands where access to digital technologies has become most widespread. Of course considerable caution is needed in projecting from current patterns to future trends. The rosy scenario suggests that digital opportunities could eventually become more socially inclusive under certain conditions: if costs continue to fall dramatically in the marketplace, if the technology becomes simplified, and if policy initiatives by the state widen Internet access, training, and keyboard skills. Through inexpensive cell phones or handheld personal assistants, use of a stripped-down version of the Internet, for example just email and some headline news services could eventually become as ubiquitous in postindustrial societies as the availability of household television sets. Genre-scrambling technologies converging broadband access, the Internet, telephony, and TV entertainment promise to alter conventional forms of content delivery and also inputting devices. The long-term process of generational replacement should eventually lead to greater familiarity with computers throughout society.

But in the short-term these rosy projections, while not impossible, involve multiple "ifs." At present, affluent households with multiple consumer durables designed for traditional forms of home entertainment and communications are also most likely to possess networked personal computers. Poorer families are excluded from digital opportunities, and hence access to online employment vacancies, educational resources, and social networks. Moreover, even if basic access to email becomes ubiquitous, say as common as public telephones in Europe and North America, the marketplace for technological innovations will continue to generate ever faster, smaller, and better machines, spawning new applications and multiple levels of functionality. The chameleon-like capacity of digital technologies to morph, converge, and reappear in different guises, as cell phones can play music files, personal digital assistants can take photos, and computers carry radio waves, makes the Internet dissimilar to earlier machines like television sets. Even if the basic digital divide shrinks gradually over time, it is naive to believe that the virtual world can overturn fundamental inequalities of social stratification that are endemic throughout postindustrial societies, any more than it is likely to overcome world poverty.

THE VIRTUAL POLITICAL SYSTEM

Part II compares the institutional context for representative democracy focusing on three issues: Where and what type of political organizations worldwide have adapted to digital technologies? What are the functions of these websites for maximizing transparent information and interactive communications? And what explains the rise of digital politics, in particular the relative significance of socioeconomic development, technological diffusion, and the process of democratization? Chapter 5 expands upon theories of cyber-democracy and considers the potential capacity of the Internet for strengthening civic society and the institutions of representative democracy around the world. Although many specific case studies describing cyber-politics in particular nations are becoming available, and a burgeoning literature is developing in the United States and Western Europe, it remains difficult to find systematic typologies and evidence comparing digital politics across a wide range of countries at different levels of social, economic, and political development. Subsequent chapters compare the way that the institutions of representative democracy have responded to digital politics, drawing on evidence about the distribution and function of websites for different types of political organizations from around the world. Chapters 6 through 9 analyze which countries have forged ahead in digital politics, where the Internet has been used for information and communication by governments and civic society, and the socioeconomic, technological, and political factors driving the adaptation of organizations to digital politics. As noted earlier, there are many reasons to be cautious in any analysis. The first decade of the emerging Internet age has seen a process of restructuring and adaptation as political institutions have learned what does, and doesn't, work using digital technologies. Yet precisely because this is a period of experimental transition and institutional change it is particularly important to draw the appropriate lessons based on the available evidence, to map the current state of play, and to consider how the Internet functions in a wide range of political systems, including but also beyond the United States and Western Europe.

The optimistic claims that the interactive capacities of digital technologies will facilitate a new era of direct democracy, characterized by widespread citizen deliberation in affairs of state, like a virtual Agora, while attractive as a normative ideal, is ultimately implausible in practice as soon as we understand who becomes involved in digital politics. As we will see, the cross-national survey evidence indicates that those who take advantage of the opportunities for electronic civic engagement are activists most likely to participate via conventional channels. As a medium of choice par excellence, it seems improbable that digital politics will reach the disengaged, the apathetic, and the uninterested, if they choose to spend their time and energies on multiple alternative sites devoted to everything from the stock market to games and music. In this regard, the Internet seems analogous to the segmented magazine market, where some subscribe to *The Atlantic Monthly, The Economist,* and *Foreign Affairs,* but others pick *Golfing Weekly* or *Playboy.* The available studies of politically oriented discussion groups, bulletin boards, and online chat rooms have found these largely fail as deliberative fora, instead serving as places to reinforce like-minded voices.[50] Claims for the potential of digital direct democracy to revitalize mass participation can find few crumbs of support from these studies. At the same time, the skeptics' claim that nothing much will change in the political system, as most established political institutions will adapt digital technologies to facilitate existing functions, while admittedly more realistic, overlooks the occasional indications that, here and there, now and then, like a faint sporadic seismic tremor, some disruptive threats to politics as usual are already becoming evident.

Rejecting the view that either everything will change as direct democracy comes to replace representative governance, or that nothing will change as the digital world merely replicates "politics as usual," this book argues that digital technologies have the capacity to strengthen the institutions of civic society mediating between citizens and the state. Established political institutions, just like major corporations, can be expected to adapt the Internet to their usual forms of communication, providing information online, but not reinventing themselves or rethinking their core strategy in the digital world, unless successfully challenged. In contrast, insurgent organizations traditionally have fewer political assets, fewer traditional advantages, but also fewer inhibitions about adapting flexibly to the opportunities for information and communication via the Internet. If this account is essentially correct, digital politics may have most impact in leveling the playing field, not completely but at least partially, for a diverse range of challengers, such as transnational advocacy networks, alternative social movements, protest organizations and minor parties, such as those concerned with environmentalism, globalization, human rights, world trade, conflict resolution, and single-issue causes from all shades of the political spectrum, ranging from genetically modified food and anti-fuel taxes to animal rights and anti-sweat shops. The Internet does not drive these movements – these causes are triggered by deeper passions – but it facilitates their organization, mobilization, and expression.[51]

Information and the mechanisms for delivering it are the lifeblood and sinews of the body politic. Some power comes out of the barrel of a gun. Some power can be bought with the resources of wealth and income. Some may be inherited by sultans and princelings. But in democratic systems the primary coinage of the realm – the resource that persuades, that influences, that swings votes – is information. "Information" comes in all shapes and forms, from the publication of official documents by government departments to brief news bulletins on the hour, from lengthy parliamentary debates to 30-second campaign ads, and from demonstrations by new social movements to informal conversations over the water cooler. Political organizations are essentially designed as control systems for the transmission of information, binding together the activities of all members within the unit and communicating priorities to the external world. Some information exchanges are brief and transitory; others use rich and well-developed channels. The explosive growth of connectivity via the Internet alters the transmission of information among networks, shrinking costs, maximizing speed, broadening reach, and eradicating distance. Potentially these changes can have profound consequences for altering the balance of resources and power between outsider challengers and established organizations within the political system. Hierarchical communication channels, typical in bureaucratic organizations like government departments and international agencies, are less effective and slower mechanisms of information transmission than horizontal networks shared by informal coalitions of alternative social movements. National boundaries to information flows dissolve, allowing global networks to flourish. Independent upstarts and multiple sources of "news," where immediacy outweighs authority, threaten the legitimacy of traditional journalism in the newspapers and television. Communication costs fall, and information costs plummet even faster. With wider and easier access to official sources, opposition groups and social movements can challenge the authority and expertise of government ministers, civil servants, and elected officials on their own turf.

The main democratic potential of digital information and communication technologies lies in strengthening organizational linkages and networking capacities in civic society. Strengthening these bonds, it will be argued, has the capacity to produce sudden disruptions to politics as usual, especially for flash coalitions mobilizing suddenly like a guerrilla army then dissolving again, exemplified by events such as the anticapitalism violent protest in the City of London in June 1999, direct-action campaigns against the World Trade Organization on the streets of Seattle and Quebec, antiglobalization protests against the World Bank/International Monetary Fund in Prague and Washington, D.C., and the poujadist fuel price revolt by farmers and truckers that swept the European continent in October 2000. Such occurrences remain relatively rare, but they can have immediate impact on the policy process, and they are important as indicators of the disruptive potential of digital politics. Some flash protests are temporary phenomenon. Other transnational advocacy networks manage to sustain longer-term electronic coalitions, such as the International Campaign to Ban Landmines that resulted in a treaty signed by 122 nations in 1997. Global protest movements and direct-action demonstrations spreading across national borders have existed for decades, such as the antinuclear movement in the 1950s and the anti-Vietnam war protests of the 1960s, or even farther back the antislavery and the suffrage movements in the nineteenth century. The phenomenon is far from new but these movements are facilitated in an environment of minimal-cost instantaneous global communications. Governments, like British redcoats lined up in perfect formations, seem unsure how to respond. They are flustered when suddenly outmaneuvered by the ad hoc coalitions of truck drivers and fuel-tax protestors, the environmental activists and animal-rights lobbies, the anticapitalists and antiglobalist forces. It is true, as cyber-skeptics claim, that most established political institutions prefer to co-opt the capacities of new technologies to preexisting functions, rather than being forced to reinvent themselves in the Internet age. But it is also true that the capacities of the Internet are adapted more easily by smaller, more flexible organizations, a process that is particularly important for the process of democratic consolidation, and for opposition movements seeking to challenge authoritarian rule around the globe.

THE IMPACT ON CIVIC ENGAGEMENT

What will be the impact of this process for civic engagement among ordinary citizens? Part III goes on to examine the nature of the cyberculture and the influence of digital politics on public participation, and then summarizes the core thesis argued in this book. Chapter 10 analyzes political attitudes in the United States and Western Europe. Many have concluded that as the Internet population has gradually normalized in America, the digital world has come to reflect the general population.[53] Nevertheless a more detailed examination of the values and attitudes of the online community in America and Europe, where we have survey evidence, suggests the existence of a distinctive cyberculture, one favorable toward the "new" left on the social agenda and the "old" right on the economic dimension. Just as Internet enthusiasts sympathize with non-regulation in the sphere of personal lifestyles, so they favor freedom from government in the economic sphere. Moreover, this cyberculture is not simply a by-product of the social profile of those who go online, since this pattern remains distinctive even after controlling for the usual demographic factors such as the age, education, sex, and income of the online population. Such a cyberculture is one broadly sympathetic to the alternative social movements that use digital technology most effectively for direct action and protest demonstrations.

Will the Internet have the capacity to revitalize public participation in conventional politics, such as levels of party membership, electoral turnout, or activism in civic and voluntary organizations? Chapter 11 suggests that digital politics reduces some of the information and communication costs for individual citizens who are interested in public affairs, but at the same time the Internet probably has the least impact on changing the motivational basis for political activism. In this way, digital politics functions mainly to engage the engaged. For those with access and motivation, the Internet facilitates opportunities for civic engagement, increasing the ability to drill down and compare multiple news sources on an issue, to forward articles and clippings to colleagues, friends, and family, to donate funds electronically to causes or election campaigns, to support groups mobilizing around particular issues, to organize within local neighborhoods, and to discuss politics online, as well as to research official documents and legislative proposals, to access government services and download official forms, and to contact public servants about particular problems of health or housing. Reduced information and communication costs lower some, although not all, of the barriers to civic engagement. Costs can only be expected to fall with the expansion of online political resources, giving grounds for optimism about the ability of digital politics to revive activism among the active. Yet the evidence also suggests that, at least in the short term, at individual level, altering the structure of opportunities and the balance of relevant resources probably has minimal impact on changing the motivational basis of political participation and interest among the mass public. Digital politics thereby contributes toward the vitality of representative democracy, but it also largely bypasses the disengaged.

In this regard, the role of the Internet is similar to the impact of traditional forms of mass media. Previous work has established a consistently positive association between use of the news media and indicators of civic engagement in the United States and Europe.[54] Those who watch the news and current affairs on television, read newspapers, and listen to radio news were found to be more politically informed, trusting, and active than average, even with the usual controls for social background such as age, gender, education, and income. The evidence in this book confirms that, along similar lines, those already most interested and involved in public affairs take most advantage of the new opportunities for information, expression, and political mobilization available via the Web. Environmentalists, for example, are most likely to surf the Greenpeace website, just as Republicans are most likely to check *www.Bush2000.org*, and women are most likely to click on *www. Oxygen.com*. Like discussing gun control or abortion over dinner with like-minded friends, reading liberal op-ed pages on problems of health care or affirmative action in schools, or attending a protest rally about genetically modified food, this experience can be expected gradually to *reinforce* political attitudes and strengthen the involvement of the participants. This process remains important, functioning to encourage the involvement of ordinary citizens in democratic government through representative channels. Yet it disappoints those who hope that the Internet will function as a deliberative public forum, drawing the less engaged into civic life, replacing representative institutions, and thereby strengthening direct, plebiscitory, or "strong" democracy.

Therefore the theory developed in this book attempts to strike a balance between more pessimistic claims that the development of the Internet will serve to reinforce the voices of the powerful, the more skeptical claims that it will merely reflect "politics as usual," and the more optimistic claims that cyber-democracy will transform governance as we know it and restore levels of mass political participation. Instead, the book concludes that the restructured opportunities for information and communication available via digital politics will potentially have positive consequences for civic society, altering the balance of relevant resources and slightly leveling the playing field. The primary beneficiaries are likely to be marginal groups such as minor and fringe parties, loose coalitions of protest organizations, and alternative social movements, particularly those advocating causes that are most conducive to the cyber-culture. Reducing the costs of information and communication minimizes some, although not all, of the significant barriers to effective political participation at individual level; it becomes easier for ordinary citizens to learn about public affairs, if they are so inclined, and to express their views and to mobilize. This process is most important in many consolidating democracies, stranded midway between an authoritarian past and stable democratic future. The wider diffusion of digital technologies can play a significant role in strengthening civic society in countries such as Taiwan, Brazil, and South Africa if e-governance improves transparency and openness in the policymaking process, if parliaments and parties use new media to strengthen their internal organizations and their links with the public, and if opposition movements develop virtual coalitions to challenge the predominance of the government's message in television, radio, and newspapers. But whether the Internet can ever encourage the less engaged to take advantage of these opportunities at mass level remains doubtful, because as the medium of choice par excellence, it becomes even easier for people to tune out from public life.

Of course, as discussed in the next chapter, there are strong grounds for caution in any prognostication about future developments. This discussion relates to the use of digital technologies during the first decade of the emerging Internet age, and the long-term consequences of these developments cannot be predicted with any accuracy at this stage. History furnishes numerous examples of the failure to foresee the ultimate uses of technologies at the time when they were first introduced. Newfangled telephones were first thought of as channels of musical entertainment, not personal communications. In the nineteenth century, modest electric shocks were believed the novel cure perfect for improving the healthy constitution. When wireless amateurs started broadcasting before World War I, most saw radio as an active medium of communication, a hobby for young boys, not a passive listening experience. Forecasts often fail to predict the weather, the election results, or the stock market for the day after tomorrow, let alone for decades from now. Contemporary estimates for the impact of the Internet may be similarly misplaced. Digital politics has evolved rapidly during the last decade, and multiple developments will probably occur within the next, such as online registration and voting. The long-term impact of digital technologies could ultimately produce different consequences to their effects during the emergent era. But despite the importance of considerable caution, the pattern of global, social, and democratic inequalities described in this study fits what we already know about the impact of traditional forms of political communications, like newspapers, radio, and television, and also receives support from the comparative evidence in the emergent Internet age, so that the evidence deserves to be examined with an open mind to contrary data and countervailing indicators. By systematically comparing the diffusion of digital politics around the world, including both the leaders and laggard nations, this account can be tested to see whether it provides useful insights into the spread of the Information Society in recent years. In conclusion, Chapter 12 recapitulates and expands on the core theory at the heart of this book, summarizes the evidence for this interpretation, and considers the broader implications for understanding digital politics in the Internet age.

CHAPTER 2

Understanding the Digital Divide

Debate about the impact of the rise of the Information Society has produced deeply contested visions predicting the future direction of trends. Optimists hope that the development of the Internet has the capacity to reduce, although not wholly eradicate, traditional inequalities between information-rich and -poor both between, and within, societies. In contrast, pessimists believe that the digital technologies will reinforce and exacerbate existing disparities. Skeptics suggest that both the fears and hopes are exaggerated, with technologies adapting to the social and political status quo, rather than vice versa. What evidence would help to settle these claims? How can we move from the Frank Capra and the Ingmar Bergman visions toward a more systematic understanding of the impact of the Information Society? It remains difficult to sort the facts from the hype, despite the burgeoning literature on all aspects of the Internet ranging from Web design, software development, and e-commerce to the sociology of the network society, group identities, and virtual culture. Studies in any discipline assessing the impact of the Internet face three main challenges: the problems of studying a phenomenon undergoing rapid change; the limitations of the available cross-cultural evidence allowing us to generalize beyond the experience of the United States; and the difficulties of developing and integrating triangulated methodologies drawn from different disciplines.

THE RAPID PACE OF CHANGE

The first challenge is the rapid pace of technological innovation and social adaptation so that studies of the impact of info-tech represent blurred snapshots of a moving bullet.[1] The genesis of the Internet was initially fairly slow but postindustrial societies are currently experiencing a sharply accelerating 'S' curve of diffusion. The birth of computer-mediated networked communication can be traced back to ARPANET in 1969, an experimental four-computer network, established by the Advanced Research Projects Agency (ARPA) of the U.S. Defense Department to develop a secure form of communication via multiple destinations in the event of nuclear war. Information was split up into "packets" that were then transmitted via several dispersed routes: if one link was unavailable then, like a delta river with numerous tributaries, information simply traveled through alternative routes before the packets were reassembled at the destination. In the 1970s, dispersed communication networks spread email among a select community of scientists and scholars at elite universities and research centers. In 1971 ARPANET linked about two-dozen computers ("hosts") at 15 sites, including MIT and Harvard, and a decade later more than 312 hosts were networked. This process was accelerated in 1986 by the National Science Foundation's development of a high-speed backbone network to link science and engineering, although, other than email, this remained mainly the domain of computer-science aficionados happy to struggle with unforgiving lines of computer programming and printouts. Data were still routinely delivered on magnetic tape mailed in large tin cans like movie reels. Beyond linking communications between research institutions and scholars, the most popular uses of the new networks were financial transactions in electronic banking and email for business.

The Internet as we know it today came about with the invention in 1989 of the World Wide Web and a hyper-text language for global information sharing, by Tim Berners-Lee at CERN in Geneva, and the subsequent release in 1991 of the first client browser software for accessing materials on the Internet. At this time about twenty countries were connected to the network, mostly in North America and Western Europe. The decisive technological breakthrough popularizing the medium occurred in 1993, when the National Center for Supercomputing Applications released Mosaic, the first graphical Web browser, made available for Unix systems, then for Microsoft Windows and the Apple Macintosh. The graphical browser removed the need for any technical expertise in accessing the Web beyond the ability to point and click, making it instantly accessible to a five-year-old. The remarkable rise of the Internet as a new mass medium came in October 1994 when Netscape Communications released the Netscape Navigator browser, built on Mosaic technology and distributed free. Microsoft awoke relatively late to the opportunities of the Internet but eleven months later, in August 1995, Internet Explorer was released, bundled with the launch of Windows 95.

In postindustrial societies, the Internet wildfire during the last decade has been, as everyone observes, remarkable. The earliest estimates suggest that in 1994 there were about 3 million users worldwide, mostly living in the United States.[2] The following year this number had risen to 26 million. The online population has subsequently roughly doubled every year since then, reaching an estimated 407 million people by late-2000 (see Figure 2.1). The first-ever American opinion poll on this issue, conducted by Louis Harris and Associates, found that one-third of the public had heard of the Internet in June 1994 but only 7 percent had ever used it.[3] Pew surveys estimate that the following year the proportion of users had doubled to about 14 percent of all Americans, but by mid-2000 more than one-half of all Americans used the Internet (54 percent).[4]

Therefore as a form of information and communications spreading beyond the scientific and technical elite, the Internet as a mass medium remains a relatively recent development. Computers have been around for about fifty years, and distributed computer networks for about thirty years, but the popular point-and-click World Wide Web, as we know it, has only existed since 1993. Predictions suggest that the familiar Internet experience of the first decade – with email and Web pages delivered through wired umbilical cords to beige desktop boxes – will probably not be the familiar Internet experience envisaged for the next decade, with at least a cut-down version enabled through wireless cell phones like DoCoMo services in Japan, pagers, digital televisions, hand-held personal assistants like Palm Pilots, even streamed in headline versions through ATM banners and screens fitted in elevators, bus stops, and airports, with online automobiles so that we are All Internet, All the Time. For technophiles, the Web is promised to arrive through everything from our toasters to our televisions. Although it is difficult to sort out the reliable estimates from the industry hype, market research forecasts suggest that by 2005 more than one-half of all Americans online, and almost three-quarters of worldwide users, may have digital Web appliances to download information.[5] Novel "killer apps" are predicted to transform information technologies.[6] Yet predictions are in constant danger of being overtaken by events ("So 1998."), as well as being exaggerated into hyperbole by the industry in its own interests. Despite predictions that smaller firms will thrive in the new economy, multiple

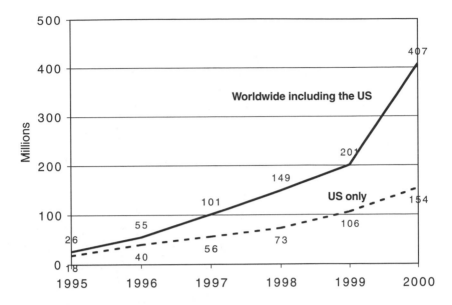

Figure 2.1. Worldwide Trends in the Online Population, 1995–2000.
Source: "How Many Online", *www.NUA.ie,* November 2000.

entrepreneurial Internet start-ups have fallen by the way, while corporate mergers producing multinational companies are more fashionable today than ever before. Like the Nasdaq, past irrational exuberance surrounding digital technology stocks may prove an unreliable guide to future performance.

One of the best ways to understand the rapid pace of change is to monitor trends during the last decade across many different nations at the forefront of the emergent information society, in order to understand how digital politics has evolved in response to the new structure of opportunities. The past decade is likely to prove atypical of subsequent developments as people learn what does, and doesn't, work. In the 1998 U.S. elections, for example, only one in ten of the major party Senate, House, and gubernatorial candidate websites facilitated online campaign donations and almost one-half did not even ask for money.[7] In contrast, just two years later John McCain's campaign raised $1 million via online contributions in the 48 hours after his New Hampshire victory in February 2000, or $2.5 million in total online.[8] In 1996, grassroots activists and individual voters for or against the major presidential candidates in America set up a handful of homegrown sites. In 2000, in contrast, there were almost 7,000 such sites. In 1996, just a handful of dedicated Internet news outlets got to the U.S. presidential party conventions. Four years later there were 80 to 100 such outlets, like *Slate* and *Salon,* as well as online coverage by almost every traditional news organization including CNN and C-Span. The key issue with these sorts of developments is how the public responds when digital politics evolves. When government departments go online, how do people use these sites to seek information? When parties, groups, and campaigns use horizontal networks via "virtual" conferences, policy discussions, and innovative feedback mechanisms, does this mobilize supporters? What new formats work, and what don't? Although future developments remain uncertain, the 1990s represents a unique opportunity to capture how the first generation of online users evolved, similar to studies in the 1950s analyzing the early television audience.

One way to think about these issues is to draw upon classic theories of technological diffusion developed by the work of the nineteenth-century French sociologist Gabriel Tarde and by the Harvard sociologist Pitirim Sorokin (1941) and advanced by communications scholars Elihu Katz and Everett Rogers.[9] These theories suggest that the adoption of many successful innovations – whether of new strains of seed corn, industrial machinery, or new medical breakthroughs – have commonly followed an S-(Sigmoid) shaped pattern.[10] New technologies have often experienced a slow rate of initial adoption, followed by a substantial surge that peaks when penetration levels reach saturation point and demand subsequently slows. Cyber-optimists suggest that the spread of the Internet will follow a *normalization* pattern, as costs fall, as the technology becomes simplified allowing plug-and-play access, and as the Web increasingly provides mass entertainment and cheap communications via streaming audio and video. In the normalization model illustrated in Figure 2.2, those who adopt the innovations at an early stage will be ahead of the curve, with the resources, skills, and knowledge to take advantage of digital technologies, but in the long term cyber-optimists believe that penetration will become saturated in these societies. Once a high proportion of households have a personal computer and access to the Internet – like owning a refrigerator, automobile, or washing machine – then demand will slow. The theory predicts that given saturated demand, prices will fall further to attract new users, allowing laggards to catch up, so that eventually access to digital technologies becomes pervasive. The initial period of adoption may therefore be expected to widen social inequalities but the normalization hypothesis suggests

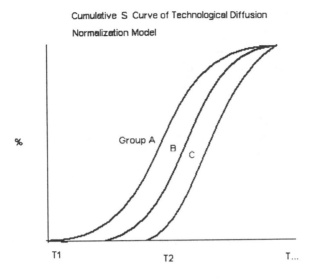

Cumulative S Curve of Technological Diffusion
Normalization Model

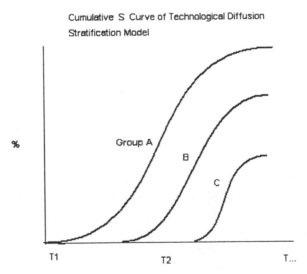

Cumulative S Curve of Technological Diffusion
Stratification Model

Figure 2.2. The Cumulative S Curve of Technological Diffusion.

that this temporary gap will eventually close. In contrast, cyber-pessimists emphasize that the *stratification* model provides a more realistic scenario where groups already well networked via traditional forms of information and communication technologies will maintain their edge in the digital economy.

31

Diffusion theory allows us to compare the growth of personal computers and the Internet with earlier technologies. In the United States, the spread of many previous innovations has usually followed a sigmoid (S-shaped) time path characterized by a slow pace of initial adoption, followed by a significant advance, and then a gradually tapering of demand (see Figure 2.3). Televisions in America experienced a rapid surge of sales in the 1950s, fueled by pent-up demand for consumer goods and the hiatus in TV production and broadcasting during World War II. VCR sales saw a similar surge in America during the late 1980s. In contrast, some other communication technologies took far longer to spread throughout the American population. Sales of radio receivers were initially held back by the technological complexity of crystal sets and the onset of the Great Depression in the 1920s, before experiencing a slow and steady rise, until today there are more radio sets than people in the United States. The telephone, which had been available as a commercial service since 1877, only took off for the majority of American households after World War II. Automobiles, as big-ticket household items, also experienced a steady climb in sales after 1945 until reaching a plateau in the 1980s. Cable TV saw slow diffusion in America from 1960 to 1980, due to the investment costs of laying cable and the number of stations available to most subscribers, before accelerating in availability. In the United States, the flood of Internet users since the early 1990s has followed an S-shaped curve, and it remains to be seen whether this curve will bottom out with two-thirds access, like cable TV, or more than 90 percent access, like TV. The pattern of American adoption so far has been closer to the rapid surge in television sets and VCRs rather than the slower diffusion of telephones and radios. Although the Internet remains a relatively new phenomenon, the diffusion patterns evident in related communication and information technologies in America provide important evidence about what we might expect to occur with the growth of the online community in future decades and in other postindustrial societies at the forefront of the knowledge economy, such as Sweden and Australia.

Worldwide the comparison of the spread of radios and televisions since the 1950s, and the rise of the Internet since 1995, shows more gradual secular trends rather than a sudden S curve (see Figure 2.4). The growth of the online community has been substantial: For comparison with previous innovations, the telephone took close to 75 years to reach 50 million users worldwide, and television took 13 years, but it took only 4 years for the Internet to reach the same number.[11]

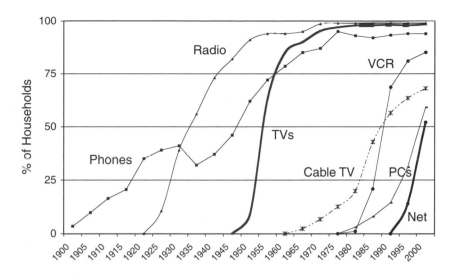

Figure 2.3. Twentieth-Century American Technology.
Sources: U.S. Census Bureau: *Statistical Abstract of the U.S.,1999; Historical Statistics of the U.S.*

CROSS-NATIONAL EVIDENCE

In addition to drawing comparisons historically over time, another major challenge concerns the difficulties of generalizing across many countries based on the limited evidence. Most studies of digital politics focus on the United States yet these findings may well be, in this, as in so much else, exceptional.[12] As an industry leader, the United States is certainly atypical in Internet use, even within the universe of postindustrial societies – containing an estimated three-fourths of all e-commerce sites worldwide, 79 percent of the world's Internet hosts, 59 percent of the world's electronic mailboxes, 54 percent of online buyers, and 38 percent of Internet users.[13] If access to digital technologies is heavily contextual, depending on the structure of opportunities available within each society, then the typical experience of Silicon Valley dot-com entrepreneurs, Harvard undergraduates, and New York lawyers will probably have little in common with their counterparts in London, Paris, and Tokyo, still less in Moscow, Beijing, and Johannesburg. A broader analysis, which examines global patterns, contrasting leaders and laggard societies, provides the basis for more reliable generalizations.

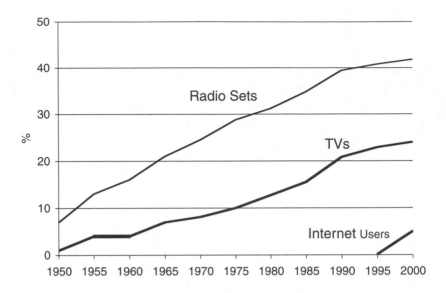

Figure 2.4. Worldwide Diffusion of Radio, Television, and the Internet, 1950–2000.

Sources: **Television sets and radio receivers per household:** annual UNESCO *Statistical Yearbooks,* UNESCO, Paris; **estimates of the Internet population:** "How Many Online?", *www.NUA.ie.*

There is another important reason why we need comparisons beyond the United States. Democracies differ significantly in their core institutions and constitutional features, most notably in terms of majoritarian or proportional electoral systems, the range of competition in party systems, whether executives are parliamentary or presidential, whether state power is centralized or dispersed, and so on. These institutional structures have significant consequences for patterns of political participation such as levels of voting turnout and types of election campaigning, as well as in rates of party membership and activism.[14] If digital technologies adapt chameleon-like to existing political systems, then we would expect to find considerable cross-national differences around the globe. The rapid adoption of the Internet as a lobbying and fund-raising tool in American election campaigns, for example, may reflect the particular form of interest group pluralism and money-driven political campaigns characteristically found in the United States, rather than a model common in many European democracies. The German SDP intranet, as a democratic mass-branch organization, may provide far more opportunities for horizontal interaction and communication among party members than is available in the Japanese leadership-dominated LDP. The online delivery of services for housing and health in Swiss local cantons, with a stronger tradition of decentralized governance, may prove more advanced than equivalent services provided by English county councils. The parliamentary website for the Norwegian Storting can be expected to be far richer and more interactive than those designed for less influential and democratic bodies such as the Jordanian National Assembly or Thai Ratha Sapha. And so on. Despite the Internet's growing importance, at present little systematic empirical research compares its spread across nations and its functions in different political systems across the globe. This raises a series of issues: Who surfs in Germany, Japan, and Mexico? Who reads online newspapers or uses broadband television and radio in the United States, Taiwan, and Italy? What information about government services is available in Switzerland, Canada, and South Africa? How is the World Wide Web utilized by parties, by networks of alternative social movements, or by lobbyists in France, Sweden, and India? How is email employed to mobilize dissident groups, human rights activists, and opposition movements to challenge the authority of authoritarian regimes in Burma, Afghanistan, and China? Scattered case studies of digital politics are available in many particular countries, and a burgeoning literature is available in the United States, but so far the broader picture across the globe remains unclear.

TRIANGULATED RESEARCH DESIGNS

Another major challenge is that research on the Internet needs to integrate research findings drawn from numerous disciplines including those of communications, sociology, anthropology, history, social psychology, market research and business studies, computer studies, and industrial design, as well as political science.[15] Qualitative methodologies deconstructing the meaning of digital communications include discourse analysis, literary criticism, rhetorical studies, and textual analysis. Quantitative approaches include the standard techniques of sample surveys representative of the general population and special surveys of the online community, content analysis, focus groups, experimental research designs, and newer market research procedures monitoring user behavior like "click stream data" from cookies measuring activity on websites.[16] Yet in the early years, the available data measuring Internet use often remain "guesstimates," even with the latest available market research techniques.[17] No single methodology can hope to capture the rich complexities of life on the Internet and this study therefore draws on hundreds of studies from different disciplines, as well as empirical evidence from aggregate data, content analysis, and cross-national surveys. The most effective research strategy is to triangulate among diverse sources of evidence, attempting to understand the Internet by piecing together a range of independent studies to see if the evidence points in a consistent direction across different countries. Where the findings conflict, we need to point out the uncertainties and consider some of the reasons leading to these different results. Where the results survive replication, this increases confidence in the reliability of the generalizations.

The book draws upon multiple databases to compare the worldwide patterns of use. Estimates of the online population are provided by NUA, a company that monitors surveys from a wide range of different market research companies.[18] Most data are collected for commercial purposes, to gauge the market for e-commerce. Although use of different surveys limits the reliability of the comparison, nevertheless this source provides the most comprehensive and up-to-date picture of Internet penetration rates worldwide. As discussed in the next chapter, evidence from independent sources serves to confirm the global pattern established in the NUA data, including information about the geographic location of Internet hosts, collected by many international agencies, and data on the distribution of telephones and computer equipment. Worldwide data on websites established by parliaments, parties, government departments, the news media, and interest groups are assembled from multiple sources, providing a comprehensive global map of digital politics. The study compares 179 nation-states worldwide, including in total 5.77 billion people living in societies at all levels of human and political development.[19]

Representative surveys in the United States and the fifteen-member states of the European Union are used to compare the social background, political attitudes, and behavior of the online community with the general population in these countries. In America, the first occasional opinion poll items on use or awareness of the Internet occurred in mid-1994 but it was only the following year that the population started to be monitored more systematically. The benchmark survey data used in this study are drawn from 1995–2000, which allows us to examine the rapid diffusion process in the emergent era as use of the new information technology penetrated the United States and Western Europe. Broader comparisons would have been desirable but unfortunately systematic and reliable cross-national surveys measuring the impact of digital politics are still unavailable in most countries, and this has to await further research. The book draws on the series of American surveys conducted since 1995 by the Pew Center for the People and the Press, and also the National Election Study since 1996. For a broader comparison with the fifteen member states of the European Union, the book analyzes the biannual series of Eurobarometer surveys since 1995. Although identical items are not always available, functionally equivalent items allow comparisons to be drawn between America and Europe.

To understand digital politics within each country, the study analyzed the contents of a selected range of parliamentary and party websites around the globe. The aim was not to develop a comprehensive mapping exercise but rather a more limited attempt to isolate and compare some of the key functions of these sites. Using standardized instruments, the coding monitored the presence and depth of *informational* features (both text and graphics), and *communication* functions (such as opportunities to email the organization and its representatives, link to listservs, bulletin boards, and chat rooms, and other ways to become active). To analyze government websites, comparable data were drawn from the CyPRG group database, which has monitored the content and functions of official departmental sites worldwide since 1997.

Finally, as discussed earlier, the analytical framework used in this study (illustrated in Figure 1.1) distinguishes three nested hierarchical levels of analysis: the *macro-level* technological and economic environment which determines the availability and social distribution of Internet access within each country; the *meso-level* context of political institutions which provides the structure of opportunities mediating between citizens and the state including parties, parliaments, government departments, interest groups, new social movements and the news media; and *micro-level* individual resources and motivation affecting patterns of online civic engagement. This approach requires an analysis of both institutional and individual data. The framework assumes that levels of technological diffusion, such as the proportion of the population online, influences how political institutions have adapted to the Internet environment. In turn, the core institutions of representative democracy that are available in the digital world provide the systematic context within which citizens have opportunities to participate online. Which citizens choose to take advantage of these opportunities is understood to be determined by their resources (like time, money, and skills) and motivation (like interest, confidence, and efficacy). To develop this framework further, we can go on to examine which nations have emerged at the forefront of the knowledge economy, and which remain laggards in Internet diffusion, and the reasons behind these disparities at macro-level.

CHAPTER 3

Wired World

The World Bank, the United Nations, and the G-8 have expressed alarm that poorer societies lacking technological investment will drift farther behind their wired rivals in the global marketplace, whereas advanced industrialized societies will surge even farther ahead on the back of dramatic productivity gains. Multiple policy initiatives have been proposed, such as investment in technological infrastructure in Malaysia, computer training and education in schools in Latvia, and innovative community-level schemes in Bangladesh. Yet understanding the role of the state and the market in this process, and predicting which initiatives will succeed or fail in widening access in poorer societies, remains difficult unless we understand the reasons for the North–South divide. To unravel this issue we need to map the global spread of the information society and analyze the underlying conditions driving the process of technological transfer.[1] Many studies by historians, development theorists, and communication scholars have attempted to characterize the mechanics of the diffusion process, and economists and marketing specialists have attempted to identify the driving factors behind the demand for new products.[2] Drawing on this literature, after discussing the theoretical debate, this chapter focuses on four interrelated questions:

- What is the global pattern of Internet diffusion?
- Does this pattern represent the particular characteristics of Internet diffusion per se, or does it reflect similar trends found in the adoption of older forms of info-tech, such as radios, telephones, and televisions?
- In exploring the reasons for inequalities of Internet access, how far do cross-national differences reflect basic economic divisions

between rich and poor societies, so that we can predict the uptake of info-tech from standard economic indicators like level of per capita GDP and investment in R&D?

• Finally, what noneconomic factors determine technological diffusion across societies, including the role of human capital and democratic development?

In all cases we are interested in mapping and exploring the patterns common across different nations to establish the underlying conditions facilitating Internet access. But we also want to understand the exceptions to these generalizations, that is, those countries that have adapted to the information society far more successfully than would be predicted by their level of socioeconomic development alone. The outliers provide important clues to successful state interventions and market conditions.

THEORIES OF THE GLOBAL DIVIDE

International agencies have sounded the alarm over worldwide inequalities in the information revolution. UN Secretary General Kofi Anan warned of the danger of excluding the world's poor from the Internet: "People lack many things: jobs, shelter, food, health care and drinkable water. Today, being cut off from basic telecommunications services is a hardship almost as acute as these other deprivations, and may indeed reduce the chances of finding remedies to them." James D. Wolfensohn, president of the World Bank, has stressed the need to bridge the technological gap between rich and poor nations. "The digital divide is one of the greatest impediments to development," he argued, "and it is growing exponentially." The poorest societies face fundamental problems of basic survival and multiple difficulties with nutrition, literacy, and health, whether Mozambique ravaged by floods, Ethiopia decimated by ethnic conflict, or Zimbabwe plagued by AIDS. But for developing countries rising above the minimum economic threshold, such as Taiwan, Malaysia, and Brazil, access to information technologies has become important for integration into the global economy.[3] Cyber-optimists believe that info-tech has become a vital engine of growth for the world economy enabling many enterprising firms and communities to address economic and social challenges with greater efficiency. In poorer villages and isolated communities, a well-placed computer, like a communal well or an irrigation pump, may become another development tool, providing essential information about storm warnings and crop prices for farmers, or medical services and legal land records for villagers.[4]

Cyber-optimists agree that the current situation shows a sharp North–South global divide but they believe that these inequalities will gradually fade over time, although not wholly disappear, under certain conditions: if access costs decline through falling prices for microprocessors and components and the growth of cheaper hand-held digital devices, mobile phones with Web-enabled technology, and community centers/Internet cafés; if the contents of the Web gradually diversify to become everybody's local radio and newspaper, community telephone exchange, and world marketplace; and if innovative programs by governments, nonprofits, and the private sector succeed in widening access to info-tech in developing nations.[5] A recent OECD report on the outlook for information technology concluded that industrialized countries account for more than 80 percent of the world market for information and communication technology, nevertheless expenditure in non-OECD countries has been growing at more than double the OECD average, with especially rapid expansion in telecommunications and IT hardware investments in Brazil and China.[6] Carlos Braga presents an optimistic scenario for developing countries' participation in the emerging knowledge economy: "Although, no doubt, income and wealth inequality may increase in the initial stages of the process, catch-up can also happen at a much faster pace than in the past. ICT spending, for example, grew more quickly in most developing regions than in high-income economies in the 1992–97 period. And countries like South Africa and Brazil already boast a higher share of networked personal computers than most industrialized economies."[7]

Numerous examples can be cited to show the expansion of digital opportunities in developing societies around the world.[8] Many Southeast Asian nations seek to emulate the Japanese model in the postwar era of reconstruction, and the knowledge-based economy in Singapore, South Korea, and Taiwan. In Malaysia, for example, the Multimedia Super Corridor has been developed to bring investment from telecommunications, multimedia, and electronics companies, and the production of silicon wafers and software. The corridor has attracted major players such as Microsoft, Sun Systems, and NTT (Japanese telecom). Under the "Vision 2020" plan, Malaysia now boasts cellular telephone penetration rates of one in every ten people, more and more wired schools, and 21 Internet hosts per 1,000 people. Revenue generated by the production of information and communication technology goods, such as office equipment, telecommunications, and consumer audiovisuals, shows that the United States leads the world but many Asian countries are close rivals, including Japan (second), Korea (third), Singapore (fourth), Taiwan (seventh), and Malaysia (eighth).[9] Southern India is most often cited as an important area of software development, producing an estimated $3.8 billion in revenues, with this figure doubling in the past few years. More than one-half of India's software services are exported to the United States.[10] The Bangalore area has attracted inward investment from many major corporations, not least from the diaspora of the Asian dot.com entrepreneurs thriving in California's Silicon Valley and Cambridge's Technology Park.[11]

In rural Bangladesh, many isolated communities lack landline telephones. An innovative program by Grameen Telecom supplies cellular mobile phones to village women, who rent calls in their community to repay the loan and sustain thriving microenterprises.[12] With this service, local communities benefit by direct links to job, weather, and health information, as well as more efficient markets for their produce. Village Telecom Centers are being developed with email and fax services, along with computer literacy projects in selected school.

In Europe, Slovenia, Estonia, and Slovakia have made great strides in getting their populations online, moving well ahead of Portugal, Greece, and Austria in levels of connectivity. Hungary's ambitious Schoolnet program has allowed students in two-thirds of all secondary schools to browse the Web from their classrooms, with extensive teaching resources, interactive discussion forums, events, and competitions.[13] The Estonian government has provided public access points for the Internet throughout the country, using schools, post offices, community centers, libraries, police stations, and health clinics. The program has been highly successful; today more than one in ten Estonians is online, with personal computer ownership well above average for Central and Eastern Europe.[14]

Progress has been slower in Africa, but nevertheless Global Crossing, Lucent Technologies, and Africa One plan for an ambitious $1.9 billion project to link up the entire continent by 2002 through a high-speed underwater fiber-optic cable, with interior countries connected through terrestrial cables, microwave, or satellite facilities, overcoming many of the current problems of the inadequate telephony infrastructure.[15] Given a high-speed backbone, and market liberalization of telecommunication services, African nations may also be able to "leapfrog" stages of industrialization through new technology by investing in fully digitized telecommunications networks rather than outdated analog-based systems. Cellular telephony is rapidly expanding as an alternative to conventional network services; the number of subscribers in the OECD region reached almost one-fourth of the population in 1998.[16] This growth has had even greater impact in the developing world. In postindustrial economies there were 20 times as many mobile phones in 1998 as there were in 1990, and in developing economies there 160 times as many, an astonishing rise.[17] More than one-third of all telephone subscribers in Cote d'Ivoire, Cambodia, and Paraguay, for instance, are now connected via mobiles, a far higher proportion than in the United States.[18] But which of these schemes for promoting access to new technologies will succeed or fail? Do international agencies, nonprofit organizations, and national governments need to intervene or will the market eventually widen access? And what are the underlying social, economic, and political factors driving diffusion? To examine these questions we first need to establish which societies have moved ahead in the Information Society and which have lagged behind.

WHERE ARE PEOPLE ONLINE?

As yet no official government statistics on the online population are collected by international agencies such as UNESCO and the International Telecommunications Union (ITU), although indirect measures of technological diffusion are available, including investment in scientific research and development, the spread of computer hardware, and the rate of telephone density. The most comprehensive worldwide guide estimating the size of the online population is provided by NUA. This organization regularly monitors and collates survey results conducted by different market research companies in each nation. The surveys ask a representative sample of the public in each country about use of the Internet from home, work, or elsewhere during the previous three months. NUA's database *How Many Online* currently collects data from 179 countries, covering 5.7 billion people.[19]

A word of caution is needed about these estimates. First, the measure of Internet use is simple and limited. Surveys only monitor whether people were online, not how many days a week, still less how long people used the Internet every day.[20] Yet patterns of use can vary widely among those who occasionally click on the Web as a reference source in a public library or Internet café, and others constantly online via a 24/7 broadband cable link from home and a high-speed LAN connection at the office. Some include "regular users," others anyone who has accessed the Internet within the past year or month. Moreover, without a common methodology, the reliability of these estimates depends on the quality of the individual surveys. Market research companies vary substantially in their fieldwork, questionnaire design, and sampling methods – for example, in how far they include rural and illiterate populations. Different responses in surveys can be produced by even modest variations in question framing, wording, or order. Some data collected by NUA may therefore represent little more than approximate "guesstimates," especially in poorer countries where market research companies have little track record. These are important limitations, but fortunately there are two ways to check the consistency and reliability of the available data. First, NUA maintains a record of all survey results within the database. This means that we can compare the estimates provided by different companies in each country around the same dates. Where two or three data points were provided within a three-month period, the results were averaged to reduce random fluctuations by outliers. Even more important, the reliability of figures can be cross-checked against independent indicators by comparing the survey estimates of the online population with the distribution of Internet hosts and computers in each country. If a high correlation exists between independent sources this increases confidence in the reliability of the estimates.

Systematic trend analysis is available from 1995 onward. Although networked computing and computer-mediated email have existed for the scientific elite since the early 1960s, the number of users was too small to monitor through mass surveys. As discussed in the previous chapter, the key historic development transforming the Internet was a series of rapid innovations: the birth of the World Wide Web (1990) and the launch of popular browsers to access materials including those by Mosaic (1993), Netscape Navigator (1994), and Microsoft Internet Explorer (1995). Subsequent technological applications, such as the easy transfer of .mp3 music files and video formats, and WAP-enabled digital telephony, while representing important innovations, cannot yet claim to have had an impact equal to the basic invention of point-and-click browsers. Rather than a slow and steady process of evolution, development of the Internet has been one of modest incremental spread for thirty years, then a punctuated break in the early 1990s, followed by a rapid surge following the 'S' time curve among early adapter nations. The NUA evidence highlights the dramatic rise in popularity of the Internet in recent years: between 1995 and 2000 the total number of Internet users surged from about 26 to over 400 million worldwide, an explosive jump within the space of a few years. The Internet became a truly global phenomenon as more and more users came online from around the world and the proportion of Americans in the online community dropped from 70 percent to 38 percent during 1995–2000 (see Figure 2.1). Despite this remarkable expansion, today about one in twenty of the world's population is online, with highly uneven diffusion worldwide.

The diffusion of the Internet today shows dramatic contrasts between and within regions of the world. Table 3.1 and Figure 3.1 display the proportion of the population online, estimated from NUA figures for November 2000 in 179 nations. Among the early adopters, Scandinavia and North America lead the world in rates of Internet penetration, followed by Western Europe, with about one in five online. Central and Eastern Europe, Asia, the Middle East, and South America fall below the world average, all with fewer than one in ten online, while minimal diffusion is evident in Sub-Saharan Africa. In terms of levels of human development, Table 3.1 highlights the stark contrasts between rich and poor nations. In 2000, most of the world's online community (84 percent) lives in highly developed nations.[21] In comparison, the thirty-five societies classified by the UNDP with low levels of human development, such as Nigeria, Bangladesh, and Uganda, contained about 1 percent of the online population, although home to half a billion people.

A finer-grained comparison of countries ranked in Figure 3.2, excluding nations where less than 2.0 percent of the population were online, reveals a pattern of widespread adoption in four clusters of societies: throughout the *smaller Nordic social democratic welfare states*, especially Sweden, Norway, Iceland, and Finland; in larger *Anglo-American and English-speaking nations* including the United States, Canada, Australia, and the United Kingdom; in the *Asian "tiger" economies* of Singapore, South Korea, and Taiwan, as well as Japan; and in a few *smaller European nations* with above-average Internet use such as the Netherlands, Belgium, Switzerland, Slovenia, and Estonia. The twenty-nine OECD member states representing industrialized nations dominate Internet users yet there are substantial contrasts even among neighboring countries within this category, for example between the United States and Mexico, or between

Table 3.1. *Internet users by region and type of society, 2000*

	Total population 1997, UNDP	Total online 2000	Total weighted hosts 2000	Number of nations
Industrialized	1,098,620,000	339,259,000	65,785,669	29
Nonindustrialized	4,672,773,000	66,237,700	2,161,528	150
North America	396,400,000	169,620,000	46,123,871	3
Asia-Pacific	3,270,250,000	99,463,200	5,950,661	35
West Europe	362,960,000	86,655,000	11,318,161	16
Central and Eastern Europe	404,180,000	16,310,500	833,419	13
Scandinavia	24,000,000	12,354,000	2,711,261	5
South America	403,893,000	13,710,000	748,279	30
Africa	685,020,000	2,956,500	21,608	52
Middle East	224,690,000	4,427,500	239,936	14
High development	1,011,650,000	340,810,500	65,517,356	43
Medium development	4,102,603,000	57,762,500	1,819,652	89
Low development	583,250,000	422,200	4,520	35
Total	**5,771,393,000**	**405,496,700**	**67,947,197**	**179**

Notes and Sources: **Total Population** 1997 from the United Nations Development Report, 1999, New York: UNDP/Oxford University Press; **Number online** in 2000 or latest date estimated from *www.NUA.ie,* "How Many Online?" and from the International Telecommunications Union Basic Indicators 1998, *www.itu.int;* **Number of weighted hosts** estimated by the International Software Consortium January 2000. The sites for .com, .net, and .org were weighted according to the location of registration and reallocated by nation according to the OECD methodology. See OECD 1999, *Communications Outlook 1999,* Paris: OECD, *www.oecd.org.* **Level of human development** defined by the Human Development Index 1999, *Human Development Report, 1999,* New York: UNDP/Oxford University Press.

Australia and New Zealand, as well as between Italy and Greece. European Union member states are all affluent, advanced economies with a large service sector, a well-trained workforce, and high levels of personal income. Nevertheless following rapid growth in Internet usage in the late 1990s, there is widespread diffusion today in Sweden, Denmark, and Finland, moderate use of the Internet in the UK, Germany, and the Netherlands, but few online in Greece and Portugal,

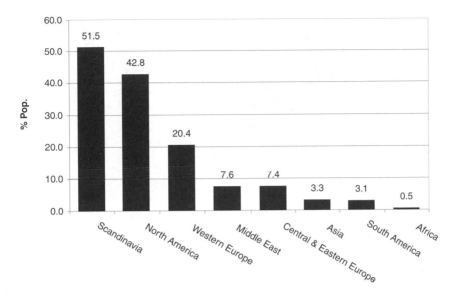

Figure 3.1. The Percentage of the Population Online by Major Region, 2000.
Source: "How Many Online?", *www.NUA.ie,* November 2000.

the latter ranking well below developing societies such as Slovenia, Estonia, and Taiwan.[22] At the bottom of the national rankings, with less than 2.0 percent of the population online, few Internet users are found throughout most of the poorer countries of Sub-Saharan Africa (with the exception of South Africa), as well as in many states in Central Europe, the Middle East, Asia, and Latin America.

The predominance of the United States on the Internet has gradually declined over time as more and more people have come online elsewhere, although still one-third of all users worldwide are American (154 out of 406 million users). The vast region of Asia-Pacific, including the massive populations of China, India, and Indonesia, contains another 99 million users, and 86 million live in Western Europe. In contrast Sub-Saharan Africa, home to more than half a billion people, contains only 3 million Internet users, or less than 1 percent of the world's online community.

To check reliability, these estimates can be compared with the geographic location of Internet hosts based on data provided by agencies such as Network Wizards, the Internet Software Consortium, and Netcraft. To function as part of the Internet all computer hosts require a domain name (like *www.yahoo.com*) and an associated Internet Protocol address record (in numeric form such as 193.51.65.17). Domain Name

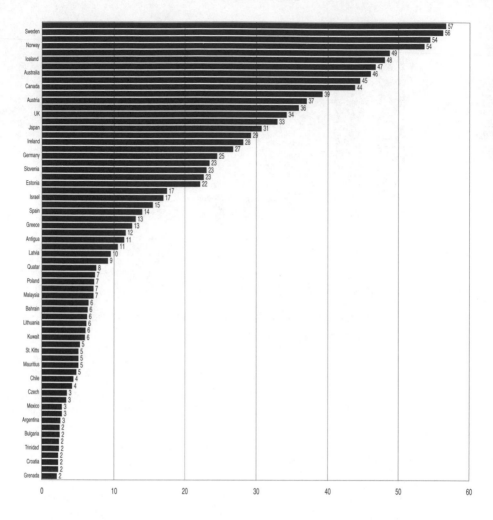

Figure 3.2. The Percentage of the Population Online by Nation, 2000.
Source: All countries with more than 0.5 percent of the population online. "How Many Online?", *www.nua.ie*, November 2000.

System (DNS) servers translate back and forth automatically between names and numbers to locate a site. Domain names are divided into two categories: *national* top-level domains such as those ending in .fr (France), .uk (United Kingdom), or .be (Belgium), and *generic* top-level domains like the dot.coms, dot.nets, and dot.orgs. The analysis of domain names provides the best available estimates of the location of Internet hosts although there are some important limitations to these data as well.

The existence of "company firewalls" means that the figures provide a minimum estimate of the number of hosts and it remains impossible to tell how many users are online via each host. Another major problem with the generic domains (like dot.coms) is that it is difficult to analyze them on a geographic basis. Following the methodology used by the OECD, this difficulty can be overcome by allocating them on a weighted basis according to the country of registration of generic domains.[23]

The maps in Figure 3.3 confirm the pattern of global inequalities already observed. The distribution of hosts according to the Netcraft data is strongly correlated with the proportion of the population online in each country provided in the NUA estimates ($R = .854$ Sig. .001), increasing confidence in the reliability of the data sources. The comparison again shows the striking predominance of a few countries including Finland, the United States, Norway, Iceland, Canada, Sweden, and Australia, and the significant absence of hosts and online users throughout large swathes of the rest of the world. There are almost as many hosts located in France as in all of Latin America and the Caribbean, and there are more hosts in New York alone than throughout Sub-Saharan Africa.[24]

RELATIVE INEQUALITIES IN THE INFORMATION SOCIETY

The fact that there are *absolute* inequalities between rich and poor nations in the virtual world is hardly surprising; it would be naive to expect otherwise given the substantial disparities in every other dimension of life from health care and nutrition to education and longevity. Despite the more exaggerated hopes of some cyber-optimists, the Internet is not going to suddenly eradicate the fundamental and intractable problems of disease, debt, and disadvantage facing developing countries. The more interesting question, with important implications for understanding the new media, concerns the *relative* inequality of opportunities. Is it easier or more difficult to go online in different societies, compared with inequalities of access to other types of communication technologies, such as telephones and televisions?

On the one hand, the pattern we have established in the distribution of the online population may represent a particular characteristic of Internet diffusion per se. If this is the case, then it would be appropriate to search for possible causes related to this particular form of technology, such as the costs of computer hardware, software, and ISP connection charges, the need for computing and literacy skills to go online, and the predominance of English-language contents. The availability of

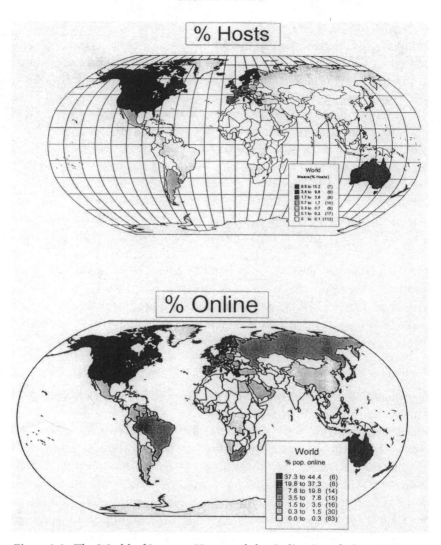

Figure 3.3. The World of Internet Hosts and the Online Population, 2000.
Sources: **Online Population:** "How Many Online?", *www.NUA.ie*; **Internet Hosts:**
www.Netcraft.com.

computers is often assumed to be one of the most fundamental barriers
to current use of the Internet for most people. Worldwide the number
of personal computers tripled in the last decade, from 25 PCs per 1,000
people in 1990 to 71 in 1998. But again the regional disparities are
marked: There are 459 computers per 1,000 people in the United States
but only 7 per thousand in Sub-Saharan Africa.[25] Most Internet con-

nections in developing countries still travel down mainline telephone lines so the rate of teledensity would also be expected to be related to patterns of Internet access. If this analysis is correct, it suggests that the solution lies in equalizing technological resources, such as through the distribution of computer hardware, skills training, and network connections.

On the other hand, the global patterns of inequality in Internet use may mirror the broader pattern of access to the Information Society. If so, we would expect to find a strong correlation between the spread of digital technologies and the availability of traditional mass media that have been around for decades or longer, such as newspapers, telephones, and television. If this is the case, it suggests that the problems of Internet access in the developing world are not particular to the nature of the medium itself – you don't need keyboard or literacy skills to switch on a radio – but instead may be due to deep-rooted and endemic problems in poorer societies such as the general lack of income, leisure time, literacy, and education that hinder use of traditional media such as newspapers. If this is the case, rather than any short-term fix, such as delivering beige desktop PCs to wired schools in Mozambique, Egypt, and Bangladesh, the long-term solution would be general aid, debt relief, and economic investment in developing countries. Understanding these issues can provide important clues to the fundamental reasons underlying the process of technological diffusion and therefore the most effective policy initiatives to overcome digital inequalities.

To analyze these questions, the different types of information and communication technologies can be divided into two categories. A standardized 100-point *New Media Index* was calculated by combining the proportion of those online within each country, as already described, with the per capita distribution of hosts and of personal computers. We would expect a strong correlation between these factors. A similarly standardized 100-point *Old Media Index* combines comparable per capita data in each country measuring the distribution of daily newspapers, radios, television sets, mainline telephones, and mobile phones (see Table 3.2). For an overall summary, multiplying both measures and dividing by two created the composite 100-point *Information Society Index*.

The results show two important findings. First, use of all forms of communication media is highly intercorrelated, meaning that countries at the forefront of the Information Society on one indicator are likely to lead on many others as well (see Table 3.3 and Figure 3.4). Info-rich countries like Sweden, the United States, and Australia are not just ahead in

Table 3.2. *Proportion of the population using new and old media*

	New Media			Old media					Info-Soc index
	Population online	Weighted hosts	PCs	Radios	TV sets	Daily newspaper	Mainline phones	Mobile phones	
	2000	2000	1998	1997	1998	1996	1998	1998	
Region									
Scandinavia	35	11	36	112	58	45	64	47	80
North America	27	10	28	118	61	16	47	15	63
West Europe	12	3	27	79	53	21	53	24	52
Central and Eastern Europe	3	0.3	6	45	32	13	21	4	30
Asia-Pacific	5	1	8	35	19	11	13	8	27
Middle East	3	0.2	6	39	25	11	19	8	22
South America	1	0.1	5	38	22	8	15	3	18
Africa	0.3	0.1	1	17	5	1	3	0.5	6
Development									
High	14	4	23	83	49	26	46	23	53
Medium	1	0.1	3	32	21	6	11	2	15
Low	0.02	0.03	0.3	14	3	1	1	.01	4
Total	**4**	**1**	**9**	**40**	**24**	**10**	**18**	**7**	**38**
No. of Nations	169	179	125	140	139	133	179	139	101

Notes: All figures are expressed as a percentage of the population. For full details see Table 3.1. Percentage of radios (1997), television sets (1998), mobile phones (1998), and PCs (1998) from *World Development Indicators 2000*, The World Bank. Level of development is classified according to the UNDP (1999). The 100-point Info-Soc Index is calculated by combining all indicators into a standardized scale.

Table 3.3. *Correlations in use of the new and old media*

	New media			Old media				
	Online	Hosts	PCs	Radio	TVs	News-papers	Phones	Mobile phones
Hosts	.854							
PCs	.806	.745						
Radio	.788	.708	.818					
TVs	.692	.614	.769	.848				
Newspapers	.725	.715	.788	.749	.734			
Mainline phones	.791	.710	.886	.837	.861	.839		
Mobile phones	.809	.827	.845	.754	.715	.830	.872	
InfoSoc Index	.883	.810	.924	.937	.917	.858	.954	.888

Note: See Tables 3.1 and 3.2 for details of the measures. The figures represent correlations (r). All are significant at the .01 level.

Sources: See Tables 3.1 and 2.2.

terms of the Internet but also in the distribution of other media such as newspaper readership, radio and television sets, personal computers, and mainline and mobile cell telephones. Correlation revealed that access to all these media fell into a single consistent dimension.[26] There was little distinction between use of old and new media; the proportion of those online in each country was most strongly related to the distribution of hosts, telephones, and PCs, but it was also significantly and strongly related to the distribution of radios, TV sets, and newspaper readership in each nation. This means that people living in poorer societies excluded from the world's flow of communications such as Burkina Faso, Yemen, and Vietnam were largely cut off from all forms of info-tech, including traditional mass media like radios and newspapers as well as modern ones such as mobile phones and personal computers. The vast majority of poorer societies, low on both indicators, cluster together in the bottom left corner of the scatter plot illustrated in Figure 3.4. At a broader level, as cyber-pessimists suggest, this analysis indicates that in the emerging Internet era, the relative inequalities between rich and poor in access to the virtual world reflect, rather than transform, global disparities in the

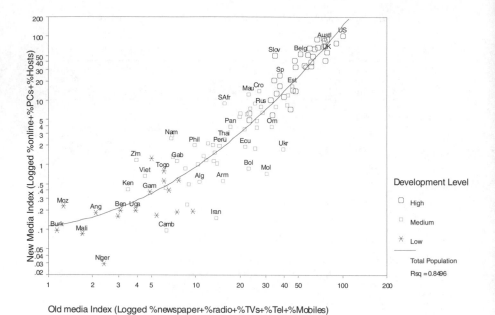

Figure 3.4. The Information Society.
Source: For details about the construction of the scales and the data sources see Table 3.2.

Information Society. Nations that already have many radios and TVs are most likely to also get access to networked computers.

The previous comparison also reveals important variations to this general pattern. Some new democracies such as Slovenia and South Africa fall above the regression line in Figure 3.4, indicating that these are more advanced in access to the digital technologies than would be expected from their use of television and newspapers. Some countries like Finland, Germany, and the United Kingdom fall exactly where predicted along the line, suggesting a balance in these societies between new and old media. The United States also falls into this category, leading the world in terms of connections to info-tech. Many less affluent societies like Bolivia, Iran, and the Ukraine, as well as Portugal and Greece, while lagging on both scales, are slightly stronger in use of the traditional print and electronic media than in access to digital technologies. Therefore although the analysis reveals that access to old and new media technologies is closely related, the outliers suggest some exceptions to the rule that may have significant implications for policy initiatives designed to broaden the spread of the wired world.

ECONOMIC DEVELOPMENT AND THE DIGITAL DIVIDE

How do we explain the diffusion of the Information Society that we observe? Many possible answers can be suggested. If the pattern reflects basic differences in levels of economic development, as many assume, then we would expect to find clear divisions between rich and poor countries. One of the most comprehensive studies seeking to explain the distribution of Internet hosts within postindustrial societies, by Hargittai, concluded that the economic wealth of a country, measured by per capita GNP, was one of the most important predictors.[27] A study for the International Telecommunications Union also found that the number of Internet hosts per country was significantly related to general levels of socioeconomic development, using the UN Human Development Index measuring the rate of adult literacy, education, life expectancy, and per capita GDP.[28] Rodriguez and Wilson's research for the World Bank arrived at similar conclusions.[29] If this pattern is confirmed in this study it would suggest that the Internet represents one more disparity reflecting the poverty of those living in developing nations, lacking access to the knowledge economy as well as basic nutrition, education, and health care.

The results of the regression analysis confirm that the relationship between Internet use and economic development, measured by per capita GDP in 1997, is indeed both strong and significant ($R = 0.77$ Sig. .000). The best-fitting model with logged data, illustrated with the scatter plot in Figure 3.5, shows that there is also a critical threshold: the online population expands exponentially once countries rise about the $9,000 level of per capita GNP. Not surprisingly, many of the poorest nations such as the Sudan, Rwanda, and Bangladesh are among the least-wired societies, whereas at the other extreme many affluent postindustrial economies such as Norway, Finland, and New Zealand fall exactly where expected on the regression line. Yet at the same time there are also some important outliers to the general pattern, and particular explanations about these countries may provide important clues to what other factors may contribute to Internet connectivity beyond economic development.

In one category, many countries, falling below the regression line, are relatively affluent yet display lower than average Internet penetration rates. This includes certain oil-rich Middle Eastern nations such as Bahrain, Kuwait, the United Arab Emirates, and Saudi Arabia, as well as South East Asian states such as Singapore, Japan, and Brunei. The reasons for this pattern cannot be established systematically here but they

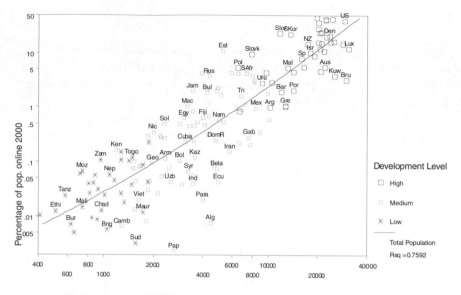

Figure 3.5. Economic Development and Internet Use.
Sources: **Per Capita GDP** in Purchasing Power Parity, United States Dollars, 1999: UNDP, *Human Development Report, 1999,* New York: UNDP/Oxford University Press; **Percentage of Population Online**: "How Many Online", *www.NUA.ie.*

can perhaps best be explained by the extreme inequalities of personal income and wealth characteristic of these societies, possibly combined with some cultural restriction on use through restricting Internet Service Providers in some Middle Eastern countries.[30]

In contrast, some other societies are above the regression line, with higher than average Internet access than would be predicted by their level of economic development, including Slovakia, Slovenia, Poland, and Estonia, as well as in South Korea and Taiwan. These exceptions to the general pattern have important implications for understanding this phenomenon, explored later in the analysis, because they weaken claims of economic determinism and highlight the significance of other factors leading to technological diffusion. Economic development certainly predicts access to the Internet, as it does to other traditional forms of information and communication, but the wider scatter of countries in the top right corner of Figure 3.5 shows that, once above a certain minimal level, economic development is not necessarily essential to greater online use.

Beyond economic development, other economic factors that might influence use of the Internet include the availability and costs of technology in different countries, including the price of computer hardware/software, connection charges through Internet Service Providers, and the provision and availability of mainline and mobile telephone services. This is not just a matter of the familiar income disparities between rich and poor nations, because the relative costs of ISP access are actually higher in many developing countries. Although some free ISP and email services are becoming available, the OECD estimates that average monthly charges for Internet access in July 1999, based on a 20-hour per month peak rate, were $24 per month in Australia but almost three times as much in Turkey ($65 per month), and almost four times as much in Mexico ($94 per month).[31] In OECD nations, the cost of ISP access was significantly correlated with the proportion online in each country ($R = -.45$ Sig. .01). Countries with relatively high Internet penetration rates (e.g., Finland and Sweden) often have lower access prices. ISP charges are gradually falling, making access more affordable for business and consumers, but the costs of local telephone connections may also be an important deterrent, especially in Europe compared with the United States. Hargittai's comparison of OECD member states concluded that telecommunications policy, notably the level of competition under deregulated systems, was significantly associated with levels of Internet connectivity.[32]

Another important reason for the spread of digital technology may lie in the broader process of research and development within each country, particularly basic investment in science and technology. One reason why use of mobile phones is so high in Scandinavia, for example, is because Nokkia and Ericsson, two leading telecommunications manufacturing companies, are located there. Expenditure on scientific and technological research and development can be gauged by many indicators, such as the proportion of scientists, engineers, and technicians employed in R&D, the proportion of science and engineering students in tertiary education, and the percentage of manufacturing exports from high-tech products. Most of these indicators are highly intercorrelated and information was not available from World Bank and UNESCO data for all the countries under comparison. In this study, therefore, the impact of the technological environment can be compared by examining the impact of per capita spending on research and development as a proportion of GNP within each country. The results are illustrated graphically with the scatter plot in Figure 3.6, which shows a consistent and significant

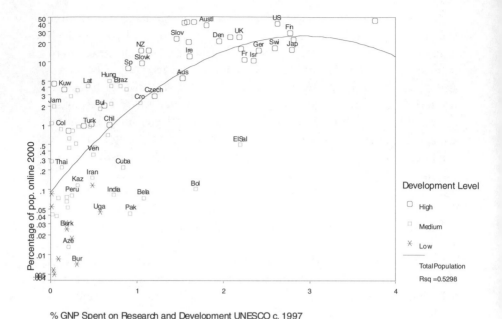

% GNP Spent on Research and Development UNESCO c. 1997

Figure 3.6. Research and Development Spending and Internet Use.
Sources: Percentage of GDP Spent on **Research and Development, 1997**: UNDP
Human Development Report, 1999, New York: UNDP/Oxford University Press;
Percentage of the Population Online: "How Many Online", *www.NUA.ie.*

correlation, confirming that R&D investments help boost the market for
digital technologies, although there are a few outliers such as El Salvador
and Bolivia, with lower than average online access given their level of
spending on research and development.

HUMAN CAPITAL AND DEMOCRATIC DEVELOPMENT

Economic development goes a long way toward explaining the global disparities between richer and poorer societies; however by itself this fails to
account for the substantial differences in Internet access between relatively similar countries, such as between the Nordic and Mediterranean
European nations. What other answers could help to explain the patterns we have found? The evidence here remains more scattered but we
can examine some common assumptions, especially the role of human
capital and democratic freedom of expression.

The development of human capital – meaning the investment in digital skills and capacities through education, training, and lifetime learn-

ing – represents one of the most important factors that might facilitate Internet access. Human capital represents the properties that allow people to live and work productively. Education is one of the most significant forms of social development, producing the skills and experiences that are most likely to contribute to using computers. Secondary and university education provide direct hands-on training in basic and advanced computing techniques, familiarity with standard software packages, and confidence in surfing the Web, as well as the general cognitive skills necessary to make sense of the online information. Academic institutions may also play an important role in spreading digital technologies because they are often among the first institutions in a nation to be wired. Studies have found that more educated people are quicker to adapt to new innovations.[33] Education also contributes directly to basic literacy, and reading and writing skills that are currently essential to using this media. The World Wide Web is rich in visual imagery, such as pictures and streaming video, and audio content is burgeoning through the easy availability of online radio and .mp3 music. These types of content are likely to surge in popularity as broadband fat-pipe delivery increases in capacity, fiber-optic cables become capable of carrying more bandwidth, and file compression continues to shrink the storage size of data. Nevertheless most material now on the Web remains closer to text-based newspapers rather than to audio or visual electronic media like television. If basic illiteracy is an important barrier to access, most of the world's poor could still be excluded from the information revolution, even if computing equipment became more widely available through Internet cafés, schools, public libraries, and community centers. One-fifth of the world's population remains illiterate, and the total rises to 40 percent or more of those living in Sub-Saharan Africa, the Middle East, and Southern Asia, with even higher figures for the female population.[34]

Social development also encompasses language skills. Wresch suggests that knowledge of English as a first or secondary language is critical: "English dominates the world of computing. Both the English and the Americans like to claim their nation as the birthplace of computing, but in one way it doesn't matter which did what – both are English speaking nations."[35] A comprehensive analysis of more than one billion unique Web pages by the Inktomi search engine found that 87 percent of all documents were in English, a language understood by an estimated one in ten people worldwide.[36] This picture is confirmed by a more limited search in 1997 by the Babel team for the Internet Society which estimated that 84 percent of all pages in English, followed by German (4.5 percent), Japanese (3.1 percent), and French (1.8 percent), Spanish (1.2 percent), Swedish (1.1 percent), and Italian (1 percent), with all other languages each below 1 percent.[37] The technology to overcome language barriers is progressing, with online translation services freely available for the major European languages such as German, Spanish, and French, but nevertheless it is striking that many of the societies at the leading edge of the digital revolution are either Anglo-American countries like Canada and Australia, or smaller well-educated welfare states like Norway, Sweden, and the Netherlands where English has become the lingua franca as the second language taught widely in schools. By most standard economic indicators, major G-8 rivals such as France, Germany, and Japan should outrank the United Kingdom in terms of Internet penetration yet they continue to lag behind; for example, there are twice as many users in Britain than France, although this may also be influenced by the checkered history of the French Minitel project. Familiarity with English as a second language among the scientific elite may also help to explain the success of software development and computer manufacturing in ex-British colonies such as India, Malaysia, and Hong Kong. Rao et al. argue that elsewhere in Southern Asia the lack of Web content in indigenous languages, as well as the limited local relevance of the available sites, limits the incentive to go online for much of the population.[38] The predominance of the English language may change in coming years, as more and more of the population moves online in China, India, and Brazil, but in the meantime those who can read English are greatly advantaged in the digital world and, although we cannot prove the proposition here with the available evidence, this could plausibly help to explain high Internet penetration rates in the United States, Canada, Australia, and the United Kingdom.[39]

Finally, broader issues of *democratic development* may also contribute to digital diffusion through the expansion of opportunities for freedom of expression and civil liberties commonly available in democratic states. Freedom House has documented many instances where authoritarian regimes have attempted to limit public access to the Internet or censor its contents and freedom of publications on the Web. The study by Leonard Sussman found that although control of the Internet was far more difficult than censorship of television or the press, nevertheless currently about twenty states restrict citizen's access to the Internet to a significant degree.[40] Cited examples include "cyber-dissidents" jailed in China, the need for Burmese owners to report computers to the government, under penalty of a fine, and restricted ISP access to information content "contrary to Islamic values" in Saudi Arabia, Syria, and the United Arab Emirates It is difficult to monitor such incidence on a systematic basis but as an indirect indicator the impact of a country's level of democratization can be compared, using the Freedom House 7-point index measuring political rights and civil liberties, which has become adopted as the standard indicator for cross-national comparisons.[41] If democratization plays a significant role, then we would expect that countries with greater civil liberties and freedom of expression would display more widespread access to digital technologies.

The relative importance of economic development, human capital, and levels of democratization on rates of Internet penetration are analyzed in Table 3.4 using simple correlations and multivariate regression models.[42] Regional dummy variables were also included to see how far these remained significant after controlling for prior levels of economic development, human capital, and the democratic background of different areas. For comparison, alternative models (not reported here) were tested before arriving at the final one based on goodness of fit, parsimony, and the prior theoretical assumptions that determined the causal ordering of the variables.[43] The models were run to determine whether similar factors that predicted Internet penetration rates also helped to predict access to new and old media technologies.

Two important findings emerged from this analysis. First, the results of the simple correlations, without any prior controls, show that all the selected indicators of economic development, human capital, and democratization proved to be strongly and significantly related to use of the Internet, as well as to use of the new media and old media, in the expected direction. In other words, the proportion of the population online in each country was significantly related to levels of per capita GDP, R&D spending, literacy and secondary education, and level of democratization, according to the available measures. The regional patterns confirmed the significance of the differences observed earlier, even after controls, with higher than average use evident in Scandinavia, North America, and Western Europe, and significantly lower than average use in South America and Africa. Similar strong correlation coefficients were evident using the composite New Media and Old Media Indexes, suggesting a robust relationship that held up to testing across all indicators. The strength of the coefficients varied slightly; for example, patterns of literacy were more closely associated with use of the old media than the new, but the overall pattern was highly consistent.

Table 3.4. *Explaining the spread of technology*

	Percent online		New media index	Old media index
	Correlation	Beta (Sig.)	Beta (Sig.)	Beta (Sig.)
Economic development				
Per capita GDP	.74 **	.37 **	.57 **	.58 **
R&D spending (%)	.46 **	.32 **	.28 **	.32 **
Social development				
Adult literacy (%)	.40 **	.03	−.05	.09
Secondary education (%)	.53 **	.07	.01	.01
Political development				
Level of democratization	.55 **	.08	−.06	.10
Region				
Scandinavia	.59 **	.26 **	.19 **	.08
North America	.34 **	.17 **	.12 **	.04
Western Europe	.25 **	.07 *	.08	−.06
Middle East	−.04	−.07	−.11	.01
Central and Eastern Europe	−.05	−.06	−.03	.12
South America	−.29 **	−.11	−.09	.01
Africa	−.29 **	.01	−.03	.01
Adjusted R^2		.80	.57	.91

Notes: The dependent variables include the proportion of the population online (spring 2000), the New Media Index (% online, % PCs, and % hosts), and the Old Media Index (% newspapers, % radios, % TVs, % telephones, % mobile phones) (see Table 3.2 for details). The figures represent correlation coefficients (R) without any controls and standardized beta coefficients from multivariate OLS regression analysis models. The regional dummy variables drop Asia. *Sig. = −.01, **Sig. = .05.

Sources: See previous tables in this chapter for data sources.

Because each of these indicators is closely related to the other, these strong associations could prove to be spurious, for example if economic development simultaneously produces a more educated and literate public, higher levels of R&D investment, and the transition to a more democratic regime. There could well be a complex pattern of interaction here. To disentangle these factors we need to turn to the multivariate analysis models that assume that economic and social development come before the process of democratization. The most important finding from the regression models in Table 3.4 is that *economic factors outweighed all others in predicting cross-national differences in access to the information society.* Economic development, measured by per capita GDP, was consistently important across all three models, indicating that more affluent societies have access to a richer range of information and communication technologies, among both traditional and digital media. The poorest developing societies such as Mali and Nigeria lack old and new technologies of mass communications. Countries with per capita GDP in the middle region of about $6,000–10,000 show a more mixed picture; in particular, African societies tend to be poor in both indicators but Central and Eastern European nations have lower than average income but higher mass media use. Finally, affluent postindustrial societies including the United States, Norway, and Japan are high in both income and information resources. Moreover, the related economic indicator of levels of technological investment, as measured by per capita spending on research and development as a share of GNP, was also confirmed to be significant across all models, for reasons discussed earlier.

Once these related socioeconomic factors were included in the models, other indicators of human capital and democratization became insignificant. This suggests that literacy, education, and democratization do not exert an independent influence on Internet penetration rates, or access to older forms of information technology.[44] This pattern lends further confirmation to the findings of Hargattai's earlier comparison of OECD states.[45] After controlling for all these factors, the regions of Scandinavia, North America, and Western Europe still emerged as significantly ahead of all other areas in levels of digital connectivity, indicating that many other residual factors in these societies not specified in these models contribute to the diffusion process, such as policy initiatives to spread the Internet through wired schools, community centers, and businesses. The economic factors predicting Internet connectivity also serve to explain the diffusion of traditional mass media, suggesting a pervasive and robust pattern irrespective of the specific type of info-tech or the particular indicators selected for analysis. Of course the interrelationship of economic, social, and democratic development does create problems for these models, since it is difficult to isolate the influence of each. The models assume that economic development leads to human capital, such as a better educated workforce, but, of course, the reverse could be equally true. In the same way, although there is no one-to-one relationship, nevertheless consolidated democracies tend to be more affluent countries.

Another major limitation of the analysis is that the Internet is a relatively recent phenomenon, so it is possible that patterns of access evident today may change considerably within the medium- to long-term. One way to explore this further is to examine the global diffusion of traditional mass media such as radio and television, to see if the gap between rich and poor nations has gradually closed over time in these technologies. Based on UNESCO data, Figure 3.7 indicates trends in the adoption of television sets and radio receivers in developing and postindustrial societies during the last three decades. The results illustrate how these media have grown in popularity worldwide during the late 1980s and early 1990s. But, most important, the trends also show that the gap in access to these media between postindustrial and developing societies has not diminished in the last thirty years – if anything the reverse. Because use of television and radio grew more sharply in postindustrial societies in the 1970s, even with a slight plateau effect, the inequalities of access today between rich and poor nations are actually slightly greater than about three decades ago. If we can extrapolate from this pattern to digital technologies, this suggests that the relative disparities between developing and postindustrial nations that we have observed today will not necessarily close as more and more people go online. The prognostication is that early-adopter countries seem likely to maintain their relative lead, leading in digital technologies, even while laggard societies attempt to catch up.

CONCLUSIONS: NEW TECHNOLOGIES, OLD INEQUALITIES

International organizations including the World Bank and the UNDP have raised concern about the growing global digital divide in the 1990s, and the need to overcome this disparity before the situation rigidifies into a new virtual Berlin Wall splitting rich and poor worlds. Potentially digital technologies may serve the needs of the developing world. As well as the direct economic benefits for trade and tourism, the Internet may accelerate the longer-term investment in human capital. Information infrastructures for distance learning and educational development can facilitate access to the most up-to-date materials for teaching and research. As the World Bank Report expressed these hopes: "ICT greatly facilitates the acquisition and absorption of knowledge, offering developing countries unprecedented opportunities to enhance educational systems, improve policy formation and execution, and widen the range of opportunities for business and the poor. One of the

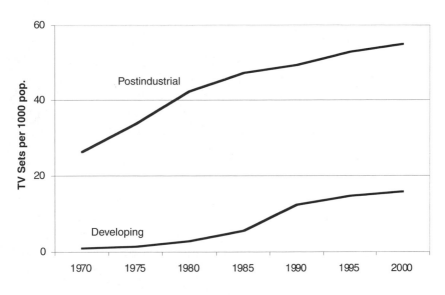

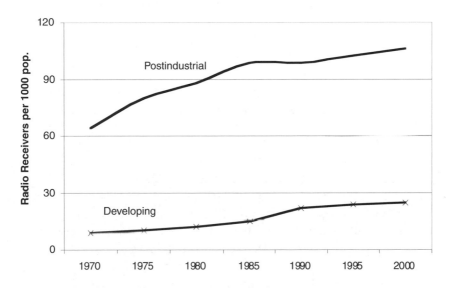

Figure 3.7. Trends in the Worldwide Spread of Televisions and Radios, 1970–2000.
Source: UNESCO Yearbooks, Paris: UNESCO.

greatest hardships endured by the poor, and by many others who live in the poorest countries, is their sense of isolation. The new communication technologies promise to reduce that sense of isolation, and to open access to knowledge in ways unimaginable not long ago."[46] Hopes about the impact of the Internet can be seen as another example in a long history of technological transfers that promise economic regeneration for poorer regions, from the industries of railroads and textiles in the nineteenth century, to the production of South Korean automobiles, Japanese Walkmans, and Taiwanese silicon chips in the twentieth century. But can these hopes be fulfilled?

Multiple factors may potentially help to explain the global divide in Internet access, as in other forms of technological diffusion, and this study has been able to focus only on a limited range of explanations. Other plausible factors that should be considered in subsequent research include the role of cultural attitudes toward science and technology, the impact of public policy initiatives in education and training, as well as interest in the available contents of materials on the Web. The structures of opportunities on the Internet, as well as the resources of particular sections of the population, are likely to prove important reasons explaining patterns of use. We are only starting to explore these cross-national differences systematically and we need to go beyond the limitations of the available national-level aggregate data to understand the reasons why, for example, far more people are online in Finland rather than France, in Malaysia rather than in Vietnam, or in South Africa rather than Sudan.

Nevertheless the results of this analysis strongly suggest that the basic reasons for the global divide in Internet access are not strongly related to the particular characteristics of this type of information technology. The problem, it appears, is less whether Namibians lack keyboard skills, whether Brazilians find that few websites are available in Portuguese, or whether Bangladesh lacks network connections. Instead, the problems of Internet access are common to the problems of access to other communication and information technologies that have been widely available for decades in the West. Many of the poor living in Namibia, Brazil, and Bangladesh lack a rich information environment in terms of newspapers, radios, and television, as well as networked computers. In the first decade, the availability of the Internet has therefore reinforced existing economic inequalities, rather than overcoming or transforming them. The reasons are that levels of economic development combined with investments in research and development go a long way toward explaining those countries at the forefront of the Internet revolution and those lagging far, far behind. The regression models successfully explain a high level of variance. If countries have the income and affluence then often (but not always) access to the Internet will follow, along with connectivity to telephones, radios, and televisions. There are some important exceptions to this generalization – both affluent countries that lack extensive Internet access such as Kuwait and Greece, and middle-income countries that have made great progress toward online connectivity, such as Slovakia and Estonia. Economic determinism does not rule our virtual fate, but worldwide, without effective public policy interventions, it goes a long way toward predicting it.

The situation may change within the next few decades. In the West, the costs of access are declining, as computers become more and more affordable for businesses and consumers. U.S. consumer prices for personal computers have dropped by 43 percent over the last two years, and the costs of information service have fallen by one-third during the same period, with slightly slower declines in the price of software and mobile phones.[47] If the costs of Internet communications plummet further in future decades – for example, if Web access becomes widely available via throwaway prepaid mobile phones, like discardable Kodak cameras, connected to inexpensive satellite services circling the globe – then the gap between rich and poor could well change. In the current era, however, general levels of economic development and research investment go a long way toward predicting which countries have widespread access to the Information Society. Although the Internet remains in its adolescence as a new technology, we do not need to discard all our old explanations. Internet penetration rates can be predicted by economic models that also explain which countries are rich in telephones, radio and television, and even newspapers. Indeed, ownership of home computers in European households was strongly correlated with possession of many other prosaic consumer durables, including electric drills, video cameras, and clock radios, as well as ownership of a second automobile and vacation home.[48] Internet technology is new; global economic inequalities explaining technological diffusion are not. The next chapter goes on to explore whether we find a similar pattern that helps to explain the substantial differences in digital access evident between rich and poor within societies, even those at the forefront of the Information Revolution.

CHAPTER 4

Social Inequalities

For many the phrase "digital divide" has become a familiar catch phrase signifying the gap between information haves and have-nots, including splits along racial, gender, and class lines. The U.S. Department of Commerce has drawn attention to these disparities in successive studies since 1993. *Falling through the Net* emphasizes the lack of access to computers and the Internet commonly found in America among poorer households, those with only high-school education, the black and Hispanic populations, rural communities and women.[1] Pew surveys in spring 2000 confirm the familiar pattern found in many American studies, with sharp inequalities of Internet access by age, education, race, and ethnicity, plus the more modest gender gap (see Figure 4.1). Three-fourths of all American college graduates use the Internet compared with fewer than one-fifth of those who failed to graduate from high school. One-half of all whites are online compared with one-third of all blacks. And two-thirds of the younger generation is online compared with one in ten senior citizens. The OECD has documented similar patterns of stratification among the Internet population in Canada, Australia, and Finland.[2]

Why does this matter? The chief concern about the digital divide is that the underclass of info-poor may become further marginalized in societies where basic computer skills are becoming essential for economic success and personal advancement, entry to good career and educational opportunities, full access to social networks, and opportunities for civic engagement. Recognizing the potential problems of a two-track knowledge economy, the EU has prioritized the need for social inclusion as one of its objectives when launching the e-Europe Action Plan. The EU's strategy involves a combination of market and state initiatives, including reducing the costs of Internet access through

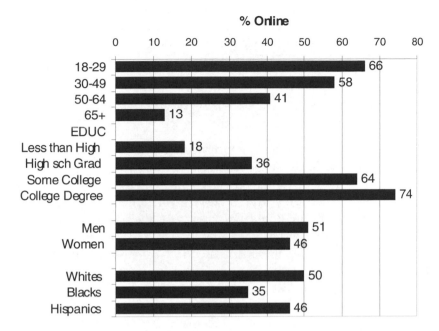

% Online

	0	10	20	30	40	50	60	70	80
18-29								66	
30-49							58		
50-64					41				
65+		13							
EDUC									
Less than High		18							
High sch Grad				36					
Some College							64		
College Degree								74	
Men						51			
Women					46				
Whites						50			
Blacks				35					
Hispanics					46				

Figure 4.1. Percent Online by Social Group, U.S. 2000.
Source: Pew Surveys, United States, spring 2000.

telecommunications liberalization as well as making terminals and on-site training available in public spaces like unemployment offices, libraries, and schools.[3] Concern about Internet access has driven initiatives taken by the Blair government. The British Department of Trade and Industry has established a network of city learning centers and distributed reconditioned computers to homes in poor neighborhoods.[4] Similar public sector and nonprofit policy initiatives designed to overcome the digital divide have been launched recently in many other European countries. To evaluate whether these initiatives are likely to work we need to understand the underlying reasons for the digital divide and the likely projection of future trends. This chapter therefore focuses on three core questions:

- What theories provide plausible accounts of Internet diffusion?
- Who is online in postindustrial societies, and, in particular, does the social profile of Internet users found in the United States reflect that found elsewhere?

• Do the social inequalities in the online population reflect the particular characteristics of Internet diffusion per se, or does this pattern reflect disparities evident in access to older media such as cable television and fax machines?

THEORIES OF SOCIAL STRATIFICATION IN THE NETWORKED WORLD

Although attracting widespread concern, interpretations of the underlying reason for the digital divide remain under debate – for example, the appropriate weight that should be given to race and income in predicting American patterns of access and use. Even greater uncertainty surrounds the projection of future population trends on the Net and two mainstream perspectives have become common. On the one hand, the more optimistic *normalization* thesis discussed in Chapter 1 predicts that, at least in affluent postindustrial societies, the social profile of the online community will gradually broaden over time, like the early audience for radio or television, until eventually it mirrors society as a whole.[5] In countries at the forefront of the information revolution, such as the Unites States, Australia, and Britain, Internet use has rippled out within the last decade from an information source networking scholars and scientists at elite research institutions to become a medium of mass communications for the delivery of news, music, video and audio programming, as well as e-commerce and home shopping. The normalization thesis suggests that in developed societies the Internet could eventually become as popular as television today, so that we can expect penetration levels to reach 90 to 95 percent of the population, encouraged by falling costs for hardware, software, and services, and the growth of online home entertainment given fat-pipe delivery and technological convergence. Popular commentators swept up in the giddy hype of new gizmos and gadgets, surrounded at home and work by easy access to all Internet, all the time, often assume that eventually most will succumb to the digital onslaught. Competition in the marketplace, some assume, will eventually correct any residual major disparities, removing the need for government intervention or regulation for the provision of universal service, beyond the minimal prevention of monopolistic practices.[6]

In contrast the more pessimistic *diffusion* theory developed by Everett Rogers provides an alternative interpretation of social stratification in technological adaptation.[7] We can draw on case studies of the impact of technological innovations ranging from the invention of stirrups and gunpowder in military strategy, to the telegraph, railway, and steam engine in the nineteenth century, and airplanes, automobiles, or telephones in the twentieth. Research has produced hundreds of case studies from the spread of new crops studied by rural sociologists to the implementation of new teaching techniques studied by educational psychologists. These studies have commonly established that, compared with laggards, early adopters of new innovations are characteristically drawn from groups with higher socioeconomic status. Education, literacy, and social status provide access to the essential financial and information resources required to adapt flexibly to innovative technologies. Moreover, diffusion theory suggests that the adoption of successful new technologies often reinforces economic advantages, like the greater productivity facilitated in agriculture by mechanized tractors, artificial fertilizers, and specialist seed-corn, so that the rich get richer, and the less well-off sectors fall farther behind. Everett Rogers emphasizes that this pattern is far from inevitable, because the conditions under which an innovations are implemented determine, in part, their social consequences. Active initiatives to level the playing field by the state and nonprofit sectors can broaden technological access. The existing social structure also plays a role; innovations in highly stratified societies will usually reinforce existing socioeconomic disparities. The type of technology can also influence this process, for example, the initial resources required for access, including both financial investments and educational skills. Nevertheless diffusion theory predicts that without successful state intervention, if the spread of the Internet follows the conventional trajectory established by many previous technologies, then the initial adoption of wired computers can be expected to exacerbate existing social divisions, at least in the early-to-middle stages of the S-shaped diffusion curve, and perhaps in the longer-term as well if the new technology produces substantial productivity gains and continuing access barriers.

The cross-national evidence on this issue remains scattered and inconclusive, but some indicators within the U.S. Internet population lend some weight to support the normalization thesis. After analyzing trends from 1995 to 1998 in Harris national surveys, David Birdsell and colleagues concluded that as the proportion of U.S. users surged from 14 to 58 percent of all Americans, the demographics of the online community broadened: "Once heavily overbalanced by male users, the Web is now accessed by men and women almost equally. And once predominantly white, the Web population now reflects a racial breakdown statis-

tically indistinguishable from Census data for the general population…
The Web reflects America much more accurately today than when the
technology was in its infancy."[8] Similarly, the 1998 Pew Research Center
study, *The Internet News Audience Goes Ordinary*, also reported greater
diversification in the American online community: "Increasingly people
without college training, those with modest incomes, and women are
joining the ranks of Internet users, who not long ago were largely well-
educated, affluent men."[9] Other research reports that the gender gap in
the U.S. Internet population has become insignificant in recent years.[10]
A Stanford Institute's study by Nie and Erbring suggests that racial differences in online access in America have become less important today
than income differentials, conclusions echoed by the Forrester Report.[11]

However, the matter has not been settled because other American
evidence points in the opposite direction. The 1999 report *Falling
through the Net* emphasized that in terms of racial, educational, and
income inequalities the digital divide between those with access to new
technologies and those without widened from the mid- to late-1990s,
not narrowed. The study by the U.S. Department of Commerce concluded that ethnic differences in the virtual world cannot be accounted
for solely by levels of affluence since in their adoption of home computers and links to the Web, African Americans lag substantially behind
white Americans within every income category. "A White, two-parent
household earning less than $35,000 is nearly three times as likely to
have Internet access as a comparable Black household and nearly four
times as likely to have Internet access as Hispanic households in the
same income category."[12] Anthony Wilhelm confirmed that racial and
ethnic differences in computer usage have not disappeared, since his
analysis of the 1994 U.S. Current Population Survey data found that
these differences persist even after controlling for education and household income.[13] A detailed study of trends in computer ownership and
Internet use from 1997 to 1998 by Hoffman and Novak also concluded
that the overall gap between whites and African Americans increased
from the mid- to late-1990s.[14] Moreover it remains uncertain whether
"normalization" of African-American participation in the online population will eventually occur even if use of the Web eventually reaches 90
to 95 percent of all Americans, because there are racial disparities in
access to far more basic and long-established technologies, such as
household telephones.

To clarify the broader pattern, and to generalize more widely beyond
America, survey evidence needs to compare Internet trends in a wide

range of societies at different levels of development. The most straight-forward approach to testing these theories would be to compare time-series data to observe whether the digital divide has widened or narrowed during the last decade. Yet benchmark survey data during this period remain limited, even in the United States. Given the rapid pace of technological change, which seems likely to continue, it remains dif-ficult to project future trends from the social characteristics of early adopters. The available evidence on the digital divide in the United States may also reflect endemic inequalities within this particular soci-ety, such as the deep-rooted cleavage of race, rather than general pat-terns characteristic of those who participate in the online community in more egalitarian societies, such as the smaller welfare state societies of Sweden and the Netherlands. Even fewer surveys have monitored trends in Internet use across many different countries, although more information is rapidly becoming available from market research com-panies, generated by the demands of e-commerce.[15] For comparative data this chapter draws on the biannual series of Eurobarometer sur-veys conducted since 1970 in the 15 EU member states by the European Commission.[16] For the United States we analyzed successive surveys conducted on a regular basis since 1995 by the Pew Center on the People and the Press, providing perhaps the most detailed continuous time-series data on Internet use available in America. The survey items are not identical in both series but functionally equivalent items allow comparison of demographic patterns of Internet use from spring 1996 to 1999. The main conclusions were cross-checked against secondary sources for comparison with other nations.

The comparison of the United States and Europe includes both lead-ers and laggard societies. This allows us to test the "normalization" claim that the size of the digital divide relates to the level of Internet dif-fusion. The fifteen member states in the European Union provide a range of postindustrial societies that are relatively similar in their levels of socioeconomic development, political systems, and cultural tradi-tions. All are established democratic states, with advanced economies and extensive welfare services. This comparison follows the classic logic of the "most similar system" design, which assumes that the factors common to relatively homogeneous types of society are irrelevant to explaining their differences.[17] Roughly equivalent levels of literacy, edu-cation, and affluence within European nations, despite the existence of poorer regions, means that these factors can be largely discounted in seeking explanations of the digital divide. The social structure remains

Table 4.1. *Trends in Internet use in Europe and America, 1996–1999*

	Spring 1996	Spring 1997	Fall 1998	Spring 1999	Increase 1996–1999
Sweden	12	26	43	61	+49
United States[a]	21	36	42	49	+28
Denmark	10	17	26	44	+34
Finland	11	16	18	39	+28
Netherlands	9	16	19	32	+23
Luxembourg	5	13	16	22	+17
Britain	9	10	11	22	+13
Northern Ireland	4	8	10	20	+16
Italy	3	5	7	14	+11
Ireland	4	5	9	14	+10
Austria	4	10	7	11	+7
Belgium	3	6	8	11	+8
France	2	4	4	9	+7
Germany West	5	8	8	8	+3
Germany East	2	4	5	8	+6
Spain	2	2	5	8	+6
Greece	1	3	3	7	+6
Portugal	2	2	3	5	+3
EU15	*5*	*9*	*12*	*20*	*+15*

[a] United States: successive surveys by The Pew Research Center for the People and the Press. See *www.peoplepress.org*.

Notes: The Eurobarometer question asks, *"Do you have access to, or do you use, the Internet or World Wide Web."*[33] The Pew survey asks, *"Do you ever go online to access the Internet or World Wide Web or to send and receive email?"*

Sources: Eurobarometer 44.2, spring 1996; 47.0, spring 1997; 50.1, fall 1998; and 51.0, spring 1999.

relatively similar, in terms of the predominance of class cleavages, although with a complex pattern in terms of ethnicity and race.[18] Moves toward removing tariff barriers, economic and monetary union, and harmonization of economic and social policy within the European Union also mean that this region shares relatively similar telecommunications policies, with market liberalization evident in most member states during the last decade. At the same time, and this is most important, the European nations under comparison vary greatly in terms of the dependent variable that we are seeking to explain, namely levels of

Table 4.2. *Trends in computer use in Europe and America, 1996–1999*

	Spring 1996	Fall 1997	Spring 1999	Increase
Sweden	43	62	73	+30
United States[a]	60	66	69	+9
Denmark	49	61	65	+16
Netherlands	54	61	64	+10
Finland	36	43	52	+16
Luxembourg	41	49	48	+7
Britain	41	47	45	+4
Northern Ireland	25	34	39	+14
Italy	31	32	37	+6
Belgium	28	32	37	+9
Austria	23	41	33	+10
Spain	25	29	33	+8
Ireland	23	27	31	+8
France	25	34	30	+5
Germany West	31	32	29	–2
Germany East	27	32	27	0
Portugal	21	20	22	+1
Greece	12	19	17	+5
EU15	*31*	*38*	*40*	*+9*

[a] United States: successive surveys by *The Pew Research Center for the People and the Press.* See *www.peoplepress.org*

Note: The Eurobarometer question asks, *"Do you have access to, or do you use, a computer?"* [34] The Pew surveys ask: *"Do you use a computer at your workplace, at school or at home on at least an occasional basis?"*

Sources: Eurobarometer 44.2, spring 1996; 47.0, spring 1997; 50.1, fall 1998; and 51.0, spring 1999.

Internet connectivity. Overall one-fifth of the European population is online, but Nordic nations have forged ahead to the forefront in the digital age while Mediterranean societies often lag behind the European average (see Tables 4.1, 4.2, and Figure 4.2). In spring 1999, almost two-thirds (61 percent) of all Swedes were online. Sweden had almost ten times as many Internet users than Portugal and Greece. Use of personal computers confirms parallel contrasts, with use ranging from three-fourths of the population in Sweden and two-thirds in Denmark and the Netherlands down to less than one-fifth in Greece. Similar cross-national patterns are evident with the distribution of Internet hosts

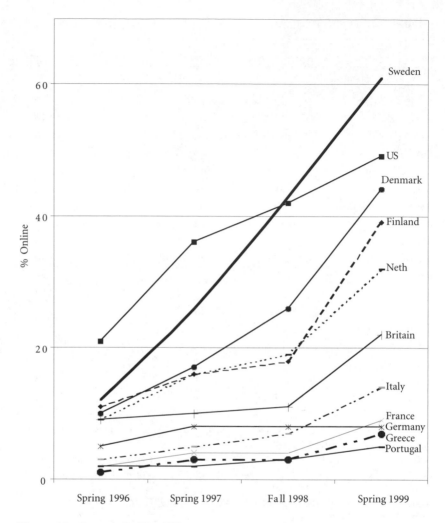

Figure 4.2. Percent Online, EU-15, 1996–99.
Sources: Eurobarometers 1996–1999; Pew Surveys, United States.

across Europe. If the "normalization" predictions are correct, we might expect to find that the *relative* size of the digital divide by social status, age, and gender would diminish most in societies at the forefront of the Information Society, including Sweden and Denmark. The social and demographic characteristics of the online community in different countries can be described first before multivariate regression analysis is used to examine the relationship among these variables.

WHO IS ONLINE?

INCOME

The digital divide is a multidimensional phenomenon tapping many social cleavages but differences of resources are commonly assumed to be among the most important, meaning the capacities based primarily on the income, occupation, and education that people bring to using new forms of info-tech. *Falling through the Net* emphasized that household income was one of the strongest predictors of Internet access in America.[19] U.S. Census data show that home ownership of PCs quadrupled from 1984 to 1997, but this period saw growing disparities in ownership among social strata based on household income, race, and education.[20] An OECD study, drawing on data from France, Japan, and the United States, confirmed the substantial disparity in the availability of personal computers in the home for different levels of household income, with the size of the gap between the lowest and highest income groups widening from 1995 to 1998.[21] Economic resources, including personal or household income, influence the ability to afford home computers and modems, related software, and the monthly ISP and telephone or broadband cable connection charges. Telephone costs can be substantial in Europe, especially where charges for local calls are metered by the minute, with these bills outweighing the initial investment in computer hardware within a few years. The OECD's *Information Technology Outlook 2000* study found that the growth in Internet demand has been driven by a combination of faster connection speeds, improved reliability and service, easier technical use, and declining access costs. Dial-up telephone modems currently remain the most popular mode of household access, used in two-thirds of all homes in OECD member states, although more advanced forms of delivery are gradually becoming more available, including cable, DSL, ISDN, and wireless.[22]

How far does household income determine Internet access? Table 4.3 summarizes trends in the social profile of Internet users within Europe from 1996 to 1999, for comparison across all major social cleavages. Figure 4.3 illustrates the size of the gap in Internet access between the most and least affluent quartile household incomes, with the nations ranked across the chart by their overall level of Internet penetration. Three major findings stand out. First, as expected, the income gap in Internet users across the whole of Europe proved sub-

Table 4.3. *Trends in the social profile of Internet users in Europe, 1996–99*

	Percent online spring 1996	Percent online spring 1999	Change
All EU-15	5	20	+15
Age			
15–25	9	32	+23
26–44	7	24	+17
45–64	5	16	+11
65+	1	3	+2
HH income category			
−	4	14	+10
−	3	14	+11
+	5	22	+17
++	10	37	+27
Age finished education			
Up to 15	1	5	+4
16–19 years	4	15	+11
20+	9	33	+24
Gender			
Men	6	22	+16
Women	4	17	+13
Occupational status			
Managers	14	44	+30
Other white collar	8	29	+21
Manual worker	3	15	+12
Home worker	2	8	+6
Unemployed	3	10	+7
Student	13	44	+31

Sources: Eurobarometer 44.2, spring 1996; 47.0, spring 1997; 50.1, fall 1998; and 51.0, spring 1999.

stantial; on average the wealthiest European households were almost three times more likely to be online than the poorest ones. Overall 37 percent, of those living in the most affluent households were online, compared with only 14 percent, of those in the poorest homes. There was a consistent and significant association between household income and levels of Internet access across all EU countries, with the single exception of Greece.[23] Moreover, across Europe the relative size

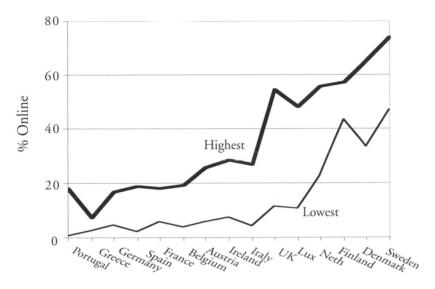

Figure 4.3. Percent Online by Household Income, EU-15, 1999.
Source: Eurobarometer 51.0, spring 1999.

of the gap between rich and poor stayed roughly constant from spring 1996 to spring 1999, rather than increasing or diminishing. During these years the EU Internet population grew at a rate of roughly 10 percent per annum but this did not lead to any closure of the digital divide by income. Finally, the comparison of societies that are leaders and laggards in the Information Age gives no support to the normalization thesis claim that income differentials necessarily diminish as Internet use widens throughout the population; if anything the reverse. Despite relatively widespread use of the Internet in Britain, for example, the most affluent households were five times more likely to be online than the poorest. The variations among European countries suggest that many factors within each nation may influence the income gap in Internet access, such as state initiatives to make wired computers widely available through community centers, unemployment offices, and schools, as well as levels of market competition driving down the financial costs of hardware, software, and access charges. But the differential between rich and poor families evident in such countries as Britain, Luxembourg, and Denmark mean that, at least during the emerging years, we would not expect the income gap to close automatically as the Internet diffuses more widely throughout society.

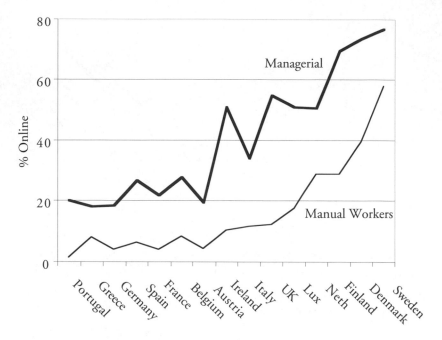

Figure 4.4. Percent Online by Occupation, EU-15 1999.
Source: Eurobarometer 51.0, spring 1999.

OCCUPATION

Related patterns in the workforce can also be expected to be important for many reasons. Professional and managerial jobs in the service sector facilitate 24/7 Internet connections at the office, often through high-speed LAN networks, as well as providing training assistance and technical support. Companies also commonly provide managers and executives with mobile equipment such as laptops, digital personal assistants, and cell phones, as well as subsidizing home access charges, to facilitate connectivity with the office. Professional, managerial, and executive salaries provide the resources to afford consumer durables like computers and high-speed cable connections for the home and family, and multiple-connection household intranets. In contrast, manual workers, although using computers as part of the industrial manufacturing process, are less likely to experience Internet access at work or to acquire the skills and experience in the workplace that breed comfort and familiarity with the Web at home. Governments in Britain, Germany, and Sweden have emphasized the need to bring the unemployed into the knowledge economy, through the provision of networked computers and training in job centers and unemployment offices. Nevertheless, even with these initiatives, those seeking work are likely to be among the most marginalized and poorest members of society. There are reasons to believe that occupational status may prove less important for Internet access as use diffuses more widely; during the last five years home access has doubled in America, with remarkably little increase in the proportion using the Internet from work.[24]

Figure 4.4 shows the distribution of Internet access by the respondent's occupation in the workforce in the fifteen member states of the EU. The pattern confirms that managers and professionals are almost twice as likely to use the Internet as those in other white-collar jobs including clerical assistants and service sector employees, and managers are almost three times as likely to use the Internet as manual workers. Access for the unemployed fell just below the level of manual workers. Again, the gap between the info-rich and poor varied across nations but it proved largest among certain leader societies including the United Kingdom, Finland, and Denmark, and slightly more marked than the disparities already observed by household income.

EDUCATION

The related divide in Internet use by educational attainment is well established in many American studies, where college graduates are among those most familiar with the Internet. Wilhelm, for example, concluded that education was a stronger determinant of connectivity in America than any other demographic or social variable.[25] Many reasons can be given for this pattern. Schools and colleges provide an environment that is exceptionally rich in all forms of info-tech and indeed these have usually been among the first institutions wired to the Net in most countries. Education can be expected to improve the general capacity for analytical reasoning and information filtering, which helps cope with the flow of information available online, as well as strengthening numeracy, literacy, English-language, and keyboard skills. Schools and colleges commonly provide students with free email and Web hosting facilities, computer labs, as well as direct hands-on experience of surfing the Internet for research, and training support or technical backup for using common software packages. College education is also closely related to subsequent occupational status and income, which we have already observed are important, as well as being linked to generational patterns of diffusion, illustrated by the popularity of programs for music sharing such as Napster on college campuses. Figure 4.5 illus-

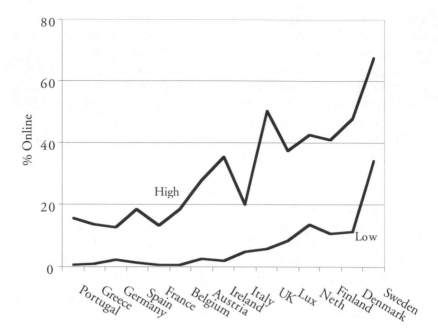

Figure 4.5. Percent Online by Education, EU-15 1999.
Source: Eurobarometer 51, spring 1999.

trates the relationship between the age of finishing education and use of the Internet in European member states. The results confirm the expected disparities by education, showing similar results to the inequalities evident in the workforce. In Europe, those with a college education are seven times more likely to be online than those who left school at 15. Indeed education proved one of the strongest predictors of connectivity: more than 40 percent of college students in Europe are online, a figure ranging up to 80 percent of all students in Sweden and Finland.

GENDER

The gender gap within the online community has been the subject of widespread study. Some surveys have reported that this difference has closed recently in America; for example the Pew Internet and American Life tracking survey suggested that by spring 2000 the surge in the number of women online had produced gender parity, although women and men continued to differ in their attitudes toward new technology and in their behavior online.[26] Nevertheless the evidence about the gender gap remains inconclusive; for example, AC Nielsen's *Net Watch* surveyed thir-

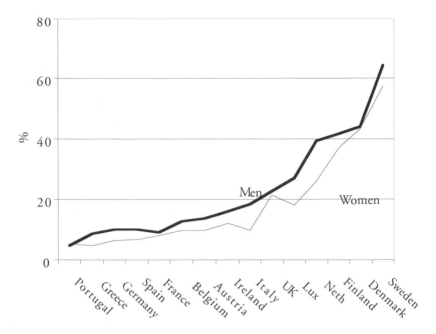

Figure 4.6. Percent Online by Gender, EU-15, 1999.
Source: Eurobarometer 51.0, spring 1999.

teen nations in North America, Europe, and Asia in spring 2000, and reported that women were less likely to be online in every country, including the United States, with almost twice as many male to female Internet users in Germany, Hong Kong, and Taiwan.[27] Many plausible reasons may account for any gender differences in use of computer technology and within the online community. Bolt and Crawford reviewed a wide range of evidence suggesting that girls and women are less likely to use computers because of their early experiences within school classrooms, reflecting long-standing gender differences in attitudes toward science and technology, as well as the typical contents of computer games and websites available for children.[28] The position of women as primary caregivers in the home and family may also play a role, since we have already observed the importance of work environments for Internet access. In Europe, the evidence on male and females within the online community in Figure 4.6 shows that the gender gap proves the weakest predictor of Internet use among all the factors we have considered so far, with the difference between women and men becoming statistically insignificant in Belgium, Denmark, France, Portugal, the United

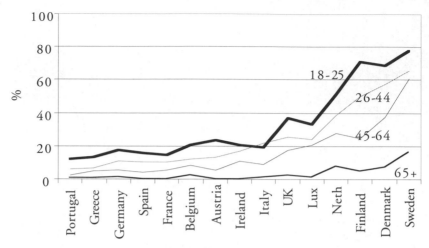

Figure 4.7. Percent Online by Age Group, EU-15, 1999.
Source: Eurobarometer 50.1.

Kingdom, and Finland. Nevertheless a significant online gender gap was evident elsewhere, especially in the Netherlands, Sweden, and Italy.

GENERATION

The generational difference in adaptation to new technologies is perhaps the most significant for the future diffusion of the Internet, and yet the most taken for granted in policy circles. The pattern in Figure 4.7 shows that early adopters in Europe were concentrated among the youngest age groups, with minimal use in most of Europe among senior citizens – this despite the fact that the Internet seems well suited to the needs of the elderly, as a fairly sedentary population with considerable leisure time, especially for social networking, hobbies, and services such as the home delivery of groceries. The typical age profile may flatten in future because there is a large potential market among the elderly if access to the Internet becomes more commonly delivered through dedicated plug-and-play email units, and services like Web-TV, rather than via more technically demanding computers. At present, the online community in Europe largely excludes the retired population. The generation gap within the Nordic region, where the Internet has penetrated most widely, proves the largest of any social cleavage observed so far. The youngest group is ten times as likely to be online than the oldest group; overall almost a one-third of all Europeans under 25 are online, compared with only 3 percent of the over-65 year-olds. The Napster

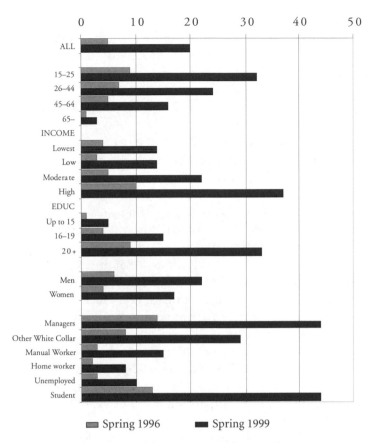

Figure 4.8. Change in the Percent Online by Social Group, EU-15.
Source: Eurobarometers 1996 and 1999.

generation is already experiencing a virtual world as they develop that is different from formative lives of their parents and grandparents.

The evidence so far suggests that the familiar social profile of online users in the United States is also evident throughout Western Europe. Trends in these societies since the mid-1990s confirm that, contrary to the "normalization" thesis, the resource-based inequalities that we have already observed grew in significance as Internet use gradually diffused more widely (Figure 4.8). Multivariate analysis predicting use of the Internet in spring 1996 and 1999 helps to distinguish the relative weight of the factors discussed so far and confirms the significance of these patterns. The order of the variables in the OLS regression models followed the standard logic of the classic "funnel of causality".[29] The demographic variables of age and gender were entered first, followed by the resource variables of household income, education, and the respondent's occupation, the latter coded as manual or nonmanual. The country variables were then entered as dummy variables (0/1) to determine if the national differences in Internet use remain significant even after controlling for social background.

The results of the models confirm that all the demographic factors discussed in this chapter were significantly associated with Internet use in Europe (see Table 4.3). In particular, the gender and age differences remained significant predictors of Internet use even after controlling for income, education, and occupation, suggesting that resources are only one part of the explanation here. Moreover the national-level country variables usually continued to be significant, even after controlling for social background. This indicates that the structure of opportunities within each nation (discussed in the previous chapter) influences Internet use even after controlling for individual-level differences in occupation and income. For example, a well-paid college-educated company manager living in Stockholm or Copenhagen would still be more likely to surf the Web or use email than an equivalent colleague working in Madrid or Athens. The macrolevel context is important, including such factors as state initiatives to widen access through education and training, and market competition in the pricing of computer hardware and ISP connectivity.

Turning to the analysis of changes over time, the comparison of the same models run in 1996 and 1999 demonstrate that, far from equalizing, the digital divide in Europe expanded during these years; the inequalities of access by income, education, occupational status, and age become stronger and only the gender gap weakened over time. It is likely that the social profile of users may possibly flatten further within the next decade, if Internet access spreads even more widely to become ubiquitous in almost all European households, as commonplace as a VCR or refrigerator. Nothing that we have said disproves the claims that the "normalization" thesis could still be true in the longer-term. But the European evidence indicates a growing digital divide between the information-rich and poor during the emergent Internet era, in addition to the widening North–South global disparities documented in the previous chapter, with no evidence to date that these gaps are starting to close or normalize in leading societies where use of the Internet has become most pervasive.

RELATIVE INEQUALITIES IN THE INFORMATION SOCIETY

The fact that there are absolute differences in access to the Internet is hardly surprising. However, the question remains whether the *relative* disparities in access to the Internet are substantially different or similar to the distribution of other common forms of information and communication technology, such as VCRs and cable TV. Like gambling at Rick's bar, some popular accounts are shocked – *shocked* – to discover social inequalities on the Internet. We should not be. As in the previous chapter, the more realistic approach compares relative inequalities in computers access and Internet use with disparities in the distribution of other common forms of information technologies. The spring 1999 Eurobarometer survey monitored whether people had access to or used ten different types of information technology, including the Internet, as well as VCRs, facsimile machines, and personal computers. If we establish that patterns of income, educational, or occupational inequalities are similar across all types of communication and information technologies, then this suggests broad explanations of this phenomenon relating to deep-rooted patterns of social stratification endemic in modern societies. Households with Internet access can be expected to possess multiple consumer durables for entertainment and communications, such as satellite or cable TVs, pagers and fax machines, home entertainment centers, and mobile phones. Conversely, if the distribution of Internet access differs from use of other types of info-tech, then we should search for explanations based on the distinctive characteristics of the Internet per se, such as the financial costs of gaining online access, the cognitive skills and computing experience required for surfing, language barriers to use of the Web in non–English-speaking countries, and the way people respond to the type of materials and services available online (e.g., music, entertainment, and shopping). Both relative and absolute inequalities can be regarded as equally important, but the analysis of the former provides deeper insights into the causes of this phenomenon and therefore also its potential solution.

The correlations shown in Table 4.4 indicate that Internet use is significantly associated with access to all forms of communication technologies, including noncomputer related machines such as VCRs and cable TV. Reflecting parallel patterns at national level documented in the previous chapter, this suggests that individuals living in affluent households with many different forms of consumer durables designed for traditional forms of home entertainment and communication are also

Table 4.4. *Explaining Internet use in Europe, 1996 and 1999*

	1996			1999		
	R	Sig.	B	R	Sig.	B
Demographics						
Age	−.085	.000	−.035	−.168	.000	−.642
Gender	.058	.000	.588	.052	.000	.327
Resources						
Education	.095	.000	.303	.153	.000	.609
Income	.055	.000	.783	.141	.000	.439
Class	.056	.000	.827	.077	.000	.574
Nation						
Greece	−.035	.000	−1.43	−.073	.000	−1.72
Germany	−.006	.849	−.035	−.067	.000	−1.30
France	−.037	.000	−.774	−.057	.000	−1.24
Spain	−.027	.000	−1.03	−.055	.000	−1.36
Portugal	−.007	.012	−.563	−.054	.000	−1.44
Belgium	−.015	.000	−.628	−.052	.000	−1.20
Austria	−.001	.923	.020	−.041	.000	−.93
Italy	−.018	.000	−.507	−.036	.000	−.91
Ireland	.010	.104	.359	−.029	.000	−.73
United Kingdom	.069	.000	.966	.000	.432	.23
Netherlands	.035	.000	.578	.021	.000	.45
Finland	.055	.000	.784	.035	.000	.65
Denmark	.038	.000	.573	.049	.000	.89
Sweden	.068	.000		.099	.000	1.77
Cox-Snell R2	.073			.278		
Nagelkerke R2	.209			.431		
Percent correct	94.5			83.8		

Notes: The table reports the coefficients predicting the use of the Internet based on binary logistic regression models. Use of the Internet is measured as a dichotomy where 1 = yes and 0 = no. Luxembourg, which is close to the Europe mean, is excluded from the standardized household income scale. Age in measured in years. Education is measured as years finished full-time education. Income is measured from the standardized household income scale. Class is based on the manual/nonmanual occupation for the head of household. Gender is 1 = male and 0 = female.

Source: Eurobarometer 47, spring 1996 (No. 65178) and spring 1999.

Table 4.5. *Use of new and old media in Europe, 1999*

	Inter-net	Com-puter	CD ROM	Modem	VCR	Fax	Sat. TV	Cable TV	Video-text
Computer	**0.61**								
CD-ROM	**0.59**	**0.70**							
Modem	**0.91**	**0.67**	**0.65**						
VCR	0.19	0.31	0.26	0.21					
Fax	0.44	0.45	0.43	0.47	0.22				
Satellite TV	0.12	0.14	0.13	0.12	0.12	0.13			
Cable TV	0.14	0.16	0.16	0.15	0.15	0.14	0.24		
Teletext TV	0.19	0.25	0.22	0.21	0.32	0.18	0.16	0.10	
Videotext	0.09	0.12	0.11	0.11	0.07	0.14	0.06	0.13	−0.02

Note: Q: "*Do you use, or do you have access to…*" The figures represent individual-level simple correlations (R) without any controls.
Source: Eurobarometer 51.0, spring 1999 EU-15.

most likely to access networked computers. As we saw in the previous chapter, ownership of personal computers is related to all sorts of other common household gadgets from deep-fat fryers to video cameras and clock radios. There can obviously be many exceptions; for example, less affluent students, low-paid service professionals, and office clerical workers are commonly in work environments where the Internet is easily available even if they lack home access. Nevertheless, the association between use of computer and other types of household consumer durables implies that broad and deep-rooted patterns of social stratification are the major explanation for patterns of Internet diffusion.

To test this further, multivariate models were run as before with three dependent variables, the percentage of the population using the Internet (% Online), a broader New Media index summarizing access to a computer, CD-ROM, and modem, as well as the Internet, and an Old Media index including access to traditional technologies, including a VCR, fax, satellite TV, cable TV, teletext TV, and videotext. Most strikingly, comparison of the results across all three models shows that similar social and demographic factors explaining online participation also help predict access to new *and* old media technologies (see Table 4.6). The digital divide is striking but far from new. The relative strength of the coefficients varied slightly across models; for example, education and occupation were slightly more strongly associated with the new

Table 4.6. *Explaining use of new and old media in Europe, 1999*

	Percent Online		New media		Old media	
	Beta	Sig.	Beta	Sig.	Beta	Sig.
Demographic						
Age (years)	−0.12**		−0.16**		−0.18**	
Gender (male)	0.06**		0.05**		0.07**	
Resources						
HH income	0.16**		0.21**		0.25**	
Education	0.12**		0.15**		0.06**	
Manual occupation	0.09**		0.12**		0.06**	
Region						
North (1) South (0)	0.23**		0.21**		0.25**	
Constant	0.21		0.81		2.19	
Adjusted R^2	0.19		0.26		0.24	

** Sig. > *p.* = .01

Notes: The figures represent standardized beta coefficients using OLS regression models. **Percent Online:** Have access to or use the Internet or World Wide Web (0 = no/1 = yes). **New Media Index:** four-point scale measuring use or access to computer plus CD-ROM plus modem plus Internet. **Old Media Index:** six-point scale measuring use or access to VCR plus Fax plus Satellite TV plus Cable TV plus Teletext plus Videotext.

Source: Eurobarometer 51.0, spring 1999.

than old media. Nevertheless the headline finding concerns the striking similarities across models. This pattern confirms that important social inequalities exist in the virtual world. Since the mid-1990s, the global divide between leader and laggard nations, and the social divide among subpopulations even within leader nations, have expanded substantially. In Europe, as in the United States, the sweeping tide of the Internet has left behind many poorer households, manual workers, the less educated, the elderly, and women. Yet, there is nothing distinctive about these social and regional inequalities in the virtual world, which also characterize access to the Information Society delivered via older media technologies such as cable or satellite TV, VCRs, and fax machines. We may be less concerned about the implications of lack of access to cable TV or VCRs than lack of access to the Internet, but this insight has important implications for policy initiatives designed to overcome the social barriers to digital access. The results suggest that such programs as training in keyboard skills or wiring schools may help to overcome the digital divide but they are likely to have limited effect given the deep-rooted socioeconomic barriers to access.

At the same time it is true that in the emerging knowledge economy the evidence of trends in Internet use remains limited, and we remain at the bottom of the diffusion curve. The situation could change in the near future and the social profile of the online community could be transformed if costs fall dramatically, driven by the proliferation of subscription-free and unmetered access services, greater competition, and the increasing availability of broadband services, as many predict.[30] Companies also forecast a proliferation of Web appliances delivering a cut-down version of the Internet outside the box. Although there are reasons to be skeptic about industry hype, eTForecast estimate that there are currently 21.5 million Web-enabled appliances in use globally, such as cell phones and personal assistants. The projected figures for 2005 are 596 million globally: 115.4 million for the United States and 126.4 million for Western Europe. Web delivery via mobile phones has proved particularly popular in Japan where home PCs are not common.[31] The popular distribution of powerful but relatively inexpensive units such as Play Station II also facilitates new ways of accessing the Internet. The consequences of these developments for the digital divide remain to be determined but their lower costs could help close the divide.[32]

CONCLUSIONS: SOCIAL STRATIFICATION AND INTERNET ACCESS

The explanation for the digital divide is often assumed to lie in certain characteristics of this technology, such as the need for computing skills and affordable online connections. The policy solutions designed to ameliorate the digital divide commonly focus on just these sorts of fixes, such as wiring schools and classrooms, training teachers, and providing community access in poorer neighborhoods. Certainly this can do no harm. But will these initiatives work in terms of diversifying the online population? The results of this analysis suggest that, unfortunately, it seems unlikely. The policy fixes are too specific, the problem of social inequalities too endemic.

The analysis in this chapter demonstrates that the heart of the problem lies in broader patterns of social stratification that shape not just access to the virtual world, but also full participation in other common forms of information and communication technologies. The results suggest that there is no need to try to explain the online gender gap, for example, by theories specific to this type of technology, such as women's supposed "computer phobia," attitudes toward computers in the classroom, or the lack of nonaggressive computer games and websites suitable for young girls. All this may, or may not, be true. But it turns out that these are flimsy general explanations for why fewer women than men are online, because women are also less likely than men to have access to technologies delivering mass entertainment such as cable TV and VCRs. Even in affluent societies, poorer families lacking such common consumer durables as cable TV, VCRs, and automobiles are likely to lack Internet access as well.

In the longer run, technological and economic developments may well alter the market for Internet access, reducing costs, simplifying technical skills, and thereby widening usage. Generational trends are likely to be particularly important in terms of the long-term patterns of use, as younger groups eventually replace the older population. Public policy initiatives such as wiring all schools are likely to contribute to ameliorating some of the major disparities in computing skills and knowledge. Nevertheless none of these developments is likely to alter long-established patterns of social stratification in the short-term. Moreover, even if the Internet eventually reaches 85 to 95 percent of the population, there are still multiple layers of access and use. TV sets essentially come in only a couple of flavors. The box can be bigger or smaller, analog or digital, single speaker or home theater, cheaper or more expensive, and so on, but basically a TV is a TV is a TV, making no demands beyond how to switch the power button, with perhaps 100+ channels but still nothing to watch. In contrast, levels of Internet access can vary substantially. Today people living in poorer neighborhoods may be able to surf the Web from public libraries, schools, and community centers, or even cyber cafés, but this is not the same as having automatic access via high-speed connections at home and the office. Nor is it the same as having all Internet, all the time, downloadable via personal appliances, digital assistants, and cellular phones for today's wired road warriors in planes, ships, and trains. Internet technology is not going to stand still as long as the market continues to demand ever smaller, faster, and improved forms of delivery. Subsequent chapters go on to explore the underlying reasons for the social inequalities established here, and the broader implications for civic engagement and political participation in the digital age.

PART II

The Virtual Political System

Early in the next millennium your right and left cuff links or earnings may communicate with each other by low-orbiting satellites and have more computer power than your present PC. Mass Media will be redefined by systems for transmitting and receiving personalized information and entertainment. Schools will change to become more like museums and playgrounds for children to assemble ideas and socialize with children from all over the world. The digital planet will look and feel like the head of a pin.
Nicholas Negroponte, *Being Digital* (1995)

Politics on the Internet is politics as usual conducted mostly by familiar parties, candidates, interest groups and news media.
Margolis and Resnick, *Politics as Usual* (2000) p. vii.

CHAPTER 5

Theories of Digital Democracy

Previous chapters have examined the technological environment, including the worldwide distribution and social profile of users, concluding that at present the Internet has provided alternative channels of communication primarily for countries and groups already rich in informational resources. In this view the Internet, like cable TV, mobile phones, and fax machines before it, connects the connected more than the peripheral. The global reach, instantaneous speed, and limitless information available via the Internet has the potential to serve a far wider and more diverse community worldwide – providing a cornucopia of textbooks for Nigerian classrooms, a rich database of the latest medical research for Romanian hospitals, and a global shop window for Balinese art and Bangalore software – but widespread popular access requires reduced financial barriers. Initiatives to wire poorer communities through public libraries, schools, and community centers can aid diffusion, as can Internet cafés, and linkages via managerial, administrative, and professional elites. But the fact that telephones, radios, and televisions have not yet become standard items in poorer households around the world casts a skeptical light on the rosier scenarios projecting widespread connectivity for ordinary citizens in developing societies.

Building on this foundation, this section of the book starts to explore the virtual political system that is emerging, meaning the way that governments and civic societies are in the process of adapting to information technologies, and the structure of political opportunities this creates for active citizenship and civic engagement. Throughout this section the study focuses on three core issues: Where and what type of political institutions are moving online? What are the functions of these political websites for maximizing transparent information and interactive communication? And what explains the rise of digital politics, in particular how far does socioeconomic, technological, and political development drive this process? The virtual political system can be understood to mirror that in the nondigital world, using a conventional system model in which civic society – including political parties, traditional interest groups and new social movements, and the news media – mediate between citizens and the state (Figure 5.1). These institutions are understood to funnel demands upward toward parliaments and government executives, in an agenda-setting and agenda-building role, as well as funneling information about government downward toward the public. Understood in this way, what will be the overall impact of the information society on governments and civic society? As with accounts of the global and social divides, interpretations offer sharply differing visions about the causes and consequences of digital politics.

THE INTERNET AND DEMOCRACY

It has become commonplace to suggest that the Western public has become more and more disenchanted with the traditional institutions of representative government, detached from political parties, and disillusioned with older forms of civic engagement and participation.[1] Putnam argues that the process of generational change in American has eroded the mass membership of voluntary associations and reduced social capital, debilitating the ability of communities to work together to solve common problems.[2] Political parties represent the core institution linking citizens and the state, yet many have seen their membership rolls wane and the public seems increasingly detached from partisan politics.[3] While a broad "crisis of democracy" has proved exaggerated, nevertheless indicators suggest increasing numbers of "critical citizens" characterized by high expectations of democracy as an ideal and yet low evaluations of the actual performance of representative institutions.[4] For advocates of direct democracy, such as Benjamin Barber, these indicators suggest that the forms of governance in the nation-state need to evolve to allow more opportunities for citizen deliberation and direct decisionmaking, with greater use of referendums and initiatives, devolution of power to community organizations, and grassroots mobilization to solve local problems.[5]

Cyber-optimists regard digital technologies as perhaps the most important development in our lifetimes that could potentially fuel this process.[6] It is hoped that the almost limitless information available via the Internet has the potential to allow the public to become more

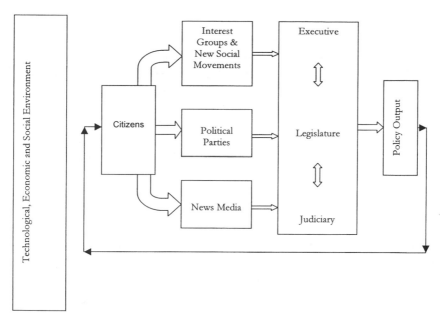

Figure 5.1. The Virtual Political System.

knowledgeable about public affairs, more articulate in expressing their views via email, online discussion lists or chat rooms, and more active in mobilizing around community affairs.[7] As a new channel of two-way communication, the Internet can function to strengthen and enrich the connections between citizens and intermediary organizations including political parties, social movements and interest groups, and the news media, as well as with public officials and agencies of local, national, and global governance. The Internet may broaden involvement in public life by eroding some of the barriers to political participation and civic engagement, especially for many groups currently marginalized from mainstream politics, facilitating the ability of citizens to gather information about campaign issues, to mobilize community networks, to network diverse coalitions around policy problems, and to lobby elected representatives. Bulletin board systems, chat groups, listservs, email, and multi-user domains represent a new public sphere available to exchange ideas, debate issues, and mobilize opinion.[8] The Internet could facilitate opportunities for direct democracy, like electronic voting for referenda and elections,[9] may help promote government accountability, as well as reviving community networks and urban neighborhoods.[10] In all these ways, the Internet offers to reconnect people to the political process and revive flagging civic energies.

In contrast cyber-skeptics suggest that in practice use of digital technologies will fail to transform existing patterns of democratic participation, and more pessimistic prognostications suggest that the Internet will even widen the gap between the engaged and the apathetic. At an institutional level, Margolis and Resnick conclude that the early hopes for an Internet-generated democratic revival have failed to be fulfilled in America as established interests including the major parties, traditional interest groups, and heavyweight media corporations have reasserted their predominance in the virtual world, producing "politics as usual".[11] Cyber-space may be dominated by multinational corporate players such as AOL, Yahoo!, and Bertelsmann, offering commercial entertainment and kowtowing to King Dollar, together with established mass media sources like CNN and the *New York Times*.[12] Putnam suggests that virtual or mediated forms of political and social communications may be an inadequate substitute for traditional face-to-face social networks in local communities, since virtual contact may preclude the face-to-face signals that build social trust, although the Internet may be a valuable supplement to traditional forms of communication.[13] The global and social divides in Internet access mean that technological resources remain far from equally distributed and online politics may thereby amplify the voice of the affluent and well educated, with the prior interest, cognitive skills, and technical ability to utilize new forms of communication, but it may also further marginalize the apathetic and underprivileged.[14] Socioeconomic biases evident for decades in conventional forms of political participation like voting seem unlikely to disappear in the virtual world, even if access gradually widens to the digital have-nots.[15] Americans who participate in online discussion groups may be an atypical minority, dominated by like-minded groups controlling the agenda, thereby reinforcing views but not exchanging ideas in deliberative mode.[16] Electronic messages may be similar to those already communicated face-to-face or through other media like newspapers and television, changing the form and medium of transmission but not its contents.[17] Plebiscitory democracy via instant electronic voting may also prove to be nothing more than simple head counting without opportunities for deliberative and thoughtful debate.[18] More political information is available via the Internet but without much prior interest or knowledge most people may be swamped by this experience.[19] The closest analogy to politics on the Web could be C-Span on

American TV, available to two-thirds of U.S. households, delivering worthy public affairs seminars, live and unedited campaign speeches, and informed commentary primarily to a small band of hard-core inside-the-beltway political aficionados. For all these reasons, although many hope that digital technologies will generate more egalitarian politics in America and Western Europe, other skeptical voices warn that in practice established interests will probably come to predominate.

The Internet and Democratization

Serious problems of civic engagement afflict established democracies but the multiple challenges currently facing newer democracies are far more serious. Many hope that in these systems the Internet can help the consolidation process by strengthening the institutions of representative democracy including parliaments and political parties, fostering linkages among new social movements and enriching community networks in civic society, as well as providing a platform for opposition parties, protest groups, and minorities seeking to challenge authoritarian regimes.[20] Since 1973 the "third wave" of democracy has transformed the geopolitical map and greatly expanded the universe of "electoral democracies." According to Freedom House, we are currently experiencing a high watermark for democracy: There are more democracies in the world today (120), and the highest proportion of democratic states (63 percent), than ever before in history.[21] Nevertheless the initial giddy optimism following the fall of the Berlin Wall has now been replaced by a more cautious ambience. During the mid-1990s the surge in the number of democratic states worldwide stabilized rather than expanded. In semi-democracies the consolidation stage proved sobering and fraught with obstacles, especially throughout much of Sub-Saharan Africa, Latin America, and Asia. Semi-democracies faced the challenge of the triple transformation of their nation-state, economic structures, and political systems. Outside of wealthy industrialized nations, the quality of democratic government often remains flawed, poorly institutionalized, and insecure. Many "incomplete," "partly-free," or "semi-democracies" remain weakly consolidated, with leaders rising to power via competitive periodic elections contested by more than one party, yet plagued by multiple and endemic problems.[22] These commonly include widespread corruption untrammeled by the weak judiciary, and the abuse of political rights and civil liberties such as government curbs on the independent media. The party system is often highly fragmented, with party organizations factionalized and lacking a grassroots electoral base. Legislatures are often poorly institutionalized, providing few effective checks on government. All this has often been accompanied by a record of economic failure and poverty, inadequate delivery of basic services including education and health care, and periodic violence against minorities arising from deep ethnic cleavages. Occasionally semi-democracies have at least faltered or even reverted back to authoritarian rule and the façade of electoral democracy has cracked, notably in Algeria, Zimbabwe, Peru, Venezuela, and Ecuador, with coups against elected governments in Fiji, Western Samoa, and Pakistan. Whether these developments constitute the normal unsteady history of democratization characterized by "two steps forward and one step back," or the start of a third "reverse wave" of democracy, remains an open question at this stage of the process.[23] Despite occasional reversions, and the continued lack of significant and sustained progress in regions such as Africa and the Middle East, the critical problem facing most consolidating systems at the end of the twentieth century concerns the flawed and incomplete quality of democratic government.

Potentially the role of digital technologies may be equally important in challenging authoritarian regimes. Governments can try to monitor and control the Internet, and Freedom House estimates that at least twenty nations have seen some attempt at censorship.[24] Problems of restricted Internet access for dissident groups are evident in authoritarian regimes such as Cuba and China.[25] Nevertheless officials normally find it far more difficult to silence critical voices on the new media compared with their ability to regulate and control the TV airwaves. Independent journalism benefits from the relatively low start-up and production costs for an online weekly newsletter or daily newspaper, compared with production and distribution costs of the printed press, or the capital investments required for radio or TV stations. Where civic society is weak, case studies ranging from the Baltic to Serbia suggest that the Internet facilitates coalitional networks linking new social movements, interest groups, and NGOs.[26] Hill and Hughes examined the contents of political messages posted on a sample of Usenet groups and found that these provide an electronic public space facilitating political discussion for antigovernment voices critical of authoritarian regimes.[27] Cases like the antilandmines campaign and the protest movements against the WTO, antifuel taxes, and genetically modified foods show the potential of computer-mediated communications for linking borderless worldwide coalitions.[28] Brophy and Halpin argue that freedom of information on the Internet may play a vital role in strengthening human rights.[29] Perhaps the strongest case is made by Christopher Kedzie, who examined the relationship between levels of democratization (as measured by Freedom House) and interconnectivity (gauged by access to email) in 141 countries worldwide in 1993.[30] The study found a strong correlation between democratization and interconnectivity, even controlling for economic development, although the direction of this relationship remains an open question.[31]

Despite this evidence, there remain fears that given the pattern of unequal access already documented, the new opportunities for civic engagement and political participation on the Internet will serve primarily to benefit those elites with the resources and motivation to take advantage of them, leaving poorer groups and nations farther behind.[32] The potential for democratization will be restricted if few have access to the World Wide Web in Nigeria, Indonesia, or Ecuador. In authoritarian regimes such as Burma, Libya, and Cuba, the Internet may serve as a traditional agency of state propaganda, strengthening the government's grip, rather than providing a channel for opposition parties and groups. Protest movements can try to utilize the Internet to network and mobilize public opinion, but multinational corporations and international agencies can fight back with all their financial and organizational muscle using the same communication channels. Like the power of gunpowder in the Middle Ages, the Internet exerts the greatest force if the battle is one-sided, which is rarely the case today. Digital technologies may appear egalitarian, a resource for alternative social movements and transnational advocacy networks, but in practice they may strengthen the power of entrenched authorities, multinational corporations, and established officials, rather than challenging them.

EVALUATING THE DEMOCRATIC FUNCTIONS OF THE INTERNET

Before evaluating the potential impact of digital technologies on democracy and democratization, and which of these perspectives seems most convincing, we need to establish suitable normative benchmarks. Many previous studies start from an unduly narrow perspective, based on the assumption that the Internet should function to maximize individual opportunities for participation and deliberation and that, if it fails in this regard, digital technologies will have minimal impact on democracy. Of course, mass public participation represents *one* important element in any conceptualization of democracy but it is far from the only, or even the most important, evaluative criteria. In contrast, in line with my previous work the theory in this book is rooted in the classical Schumpeterian tradition that defines representative or liberal democracy in terms of its structural or institutional characteristics.[33] Understood in this way, representative democracy involves three dimensions:

- **Pluralistic competition** among parties and individuals for all positions of government power;
- **Participation** among equal citizens in the selection of parties and representatives through free, fair, and periodic elections; and,
- **Civil and political liberties** to speak, publish, assemble, and organize, as necessary conditions to ensure effective competition and participation.

This conceptualization focuses particularly on how representative democracies function through free and fair elections, as the primary mechanism for holding governments accountable for their actions. Representative democracies require competition for elected office allowing citizens to choose from among alternative candidates and parties. Multiple sources of information should be available in civic society so that citizens can understand the alternative electoral choices, can evaluate the performance of those in authority, and can predict the consequences of casting their ballot. In elections, citizens need opportunities to formulate their preferences, communicate their preferences, and have their preferences weighted equally in the conduct of government. Transparency in government decisionmaking, where it is clear who is responsible for what, promotes accountability via the ballot box. Free and fair elections need to occur at regular intervals to translate popular votes into positions in elected office, and to allow alternation of government authorities. If these conditions are met, citizens can exercise an informed choice, hold governments, parties, and representatives accountable for their actions and, if necessary, "kick the rascals out."

Of course, many other definitions are available, especially those based on alternative conceptions of "direct," "strong," or "plebiscitory" democracy which envisage a direct role for citizens in the decisionmaking process, so why adopt this one? The Schumpeterian perspective reflects one of the most widely accepted understandings of how representative institutions should function in a democracy, thereby providing important insights into the role of parties, legislatures, and civic society, as well as the individual role of citizens.[34] It has the advantage of being widely used for cross-national and longitudinal comparisons attempting to measure and operationalize democratic indicators, for example as measured by the Gastil Index which Freedom House has published annually since the early 1970s, ranking countries worldwide.[35] Moreover, most important, in contrast to many other accounts, this view weighs the value of mass participation as only *one* of the core democratic functions of politics on the Internet. Promoting the conditions of party and candidate competition, facilitating the public sphere via the news media, mobilizing civic society, promoting transparency and accountability in the decisionmaking process, and strengthening the effective delivery of government services to citizens, are regarded as equally valuable potential functions of the Internet that can strengthen representative democracies. Indeed, these may prove even more important functions than levels of mass participation, especially in nations ruled by authoritarian and transitional regimes. Electoral democracies may mobilize high levels of voter turnout, but other political rights and civil liberties will fail to flourish if civil society is fragmented and weak, if representative institutions are poorly consolidated, if there is minimal competition between parties providing voters with a real choice at elections and the alternation of those in power, if there is widespread government corruption and the breakdown of the rule of law, or the suppression of opposition movement and dissident voices among NGOs. Insurgent challengers must be able to compete against established authorities.

This study therefore departs from much of the previous literature in the United States and Western Europe, which often assumes that the Internet will only strengthen democracy if it expands opportunities for political participation, such as direct citizen decisionmaking and deliberation in the policy process, or electronic voting. Many conclude that if the Internet fails in these regards, then digital technologies will have minimal impact on democracy and democratization. But this is an unduly limited, and thereby misleading, normative yardstick. A broader vision about the ways that digital technologies can strengthen the institutions of representative government and civil society seems more appropriate as soon as we look beyond the rather narrow navel gazing of rich established Western democracies to many polities such as Russia, Indonesia, and Peru struggling, (with mixed success) to establish effective party competition. Such competition allows for the stable rotation of power between government and opposition, opposition parties, interest groups, and new social movements capable of organizing, mobilizing, and articulating public opinion through multiple channels connecting citizens and the state, and the basic conditions of human rights and civil liberties to facilitate the open expression of dissenting viewpoints critical of the authorities. In most societies throughout the world it is the core institutions of representative government and civic society that urgently need to be nurtured and strengthened.[36] The extensive debate about the role of digital technologies for direct or strong democracy in the United States and Western Europe can be regarded as a distracting irrelevance, a buzzing mosquito, deflecting attention from the potential function of Internet in strengthening the institutions of representative governance and civic societies worldwide.

This understanding of representative democracy is outlined schematically in Figure 5.1, which uses a basic systems model to conceptualize the role of intermediary organizations linking citizens and the state. Working within this framework, the key issue when evaluating the role of digital technologies for democracy is how much governments and civic society learn to use the opportunities provided by the new channels of *information* and *communication* to promote and strengthen the core representative institutions connecting citizens and the state. In this regard, opportunities for public participation and civic engagement generated via new technology are important, as is the ability of the Internet to provide information promoting the transparency, openness, and accountability of governing agencies at national and international levels, and to strengthen channels of interactive communication between citizens and intermediary institutions. These functions remain distinct, and the emerging structure of political opportunities via the Internet may prove better suited for some functions rather than others. For example, the Internet could plausibly provide a better tool of campaign communications for minor parties than the traditional mass media such as newspapers, radio, and television, or it could facilitate more effective means of global networking and cooperation linking transnational NGOs across borders. It could also provide journalists more extensive and timely access to information such as official documents and current legislative proposals, or it could strengthen internal party organizations and communications for middle-level party activists – all functions that could ultimately benefit representative democracy – without necessarily promoting greater activism and civic engagement among ordinary citizens and the general public.

WHAT EXPLAINS THE RISE OF DIGITAL POLITICS?

DEVELOPMENTAL THEORIES

Determining why some countries have moved ahead in digital politics while others lag behind raises complex issues, and developmental, technological, and democratic theories provide alternative frameworks for interpreting this phenomenon. There are multiple strands within developmental accounts but the classic work is Daniel Bell's theory of the rise of the postindustrial Information Society.[37] Explanations emphasizing the role of development emphasize long-term secular changes in the economic structure that drive social and political change. The rise of the knowledge economy is associated with the shift in the labor force from agriculture and manufacturing industry toward the service sector, and the parallel shift in resources from the importance of raw materials and financial capital toward information and know-how. The knowledge economy is heavily dependent on modern global communications, such as the multinational corporations in financial investment, banking, and insurance. As computers, high-speed LAN networks and wireless communications become ubiquitous throughout service work in the private sector; for example in advanced economies such as Sweden, Australia, and the United States, use of digital technologies gradually spreads from offices to homes, facilitating such services as home shopping, banking, and entertainment. Moreover, the rise of the knowledge economy is dependent on widespread computer literacy and a large, well-educated professional and managerial middle-class in a broad array of jobs related to information, ranging from programmers and software engineers to teachers, researchers, and financial analysts. Computing skills and training are spread through higher education. In this account, structural changes in the workforce and society associated with socioeconomic development will therefore provide the underlying conditions most conducive to widespread access to, and use of, digital information and communication technologies. In turn, as the general population gradually becomes wired, greater incentives are created for public-sector institutions to invest in forms of service delivery and communications via digital channels. If socioeconomic development per se creates the underlying conditions most conducive to the networked world, then according to this theory we should expect to find that political institutions such as government departments, political parties, and interest groups have moved online most extensively in affluent postindustrial societies.

TECHNOLOGICAL THEORIES

Developmental explanations are common but they are problematical, because, by themselves, they cannot plausibly explain certain apparent anomalies; why, for example, relatively similar postindustrial societies currently show strikingly different levels of Internet access and use in the general public, such as the contrasts between Finland and France, or Greece and Sweden, or Japan and the United States. Nor can they provide convincing accounts of even greater differences in the spread of digital politics, shown in subsequent chapters; for example, the way that some developing countries such as India, Taiwan, and Brazil have moved ahead so rapidly in e-governance, overtaking many postindustrial societies in the process. An alternative interpretation is provided by accounts which emphasize that political and social organizations are responding to adaptations and uses of digital communication and information technologies that are, at least to some extent, autonomous of levels of socioeconomic development. This perspective reflects a long tradition of theories based on the assumption that technologies shape society more than society shapes technologies. Again there are multiple perspectives within this interpretation, including both stronger and weaker versions of technological determinism, and accounts such as that by Nicholas Negroponte exemplify this viewpoint.[38] These theories emphasize that governments and civic society have ventured online in countries where a suitable technological infrastructure has developed – such as the widespread availability of landlines and cellular telephones, facilities for broadband delivery via cable television, high levels of investment in science and technology research and development, and the location of high-tech industries and companies – all of which facilitate the networked society. As established in earlier chapters, countries with an environment rich in access to many traditional forms of communication technologies, such as telephones, televisions, and fax machines, are also most likely to experience the diffusion of the Internet. Technological development directly influences how far political organizations can go to provide online services and information, and indirectly produces greater incentives for political organizations to do so, as the general public gradually becomes wired. If this account is correct, then studies should expect to find that digital politics has spread most fully in countries with high levels of technological infrastructure, at whatever level of socioeconomic development. In this case, the proportion of government and civic society organizations that have moved online should be predicted by technological indicators such as the distribution of Internet users and hosts.

THEORIES OF DEMOCRATIZATION

Both the developmental and the technological accounts regard the virtual political system as the superstructure based on and driven by more deep-rooted structural phenomena. Such theories suggest that, for example, e-governance will be as advanced in Singapore as in Sweden, or that community groups and grassroots civic associations will be as active and prolific on the Web in Malaysia as in Mexico. Yet there are multiple critiques of strong versions of technological determinism, on the grounds that social and political choices shape the uses of the Internet far more than the hardware and software.[39] As already discussed, new technologies allow greater transparency in the policy-making process, wider public participation in decisionmaking, and new opportunities for interaction and mobilization in election campaigns, but, critics argue, whether these potentialities are realized depends on how the technology is employed. If the process of democratization plays an important role, as political theories suggest, then the type of political organizations found on the Internet, and in particular the function of these websites in promoting transparent information and interactive communications, can be expected to reflect levels of pluralistic competition, political participation, and political rights and civil liberties within each political system. In this account, virtual politics will mirror the traditional political system, so that there will be far more opportunities for civic deliberation and public debate, for group mobilization and for party activism on the Internet in established democracies and open societies with a long tradition of civic engagement and pluralistic competition than in authoritarian regimes that suppress dissident voices (such as opposition movements, the independent press and protest groups), or in consolidating democracies that are still struggling with weak and fragmented civic societies, poorly institutionalized legislatures, factionalized party systems, and the lack of a flourishing independent news media. If this account is correct, then the diffusion and functions of digital politics within each country should be able to be predicted by overall levels of democratization.

Although each of these accounts emphasizes different factors, it remains difficult to test these theories owing to the strong relationship between levels of economic and political development. Theoretically, even with the most rigorous statistical models, with cross-sectional rather than time-series data it is difficult to disentangle the causal sequence involved in this relationship, and a full exploration of this issue would carry us well beyond the scope of this study.[40] As Seymour

Martin Lipset, among others, has long suggested, there are many reasons why rising affluence is commonly associated with the growing strength of democratic forces. Economic development is often associated with increased literacy and education that facilitate civic engagement in public affairs; a growing middle-class service sector that buffers between the extremes of rich and poor; the spread of the mass media providing information independent of the government; the development of civil society such as networks of professional and trade associations; and the growth of the welfare state to alleviate absolute poverty.[41] An extensive literature has demonstrated that the association is not perfect, since power is retained in the hands of the elite in many affluent societies in the Middle East and South Asia, in states characterized by ineffective and fragmented opposition movements, limited party competition, and restricted political rights and civil liberties. There are also some long-standing poorer democracies, such as India. Nevertheless, despite these exceptions, a simple correlation in the 179 countries under comparison demonstrates a relatively strong, significant, and consistent relationship between levels of democratization and real per capita income ($R = 0.462$ Sig. p. 001), and an even stronger relationship between democratization and human development ($R = 0.757$ Sig. p. 001). Real per capita income averages about \$4,760 in authoritarian regimes, compared with about \$11,630 in established democracies.

Based on Lipset's theory, and the analysis in earlier chapters, the analytical models used in this study assume that human development helps to drive both levels of democratization and the diffusion of digital technologies. Many models were examined, to see whether alternative indicators produced different results, but after testing three independent variables were selected for consistent comparison throughout this study. *Socioeconomic development* was measured using the United Nations Development Program standard human development index, combining measures of the standard of living, educational attainment, and longevity in a country, providing a broader and more reliable indicator than income alone.[42] *Technological diffusion* was gauged by the percentage of the population online, derived from the NUA database discussed earlier. This was selected as the simplest and most relevant measure from all the available indicators, although similar results were produced when models were replicated with alternative yardsticks of diffusion such as the per capita distribution of personal computers and hosts, or the composite information society index. *Political development* was measured by the level of democratization, using the standard

Freedom House index, a seven-point scale that is based on an annual review of the political rights and civil liberties within each country.[43]

MAPPING DIGITAL POLITICS

To proceed we need to explore systematic evidence analyzing the structure of digital politics, including where and which type of institutions have ventured online, and the functions of this process for information and communications in democracies. Digital technologies have generated multiple opportunities for political information and communication. A rough and ready yardstick of the popularity of politics on the Web can be gauged using common search engines. Yahoo, Alta Vista, and InfoSeek were searched to monitor the frequency that certain popular keywords are located, with eight terms selected as common topics on the Web including "politics," "computers," and "sex." For comparison, this search replicated a similar study conducted by Hill and Hughes in 1997, to monitor any significant changes over time.[44] The search in mid-2000 identified in total 56 million websites or pages indexed under the selected keywords. Each of these engines uses slightly different techniques for searching, so the proportion rather than the absolute number of hits provides the most reliable comparison across keywords. The results in Table 5.1 illustrate that the rank order of topics, and the rough proportion of websites and pages about politics, have remained fairly stable in recent years. Overall, reflecting the culture of the Web, the terms "computers," "sex," and "television" proved the most popular keywords on the list. But "politics" ranked fourth most common from the list, slightly outweighing the number of Web pages devoted to the topics of "movies," or "religion," or "investing." Moreover in the ranking of topics, while one-fifth of the sites referred to "sex," perhaps surprisingly one in ten referred to politics in some shape or form, representing in total almost two million Web pages or sites identified by each of the separate search engines.

This approximate estimate probably represents a conservative indication of the full range of political resources available on the Web because many sites are indexed under other terms. To provide an approximate estimate of the universe of political websites, Table 5.2 shows the frequency that these search engines hit a range of five politically related keywords. The term "government" was easily the most common, producing 12.6 million combined hits across Yahoo, Alta Vista, and InfoSeek. "Interest groups," "political parties," and "elections"

Table 5.1. *The popularity of politics on the Web*

| | 1997 | | | | 2000 | | | |
	Yahoo (%)	Alta Vista (%)	InfoSeek (%)	Total (%)	Yahoo! (%)	Alta Vista (%)	InfoSeek (%)	Total (%)
Computers	26	21	66	43	47	22	47	26
Sex	11	36	6	22	6	23	11	21
Television	17	11	9	10	14	17	13	16
Politics	*19*	*11*	*6*	*9*	*11*	*9*	*11*	*10*
Movies	10	7	5	6	5	9	5	8
Religion	6	7	4	6	10	8	6	8
Recipes	9	4	2	3	6	6	5	6
Investing	1	2	1	1	1	5	3	5
Total	100	100	100	100	100	100	100	100

Note: The percentage frequency of sites and pages identified by these keywords using Yahoo!, Alta Vista, and InfoSeek search engines, July 1, 1997 and June 20, 2000. The search identified in total 56 million counts in 2000 and 14.5 million in 1997.

Source: 1997 data from Kevin Hill and John E. Hughes. 1998. *Cyberpolitics: Citizen Activism in the Age of the Internet.* Lanham, MD: Rowman and Littlefield, Table 1.2, p. 25.

Table 5.2. *The estimated universe of political websites*

	Total (*n*)	Yahoo! (%)	Alta Vista (%)	InfoSeek (%)	Total (%)
Government	12,651,340	77	81	25	58
Interest groups	4,748,698	9	2	51	22
Political parties	1,880,572	3	2	18	9
Elections	1,618,668	9	10	4	7
Parliaments	887,659	2	6	2	4
Total	21,786,937	100	100	100	100

Note: The percentage frequency of sites and pages identified by these keywords using Yahoo!, Alta Vista, and InfoSeek search engines, June 20, 2000.

also each produced from one to five million combined hits, whereas there were just under one million hits for the term "parliament." These sorts of counts can only produce extremely rough and ready indicators of the contents of the World Wide Web, at best, but clicking on any common search engine quickly confirms no shortage of websites and discussion groups on the Internet devoted to politics and public affairs in all its glorious and multiple diversity, ranging from the Anarchist Action Network to the Zimbabwe Labour Party. We need to develop a systematic analysis of the informational and communication function of these sites, and their potential for strengthening representative democracy. No single source of data is wholly reliable, but replication of different sources – examining the distribution and function of websites identified though multiple databases – strengthens confidence that the patterns established in the analysis survive repeated testing. The study starts by analyzing the rise of e-governance in national-level departments and official agencies, and moves on through national parliaments to civic society, including political parties, the news media, interest groups, and new social movements.

CHAPTER 6

e-Governance

Cyber-optimists are hopeful that the development of interactive services, new channels of communication, and efficiency gains from digital technologies will contribute to revitalizing the role of government executives in representative democracies, facilitating communications between citizen and the state. In contrast, cyber-pessimists express doubts about the capacity of governments to adapt to the new environment. After reviewing theories about these issues, this chapter will examine the evidence and compare the causes and consequences of the rise of e-governance in terms of three core questions:

- Where and what type of government departments are online around the globe?
- To evaluate the consequences of the rise of e-governance, what are the democratic functions of government websites; in particular how far do they provide *transparent information* about government activities and opportunities for *interactive communication* between citizens and the state?
- What explains the growth of e-governance and, in particular, how far does democratization drive this process, or is socioeconomic or technological development more important?

THEORIES ABOUT THE IMPACT OF E-GOVERNMENT

Like other political institutions, government departments and official agencies have adapted to the Information Society during the last few years, albeit at a more cautious pace than the private sector. The main potential of digital technologies for government, cyber-optimists suggest, lies in strengthening policy effectiveness, political accountability, and, to a lesser extent, public participation.[1] E-governance holds great promise for the delivery of many types of public services from housing and welfare benefits to community health care and the electronic submission of tax returns, reconnecting official bureaucrats with citizen-customers.[2] The Internet can serve multiple functions: disseminating information about the operation of government as well as public services, facilitating public feedback mechanisms such as emails to government agencies, enabling more direct participation into the decision-making process including consultation exercises at local level, and providing direct support for the democratic process, such as the efficient administration of electoral registration or online voting.[3] There is widespread concern that the public has lost faith in the performance of the core institutions of representative government, and it is hoped that more open and transparent government and more efficient service delivery could help restore public confidence.[4] In developing societies, the Internet can potentially help with the multiple challenges facing the effective delivery and administration of basic government services such as health and education, especially given the global reach that the technology provides, connecting medical professionals, local officials, and university teachers in Oslo, Cambridge, and Geneva with those in Nepal, Bangalore, and Havana.

For all these reasons, cyber-optimists have high hopes about the democratic potential of digital technologies. Yet such visions are tempered by more cautious voices stressing that it is naive to expect technology to transform government departments as organizations that are inherently conservative, hierarchical, and bureaucratic. Official documents can be published online, but it often requires considerable knowledge and technical skills to negotiate the complexities of these information resources. An OECD study of e-governance, based on a series of interviews with information specialists, public officials, and the policymaking community in eight postindustrial societies in 1996–1997, presents a pessimistic scenario. The report found that new technologies had had little impact on the way that governments gathered information for policy analysis, since traditional methods including letters, written submissions, and informal meetings, continued to predominate.[5] Digital technologies such as email have had greater impact in the dissemination of information to senior decisionmakers and policy elites, although even here traditional channels remained most popular, including press releases, official gazettes, and face-to-face meetings. The report concluded that the overall impact of the Internet has failed to increase access to policymakers, to improve the transparency of government decisionmaking, or to facilitate public participation in policy making.

Similar concerns have been expressed elsewhere. Many observe that although governments have developed websites to promote "top-down" publicity, and even state propaganda, there are few opportunities so far via these media for genuine "bottom-up" interaction, public criticism, or discursive deliberation.[6] Advocates of direct or "strong" democracy frequently critique the "failure" of the reality of digital politics to live up to their expectations and then conclude that because political participation has not been transformed, the Internet represents "politics as usual" and nothing significant has changed.[7] But the key issue here is whether the Internet provides an effective means of government communication and information supplementing traditional channels. In terms of the overall opportunities for political information and communication, are we better off or worse off in the Internet age than say ten, twenty, or thirty years ago? To evaluate these issues, this chapter starts by mapping where government departments have moved ahead into the Internet age and where governments continue to lag behind around the globe.

THE RISE OF E-GOVERNANCE

The full range of new information technologies may serve multiple internal administrative and organizational functions for governments, linking horizontally as well as vertically. These technologies include the proliferation of fax machines, beepers and mobile phones, email, list-servs, and Intranets binding together internal communications between departments or branches, as well as the use of computers in government offices. Email communications are particularly important for strengthening one-to-one communications and group networks within established political organizations, as in the corporate world and local community, as well as linking citizens and government.[8] But technologies such as fax machines and mobile phones usually serve to supplement or replace older machines, just as photocopies replaced roneoed stencils, and stencils replaced carbon paper, altering the speed and convenience without essentially changing the function or contents of communications. Being able to communicate faster does not necessarily mean that this will be to greater effect. Detailed case studies and network analysis are useful tools to study the internal use of these private forms of communications within government departments, drawing on the growing literature in organizational theory and management studies on the use of digital technologies in business and the nonprofit sector.[9] Initiatives in e-governance by local, state, and national agencies have attracted considerable interest in public administration and management studies, such as comparisons by the twenty-nation Government Online (GOL) survey and OECD Public Management report.[10] Much of the interactive government activity conducted via digital means, including the most effective forms of interpersonal persuasion and deliberation, may be underestimated because it occurs within communities behind closed doors.

Government websites – the primary focus of this chapter – are the most important public face of the Internet. Building on the literature, a simple mapping exercise helps to establish where e-governance has developed most fully. Two sources are used. The first estimate of the total number of all government websites in 179 countries, excluding dependent territories, is derived from *Governments on the WWW*. This source provides the most comprehensive list worldwide, and the accuracy of the list was confirmed and checked using common search engines like Yahoo!.[11] The analysis based on this list summarizes the total number of all official government websites in each country, broadly defined to include those for the national executive (such as ministries, departments, offices, agencies, institutes, councils, and committees), as well as for the legislative branch, state and local governments, all political party websites (including at regional as well as national levels), the law courts, government representatives in foreign countries including embassies and consulates, and other official institutions. Some of the cross-national variations may be due to specific administrative policies, such as whether government websites are hosted from one central server or dispersed across more autonomous agencies at different levels.

This initial estimate provides a comprehensive overview of all official sites but it does not distinguish between different agencies, although politically it is far more important for the transparency of government and the accountability of officials that citizens can learn about central government ministries and the core executive rather than, say, travel and tourism information from embassies. To focus on national-level government agencies such as Cabinet ministries the chapter draws on a second source of data, from the Cyberspace Policy Research (CyPRG) group.[12] This database has systematically monitored ministerial-level national government departmental websites around the world since

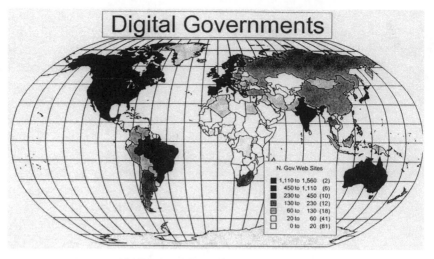

Figure 6.1. The World of e-Governance.

1997. The latest year of data that is available (1999) identified 2,941 such websites in 105 nations.

The map of e-governance around the globe is illustrated in Figure 6.1. Worldwide, more than 14,000 government agencies were found online in mid-2000, a remarkable number given that the World Wide Web is a relatively recent development. North America and Western Europe led the world in the spread of e-governance, followed by Scandinavia, with the Middle East and Sub-Saharan Africa ranking last. The comparison of the total number of government websites ranked by individual countries shows that Germany tops the list, in part because of the extensive development of websites at Lander level in the federal system. Other leading countries include the United Kingdom, United States, France, Italy, Spain, and Sweden, all affluent postindustrial societies, but also, perhaps more unexpectedly, India (ranked seventh) and Brazil (ranked ninth). These exceptions strongly suggest that government priorities, telecommunication strategies, and the structure of federalism in the political system may help to drive this process, because some developing societies with relatively low levels of connectivity but a decentralized political system have forged ahead in digital government. Farther down the rankings, Mexico, Taiwan, and Malaysia also have many more government websites than would be expected by their levels of socioeconomic development alone. Yet the presence of these outliers should not be exaggerated, since the overall contrasts between developing and industrialized nations are marked; on

Table 6.1. *The world of e-governance, 2000*

	All government websites (i)		National-level government websites (ii)
	Total number	Mean number per nation	Mean number per nation
All	14,484	82	27
North America	1,283	428	132
Western Europe	6,060	404	45
Scandinavia	1,156	231	41
Asia-Pacific	2,555	75	33
South America	1,378	46	17
Central and Eastern Europe	1,015	41	8
Middle East	446	32	22
Sub-Saharan Africa	599	12	11
High human development	10,073	240	45
Medium human development	3,788	43	16
Low human development	272	8	3
Established democracies	11,771	163	39
Consolidating democracies	2,294	32	15
Nondemocracies	419	13	12

Notes and sources: Columns (i) in the table summarize the distribution of 14,492 official government websites for the national executive (ministries, departments, offices, agencies, institutes, councils, and committees), the legislative branch, state and local governments, political party websites at national and regional level, the law courts, government representatives in foreign countries including embassies and consulates, and other government-related institutions found in 179 nations as of June 2000, according to *Governments on the WWW, www.gksoft.com/govt/.* Column (ii) in the table summarizes the distribution of 2,941 national-level government agency websites in 105 nations in 1999, according to Cyberspace Policy Research Group, 1999, *www.cybrg.org.* **Level of human development** was derived from the UNDP Human Development Index 1999: UNDP, *Human Development Report, 1999.* New York: UNDP/Oxford University Press. **Type of Democracy:** The level of democracy for each country was classified according to Freedom House seven-point scale of political rights and civil liberties. Countries were then classified as established democracies (1.0 to 2.5), consolidating democracies (3.0 to 4.5), and nondemocracies (5.0 to 7.0). Freedom House Survey of Political Rights and Civil Liberties 1999–2000, *www.freedomhouse.org.*

average, only eight government department or agencies maintain a website in each of the poorest nations whereas in contrast 240 such sites were found in each of the more affluent societies.

The more limited comparison of ministerial or national-level government websites from the CyPRG data confirms a similar pattern, with almost 3,000 departmental websites online, representing on average about 27 per country. Again there are marked contrasts by levels of human development, with only three departments online in the poorest nations compared with 45 in the most developed. The disparities by level of democratization are also clear, with a dozen departments online under nondemocratic regimes compared with more than three times as many (39) in the most democratic states. The regional comparison displays a familiar picture although fewer central departments in Central and Eastern Europe have ventured online than might be expected from other indicators of technological diffusion, and in contrast more government ministries in the Middle East have moved into e-governance.

THE DEMOCRATIC FUNCTIONS OF
GOVERNMENT WEBSITES

The government websites that have been launched vary substantially in their levels of information and interactivity, as well as to what extent there has been an attempt to link all the available official sources into a client-oriented portal. As illustrated in Figure 6.2, some websites such as that illustrated for the Norwegian government continue to be organized traditionally by ministries or agencies, which requires users to understand the responsibilities and functions of different institutions. Countries like the United Kingdom have adopted a "one-stop shop" approach attempting to tie together multiple government departments and agencies at all levels. The aim is to allow citizens to find the information and transactions they need in one searchable integrated database, as well to strengthen linkages between departments, and to encourage "joined-up" government.[13] Other innovative designs, such as *FirstGov.gov* site in the United States and the Singapore government website, aim to provide a more customer-oriented approach organized by topics and issues, stressing how to deal with government services and regulations, such as those concerning jobs, health, or taxes.

To analyze which departments were online, and to consider the role of these websites more systematically, this study can draw on the content analysis data collected by the Cyberspace Policy Research group.[14]

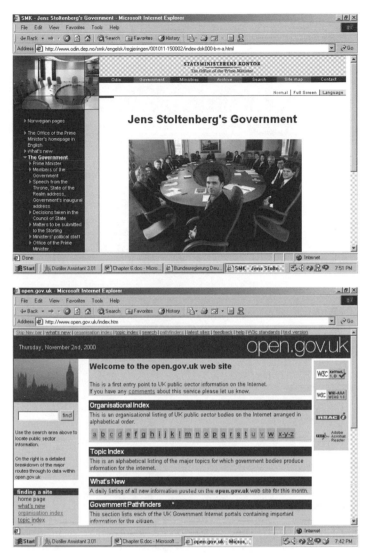

Figure 6.2. One-stop e-Governance in the United Kingdom, Norway, Singapore, and the United States. *(Figure continues)*

The database has systematically examined the contents and format of national-level government department websites around the world. The analysis classifies the contents according to two principle criteria: the *informational transparency* of the website based on indicators such as the site ownership, contact details, organizational information, and

Figure 6.2 Continued

freshness of updated material, and the *communication interactivity* of the website based on the provision of links and opportunities for input. Table 6.2 shows the worldwide distribution in 1999 of almost 3,000 government department websites classified by policy sector, as well as the standardized 100-point scores for different types of departments on the measures of information transparency and communication interactivity.

Table 6.2. *e-Governance by policy sector, 1999*

Policy Sector	Number of departments online	Mean transparency index (information)	Mean interactivity index (communications)
Science and technology	236	42	25
Finance	200	43	24
Trade	193	40	21
Defense	172	36	17
Government operations	141	37	19
Justice	139	36	20
Interior	138	37	18
Culture	135	37	23
Health	134	42	24
Environment	133	37	21
Industry	132	39	18
Education	121	39	21
Agriculture	118	41	23
Social Services	115	41	22
Telecommunications	112	40	22
Transportation	107	36	20
Miscellaneous	101	35	21
Executive	95	32	16
Foreign	94	41	22
Legislative	84	40	23
Regional/Local	77	39	26
Labor	77	39	22
Energy	66	43	22
Library	26	36	22
Immigration	19	41	22
State	11	36	20
Total	*2,976*	*39*	*21*

Note: All indices have been standardized to 100-point scales for ease of interpretation. For the methodology classifying the Transparency and Interactivity Indexes see *www.cyprg.org*.

Source: Cyberspace Policy Research Group, 1999, *www.cyprg.org.*

The results show certain significant differences by policy sector. Not surprisingly, science and technology departments were most commonly found online, followed by finance and trade, all departments that can be expected to need to maintain a high international profile in dealing with governments from many other countries. Yet there was no apparent logical pattern in the distribution of other departments, in terms of their type of dealings either with other governments or with the public. For example, despite their global responsibilities, relatively few departments dealing with foreign affairs and immigration had established a website. Despite the potential of the Internet for research, official library websites were rare, while telecommunications departments were found in the middle rank. Part of the variations could be attributed to the structure of government in different countries, for example whether immigration was dealt with by a separate department or integrated into the Department of Justice or home office. Another factor that is likely to prove important concerns the centralization or dispersion of websites within government, because some countries have adopted a "one-stop shopping" approach for citizens, whereas others have encouraged multiple independent websites.[15]

The pattern by the function of government websites was clearer: Most strikingly, across all policy sectors, departmental websites scored almost twice as well in their information transparency rather than their communication interactivity functions. Departments used their websites far more extensively as "top-down" mechanisms for posting information such as mission statements, details about the structure and activities of the organization, and official reports and documents, rather than providing clickable links to email officials, opportunities to subscribe to an electronic newsletter, or facilities to download and upload official forms. In this regard, the Internet was used conservatively, as predicted, to replicate existing channels for the publication and distribution of official documents like reports, providing information through different channels, rather than to "reinvent government," to rethink the nature of the relationship between departments and the public, or to open bureaucratic organizations to interactivity with customer–clients. Moreover there was little variation across policy sectors: the functions of the websites were relatively similar whether for departments that might be expected to generate considerable interaction with the public in service delivery, such as those of health, education, and social services, or those generating minimal direct contact, such as departments concerned with the management of internal government operations or defense. While the design usually proved conservative, the provision of electronic information resources may have certain important consequences, since the distribution of electronic information resources becomes equally available to all actors, whether professional lobbyists or activist volunteers, the costs of access are sharply reduced, resources are searchable, and the information is in real-time for pending proposals. Those seeking to challenge the authorities on current issues of concern – including think-tank policy analysts, professional advocates, backbench politicians, small opposition parties, journalists, and organizational activists – can use these resources to be as well briefed as government ministers and civil servants about official reports, government proposals, administrative decisions, and pending legislation. Making sense of the materials remains a demanding process, but the provision of more official documents and search facilities via the Internet loosens some of the government's control over information resources and augments the transparency of the decisionmaking process.

EXPLAINING THE RISE OF E-GOVERNANCE

What helps to explain the rise of e-governance? It might be anticipated that the type of political system would be one of the leading candidates, in particular e-governance could plausibly be expected to have developed furthest in long-established democratic states that are committed to open government and freedom of information, such as Norway, Canada, and Australia, rather than in consolidating and transitional democracies such as Russia, Sri Lanka, and Tanzania. The contrasts are likely to be even stronger with the availability of official information online in one-party regimes and authoritarian states. Yet there may also be many exceptions to this pattern because general levels of socioeconomic development and the broader process of technological diffusion may also influence the rise of e-governance. Government departments may have developed few websites in many poorer societies lagging behind the Internet revolution in Sub-Saharan Africa and Southeast Asia, including democracies like Mali and Bangladesh, while in contrast more public services may have transferred online to streamline administrative efficiency and maximize bureaucratic control in affluent but nondemocratic countries, such as Singapore, Malaysia, and Saudi Arabia. Therefore levels of democratization, technological diffusion, and socioeconomic development are all factors that may plausibly explain the distribution of government websites worldwide. Following

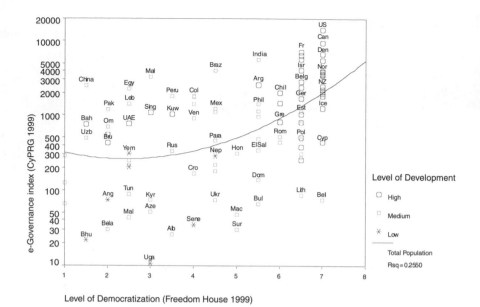

Figure 6.3. E-Governance and Democratization.

Notes and Sources: **e-Governance Index:** This is calculated as the number of national-level government websites multiplied by the content analysis measures of their informational transparency and communication interactivity. Calculated from CyPRG 1999, *www.cyprg.arizona.edu.* **Levels of Democratization:** Reversed Freedom House seven-point scale of political rights and civil liberties, 1999, *www.freedomhouse.org.*

the logic discussed in the previous chapter, the models in this study are based on the assumption that socioeconomic development precedes and thereby helps to drive the process of democratization and technological diffusion. To examine these relationships, the standard measures were incorporated into models, including indicators of socioeconomic development, technological diffusion, and levels of democratization. Five dependent variables were examined: the total number of all government websites, the number of national-level government websites, the content analysis indicators of government information transparency and communication interactivity, and the overall e-governance index. The summary index was developed by multiplying the number of government agencies with the combined indicators of informational transparency and communication interactivity.

The results given in Table 6.3 show that even after controlling for socioeconomic development, technological diffusion measured by the spread of Internet use proved the single most significant predictor of the distribution and functions of e-governance across models, with the

Table 6.3. *Explaining e-governance*

	Total number of government websites		Number of national-level government websites		Information transparency scale		Communication interactivity scale		e-Governance index	
	Beta	Sig.	Beta	Sig.	Beta	Sig.	Beta	Sig.	Beta	Sig.
Human development	.154	.079	.071	.521	.206	.115	.187	.082	.088	.398
Technological development	**.381**	**.000**	**.502**	**.000**	**.154**	**.224**	**.376**	**.000**	**.535**	**.000**
Political development	.106	.203	.054	.598	-.002	.988	.167	.095	.094	.404
Constant	-106		-2.16		24.1		-.17		-775	
Adjusted R²	.288		.314		.076		.371		.404	
Number of nations	179		108		106		105		105	

Notes: The standardized beta coefficients represent the results of OLS regression models predicting the distribution and function of government websites in June 2000.

Sources: **Socioeconomic development:** measured by UNDP Human Development Index 1999, UNDP *Human Development Report 1999*, New York: UNDP/Oxford University Press; **Percent online:** Calculated from "How Many Online," *www.nua.ie* (see Table 3.2 for details); **Level of democratization:** Freedom House, *Annual Survey of Political Rights and Civil Liberties 1999–2000, www.freedomhouse.org/survey/2000/*; **All government websites:** Governments on the WWW, June 2000, *www.gksoft.com/govt* See Table 6.1 for details of the classification; **All national-level government websites:** CyPRG 1999, Cyberspace Policy Research Group, *www.cyprg.org* ; **Government website transparency and interactivity scales:** CyPRG 1999, Cyberspace Policy Research Group (website as above); **e-Governance index:** Number of national-level government websites times transparency plus interactivity.

exception of government transparency, where none of the factors proved significant. This pattern suggests that much of the impact of socioeconomic development comes not from patterns of literacy and education per se, but through its close association with technological development. As Chapter 3 established, affluent postindustrial societies characteristically have the widest access to multiple forms of communication technologies, including such traditional media as telephones and televisions, and digital media like computers and Internet hosts, and this environment is most conducive to the spread of e-governance as well. Government organizations respond to the opportunities for interaction within their broader socioeconomic and technological environment. Like a political version of Metcalfe's law, the incentive for departments to communicate via the Internet expands at an exponential rate as society moves online. The replication of the results across the two alternative indicators of the spread of e-governance, derived from different sources, increases confidence in the reliability and robustness of the models. Equally important, the results indicate that once models have already controlled for prior socioeconomic and technological development, the level of democratization fails to explain the distribution and functions of e-governance. Although it is plausible to imagine that freer societies generate more open and transparent e-governance, once controls are introduced for the Internet population, this turns out not to be the case. The overall results suggest that technological diffusion proved the most important single factor driving the spread of e-governance: Departments and official agencies have taken to the Internet in societies leading the digital revolution. E-governance may help to strengthen democratization, but the process of democratization does not appear to be its primary cause.

To confirm that this interpretation was not just a statistical artifact, or a by-product of the sequential ordering of the variables in the models, and to identify any particular anomalies to this pattern, the main relationships were also examined graphically by using scatter plots. The pattern comparing the level of democratization with the index of e-governance shown in Figure 6.4 confirms the models, and explains some of the reasons for the poor fit. It is true that established democracies such as Germany, the United Kingdom, and the United States are ahead in e-governance, yet some comparable democracies such as Greece and Belgium continue to lag far behind. The most plausible reason is that the broader structure of the Information Society is poorly institutionalized in democracies like Greece, where relatively few people

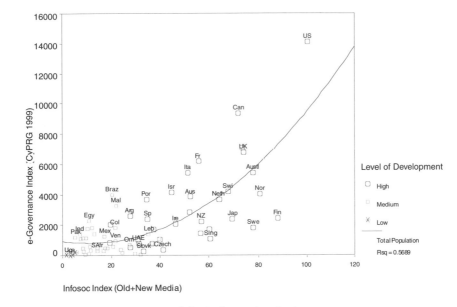

Figure 6.4. E-Governance and the Information Society.

Notes: **e-Governance index:** This is calculated as the number of government websites multiplied by the content analysis measures of informational transparency and communication interactivity. **Infosoc Index:** For details of the construction and data sources see Table 3.2.

Source: Calculated from CyPRG 1999, *www.cyprg.arizona.edu.*

are online, and, given Metcalf's law about the value of networks, this context creates minimal incentives for official departments to venture online. Similar contrasts can be drawn within every category of democratization, such as between India and the Philippines, between Brazil and the Ukraine, between Egypt and Algeria. In contrast, the scatter plots of e-governance compared with the Information Society index display a closer, although admittedly far from perfect, fit to the data. The relationship proved robust since similar patterns were found if the number of government agencies online was compared, rather than the composite index of e-governance.

To check further, the overall pattern was also examined using a simple cross-tabulation of the density of e-governance in rich and poor democracies (in Table 6.4). The results show that government websites were by far the most common in the richest established democracies. The poorest societies had few such websites and there was little difference in this between countries ruled by despots or democrats. The com-

Table 6.4. *e-Governance by the type of society and democracy*

	Low development	Medium development	High development
Nondemocracies	**5** (9)	**17** (18)	**10** (2)
Consolidating democracies	**9** (25)	**46** (40)	**40** (4)
Established democracies	**4** (1)	**56** (29)	**275** (36)

Notes and sources: The figures in bold represent the mean number of government websites and those in parentheses represent the number of nations within each category. **Type of democracy:** Classified from the Freedom House Annual Survey of Political Rights and Civil Liberties 1999–2000, *www.freedomhouse.org/survey/2000/*. See Table 6.1 for details; **Level of Development** is measured and classified by the UNDP Human Development Index 1999, UNDP. *Human Development Report 1999.* New York: UNDP/Oxford University Press; **Total number of government websites:** Governments on the WWW, *www.gksoft.com/govt.* See Table 6.1 for details of the classification.

parison of all these different indicators strongly suggests that the distribution and functions of e-governance reflect levels of technological development first and foremost: This is the single-most consistent pattern to be found across all the data. Countries that have forged ahead with the distribution of computer access and online use are also the foremost societies in e-governance. The gradual diffusion of the Internet into people's everyday lives is the bigger ocean within which government organizations swim. Without wishing to suggest a strong version of technological determinism, the analysis leads to the conclusion that so far the rise of the Information Society has had important consequences for the ability of citizens to communicate with government via the Internet, and therefore for how far digital technologies promote the process of democratization, more than democracy has driven the rise of e-governance.

CONCLUSIONS

The importance of transparency in government is widely acknowledged, both to promote greater public confidence in the policymaking process and to maximize accountability. The evidence demonstrates that more and more government departments and public sector agencies are using the Web to publish and distribute official information and, to a lesser extent, to facilitate the delivery of online services. As noted earlier, the full consequences of this process remain under development. At present, societies are experiencing a transition process where governments work simultaneously with paper and electronic formats, duplicating rather than replacing channels of information and communication. Potentially the gains in administrative efficiency, effective service delivery, transparency, and accountability could be substantial, although governments are still learning by trial and error how best to employ digital technologies.[16]

What will be the consequences of these developments for representative democracy? Any evaluative judgments relate to broader visions of democracy and the appropriate functions of governments. Many accounts assume that the Internet can by itself reinvent government, transforming old-fashioned bureaucracies into agencies of direct democracy, which, most authors conclude, it fails to do. It seems more appropriate and realistic to start from the premise that governments are core institutions of representative democracy, and to compare their online activity with their role in the nonvirtual world. In this regard, government websites should be evaluated in terms of the quality and effectiveness of their informational and communication functions.

The criteria of transparent *information* is important to representative government because citizens can only make effective electoral decisions if they can evaluate the record and performance of the government, as well as the programs of the alternative parties and candidates competing for office. People can thereby cast informed ballots that accurately match their political preferences. Information can and does come from multiple sources, more commonly the news media, as well as many unmediated channels of political communications such as political advertisements and personal discussions. This comparison shows that the most effective government websites provide detailed and comprehensive policy-relevant information and the ability to research the most abstruse legislative proposals, White Papers, and official reports. The content analysis found that government websites scored roughly twice as well on the criteria of the transparency over interactivity. For those who are interested, more timely unmediated information about the public policymaking process is more easily available via the Internet than ever before. The ability to research policy issues in real-time potentially strengthens organizations seeking to challenge those in authority, such as nonprofit advocates, journalists, policy think tanks, challenger parties, and opposition movements. Insofar as much of this information is often not readily available elsewhere, and so long as the information can be compared across a variety of alternative sources, this process can strengthen the intermediary institutions of civic society in representative democracies, and therefore, in a two-step trickle-down process, ordinary citizens as well. Departmental transparency in the timely and equitable release of official records, policy proposals, and administrative decisions serves the public interest. Ordinary citizens will rarely make direct use of most of these facilities, but the potential for more efficient and targeted service delivery is illustrated by the popularity of online electronic filing of routine forms, such as for taxes or auto registration.

Yet representative democracy requires two-way *communication* as well as information, at regular intervals beyond elections, so that political leaders receive feedback and maintain contact with the grassroots. Many commentators who advocate "strong" or "direct" democracy commonly argue that these functions are not well served by e-governance, and this criticism has some value if judged by government websites alone. The opportunities for "bottom-up" interactivity in communicating with official departments are far fewer than the opportunities to read "top-down" information. It is possible that at present communications between citizens and officials is more easily facilitated through more private electronic communications, such as one-to-one or small group emails. Government websites rarely facilitate unmoderated public feedback, for example, few published public reactions to policy proposals, or used discussion forums, listservs and bulletin boards, although there have been occasional experiments with interactive formats. In the United Kingdom, for example, the Central Computing and Telecommunications Agency (CCTA) established a number of open discussion groups to discuss issues ranging from open government to ethics, the family, and women. E-governance is open to criticism that agencies have been more willing to carry out traditional functions via electronic means, rather than using digital technologies to reinvent how they conduct business, to reconnect with citizens as customers, and to strengthen public participation in government. However, given the multiple demands on the executive branch, should forms of public interactivity be the primary function of official government departments or of the broader public sphere? Public deliberation may well be more effectively organized and run by the extensive network of nongovernmental nonprofit organizations that host policy discussion groups, such as UK Citizens Online Democracy or the Minnesota Electronic Democracy Experiment, not to mention the thousands of political listservs and multiple chat rooms that exist in cyber-space. Later chapters consider the potential impact of the new communication processes for civic society, including the major intermediaries between citizens and the state – namely parties, interest groups, new social movements, and the news media. Before considering these issues, Chapter 7 considers to what extent parliamentary institutions have adapted to the digital age.

CHAPTER 7

Online Parliaments

Government department and official agencies may have adjusted conservatively to digital politics but, given the electoral incentives to maintain stronger links with citizens, have elected bodies adapted at a faster rate? To map the virtual political system around the globe, and to understand the democratic potential of digital technologies for national legislatures, this chapter focuses on three questions:

- Which national parliaments are currently online?
- What is the function of parliamentary websites; in particular how do they provide opportunities for *comprehensive information* to allow public scrutiny of their activities and *interactive communications* to facilitate public feedback?
- To explain the pattern we establish, how far does the process of democratization, technological diffusion, or socioeconomic development drive variations in the quality of parliamentary websites?

WHICH PARLIAMENTS ARE ONLINE?

Potentially, digital technologies can affect the internal workings of legislatures in multiple ways, from the widespread use of computers for administrative, research, and communication functions by elected members and officials to electronic voting in the chamber.[1] Electronic databases maintained by parliamentary library services, such as Thomas in the U.S. Congress, facilitate more effective and targeted research by members, lobbyists, and policy analysts. Email is likely to have important consequences once it is more widely used by representatives to connect to constituents, with the capacity of replacing or supplementing conventional channels of correspondence and local newsletters, although studies show that many members have problems in responding to quantities of electronic mail.[2] But websites are the chief public face of parliaments, with the greatest potential for external effect in how citizens see the institution and how they interact with their representatives, and therefore the one this chapter focuses on.

Worldwide, recent years have seen more and more elected assemblies at national, regional, and local levels launch themselves online. The most comprehensive list of all such official parliamentary websites in 179 nations worldwide is maintained by the Interparliamentary Union (IPU) in Geneva.[3] By mid-2000, national parliaments in 98 countries had established websites, representing slightly more than one-half of all nations, and the IPU estimates that the overall number of such sites has tripled within the past two years.[4] The regional analysis shows that parliamentary sites have become universal throughout Scandinavia and North America; they are found in every country in Western Europe except one (Cyprus), and in three-fourths of all nations in Central and Eastern European and the Middle East. The region lagging farthest behind these trends is Sub-Saharan Africa, where only 15 of 50 parliaments had developed an online presence, reflecting the low level of technological diffusion already observed in this area. In line with these patterns, Table 7.1 shows that parliamentary websites were most common in established democracies, as well as in developed economies.

THE FUNCTIONS OF PARLIAMENTARY WEBSITES

So far the comparison tells us nothing about the quality or functions of the parliamentary websites. A glance through these sites quickly reveals wide variations: some include just a few rudimentary pages containing largely outdated official information, commonly including a photo of the building and the names of the chief officials, but little about current activities such as pending legislation or forthcoming debates. In contrast, others provide a wide array of rich and dynamic interactive resources, functioning as a sort of combined official bookstore and public records office, parliamentary TV channel, political almanac, and civics schoolroom. Do you want to watch the Australian Senate in action? Do you want to read the speech on spending proposals by the British Secretary of State for Education? Do you want to tour the U.S. Congress? You can do all this, and more. The most comprehensive sites include such facilities as the daily schedule of official business, the full searchable text of pending legislation and government proposals, the full text of updated

Table 7.1. *The world of parliamentary websites*

	All Nations		
	Percent with a parliamentary website	Number with a parliamentary website	Total number of nations
All	55	98	178
Scandinavia	100	5	5
North America	100	3	3
Western Europe	93	14	15
Central and Eastern Europe	76	19	25
Middle East	73	8	11
Asia-Pacific	57	17	29
South America	59	17	29
Sub-Saharan Africa	30	15	50
High human development	95	38	40
Medium human development	51	43	85
Low human development	42	14	33
Established democracies	76	54	71
Consolidating democracies	59	26	44
Nondemocracies	35	18	51

Notes and Sources: The data indicate whether a parliament had established a website as of June 2000. **Type of Democracy:** The level of democracy for each country was classified according to Freedom House seven-point scale of political rights and civil liberties. Countries were then classified as established democracies (1.0 to 2.5), consolidating democracies (3.0 to 4.5), and nondemocracies (5.0 to 7.0); **Parliamentary websites** were identified using the list maintained by the Inter-Parliamentary Union. May 2000. *http://www.ipu.org/cntr-e/web.pdf;* **Level of human development** was derived from the UNDP Human Development Index 1999.

press releases, audiovisual streaming virtual tours of the building, detailed personal websites for individual members, electronic newsletters available on subscription, sections with civic education resources for schools, as well as live multimedia streaming audio and/or video coverage of parliamentary debates and subcommittee hearings.

To explore these contrasts more systematically we need to evaluate the function, structure, and contents of the websites, a process that

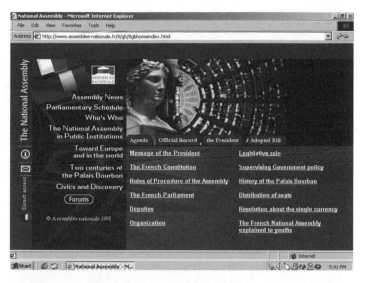

Figure 7.1. Examples of Parliamentary Websites in France, Australia, India, and Brazil. *(Figure continues)*

requires an understanding of the appropriate functions of parliaments, which in turn rests upon broader visions about the ideal workings of representative democracy. Too often parliamentary websites are critiqued for not fulfilling certain functions, when these functions are actually inappropriate for their role in representative democracies,

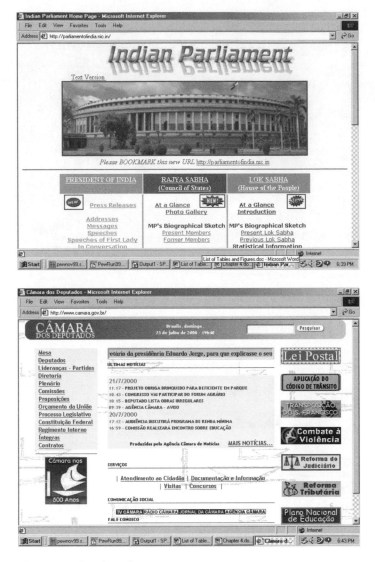

Figure 7.1 Continued

reflecting inadequate conceptualizations of the normative assumptions underlying these judgments. This study assumes that parliamentary websites should ideally serve two primary functions in a democratic political system: the "top-down" provision of *information* from the legislature to the public and a "bottom-up" channel of *communication* from the public to the elected members. These functions reflect the classical liberal notion of the role of parliament in representative democracy articulated by those such as John Stuart Mill. In this view, for strong and effective government, capable of making difficult decisions, considerable power should be delegated to elected representatives during their period of election, particularly to the party or parties in government. But ultimately power should be trammeled by electoral accountability. Parliament's prime function should be one of scrutinizing government actions – critiquing legislative proposals, examining public accounts, debating major initiatives, controlling the executive, demanding full disclosure of information justifying proposed actions – but not governing per se. Just as the government is accountable to parliament, so parliament is accountable to the public. Comprehensive and accurate information is essential for the public to be able to scrutinize those in authority and hold them responsible for their actions, collectively and individually, throwing the rascals out in periodic elections if dissatisfied with their performance. Moreover, communication is essential so that elected representatives reflect the views of their constituents and take up particular administrative grievances on their behalf, where there is a tradition of constituency service. In John Stuart Mill's words:

> Instead of the functioning of governing, for which it is radically unfit, the proper office of a representative assembly is to watch and control the government: to throw the light of publicity on its acts: to compel a full exposition and justification of all of them which any one considers questionable; to censure them if found condemnable, and, if the men who compose the government abuse their trust, or fulfill it in a manner which conflicts with the deliberate sense of the nation, to expel them from office... In addition to this, the Parliament has an office, not inferior even to this in importance; to be at once the nation's Committee of Grievances, and its Congress of Opinions; an arena in which every person in the country may count upon finding somebody who speaks his mind, as well or better than he could speak it himself.[5]

Parliamentary websites can prove particularly effective mechanisms for providing the public and intermediary organizations with detailed and comprehensive information about legislative procedures and activities, allowing greater transparency and public scrutiny of the policymaking process, and promoting the accountability of elected members to their constituents.[6] Many other channels of information about parliamentary business are available, ranging from unfiltered and unedited televised debates on channels such as C-Span to newspaper and television news coverage of parliamentary debates and leadership speeches, committees and legislation, as well as the traditional publication of official government documents like Hansard. Yet official documents can be expensive and publication creates inevitable delays. The potential advantage of the Internet as a medium is that it allows legislative bodies to freely distribute many different types of information, particularly lengthy official publications like the full searchable text of pending legislation and government reports, directly and simultaneously to a wide community of users in an efficient, timely, and equitable manner. Thus every citizen has the same access to a document as the highest paid lobbyist. The Internet allows transmission of everything from the complete version of official documents and the daily agenda for parliamentary business to streaming audiovisual feeds of the debating chamber during parliamentary sessions and "virtual" tours of the buildings. Moreover unlike public records and official government document offices, the search and retrieval facilities in digital formats easily facilitate prompt, detailed, and targeted policy research by those interested in tracking the progress of specific legislative bills, government proposals, or members' voting records on contentious issues. Many parliaments also recognize the value of websites for broader "civics education," devoting specific sections of information for students and teachers. All this material, if well planned and presented, should help to make the policymaking process, and even the more arcane minutiae of parliamentary business, more open to outsider scrutiny, allowing the powerful disinfectant of publicity against the possible abuse of power.

Equally important, as well as "top-down" information, parliamentary websites can also provide additional "bottom-up" channels of communication for citizens, interest groups, professional lobbyists, and community associations seeking to contact elected representatives. In this regard email is only one mechanism, supplementing traditional communications such as letters and phone calls, organized petitions, constituency surgeries, and local rallies or meetings. Nevertheless, the advantage of email for senders lies in its timeliness, minimal cost of transmission, the ability to attach full documentation and links, and the potential simultaneous distribution to multiple recipients. Parliamentary websites can also be designed to encourage online discussion groups, straw polls, and other feedback mechanisms including comments pages and guestbooks, which advocates of direct democracy regard as important mechanisms of public deliberation and participation.

To what extent do parliamentary websites serve these functions by providing effective channels of information and communication for citizens? A study conducted by the Inter-Parliamentary Union examined the contents of websites for 125 parliamentary chambers in 82 nations in August 1998. The IPU found that certain features are becoming more standardized so that the website for the U.S. Congress shares certain design features with the ones for the Australian House of Representatives, the German Bundestag, and the South African parliament.[7] As shown in Table 7.2, parliamentary websites commonly provide contact details and basic biographical information about members and officers, information about the composition, schedule, and activities of parliamentary committees, materials about the history and procedures of the institution and the basic constitutional document, a calendar of current parliamentary business, access to draft bills and official government documents, and general information about the parliamentary and the electoral system.

To analyze this pattern further and to compare nations more systematically, content analysis was used to examine the 98 websites for all parliaments that the Inter-Parliamentary Union identified as being online worldwide in May 2000. In bicameral legislatures with dual websites, only the lower house was included in the analysis. The sites were classified in accordance with the evaluative criteria already discussed, namely, the richness of the *informational* contents and the opportunities for interactive *communication*. Nine indicators were selected and each was recorded as present if it was listed on the home page or appeared within the top three levels.

The *Information Index* was classified by summing five indicators measuring whether the website included the following types of contents:

- The entire text or abbreviated version of the nation's constitution.
- The background history of parliament and government.
- The organization, structure, and functions of parliament.
- The rules, standing orders, and procedures of parliament.
- The provision of official documents such as the text of legislation, publications, and reports.
- Press releases or other news issued on a regular basis.
- The status of pending legislation.
- The calendar of parliamentary business and current events.

Each of the first five categories was coded on a simple "present/absent" (1/0) basis. The last three categories reflect more current information

139

Table 7.2. *The contents of parliamentary websites*

Type of Information	Percent
English-language pages	76
List of Members ordered by alphabetical surnames, party, or constituency	75
Presiding officer of parliament	71
Parliamentary committees, subcommittees, and commissions	70
Complete constitutional text	65
Parliament's email address	65
Information about the parliamentary or electoral system	63
Chairs of parliamentary committees	63
Brief history of parliament	54
Breakdown of seats by party	52
Links to international and regional parliamentary bodies	50
Biographical data on MPs such as date of birth, education, and prior occupation	49
Information about current legislative business	47
Links to the websites for other national parliaments	44
Summary of parliamentary session	43
Text of Standing Orders or parliamentary Rules of Procedure	37
Description of parliamentary bodies, functions, and working procedures	36
Text of pending legislation	34
Opportunities for a "virtual" visit	33
Postal address, telephone, and fax number to contact parliament	33
Email addresses of some members and/or links to members' home pages	30
What's new section	28
Links to party websites	27
Calendar of parliamentary business	22
Full results of current and past general elections	22
Search facility	21
Opportunity for sending feedback, comments, or questions to the Web page	17
Full record of parliamentary proceedings	14
Links to the websites for state and provincial elected bodies	14
Site map	13
Opportunity to subscribe to mailing lists for receiving regular e-mail updates	5
Regular online discussion forums involving the public	3
Opportunity for public participation in online polls	2

Note: The content analysis by the IPU examined websites for 125 parliamentary chambers in 82 nations in August 1998. Each site was classified on a yes/no basis according to 48 categories of types of content.

Source: Inter-Parliamentary Union, May 2000, "Guidelines for the Content and Structure of Parliamentary websites," *http://www.ipu.org/cntr-e/web.pdf.*

that needs to be updated on a regular basis to be valuable. These items were each classified on a three-point scale according to whether the information had been updated within the previous week (3 points), more than a week ago but within the previous month (2 points), or later than a month (1 point).

The *Communication Index* was classified by summing four indicators using a simple "yes/no" (1/0) count for each according to whether the site included the following:

- Hypertext links to external sites such as to state or regional assemblies, government agencies, or political parties.
- Feedback mechanisms such as pop-up email forms, guest books, online discussion groups, and chat rooms.
- Search facilities such as a Web-based engine looking for topics under keywords.
- Email facilities to contact some or most individual members of parliament.

The Information Index and the Communication Index were each produced by adding the separate indicators and standardizing the results to 100-point scales. These two indexes were then summed into an overall Total Score. The exercise was strictly limited in the sense that priority was given to a broad global overview across all countries rather than more in-depth analysis. No attempt was made to evaluate the quality, accuracy, or even depth of the information provided, which could be done in a more comprehensive study. For example, continuous scales could be used for each indicator, rather than the simple dichotomous coding scheme, although this could produce less reliable results if these measure not just the amount of information but also coder judgments about its quality. Three-fourths of the websites provided an English-language section that aided the classification, and language translation programs helped elsewhere, but some features of the website could have been overlooked in this process. A single coder was used to ensure consistency in the content analysis schema. Websites were downloaded in May 2000 for coding but since the contents are rapidly changing, the analysis can only provide a snapshot of websites at one point in time. The exercise should be repeated in the future to monitor how far parliamentary websites adapt to new technological developments, for example if streaming audio and visual coverage of parliamentary debates become more common and if more members develop home pages. Nevertheless, the

Table 7.3. *The functions of parliamentary websites*

	Mean information index	Mean communication index	Mean total score	Number of nations
All	43	57	45	98
North America	74	83	75	3
Western Europe	69	87	72	14
Scandinavia	53	70	56	5
South America	45	69	50	17
Central and Eastern Europe	38	47	40	19
Asia-Pacific	35	51	38	17
Sub-Saharan Africa	36	33	36	15
Middle East	16	34	20	8
High human development	57	79	62	38
Medium human development	35	47	37	43
Low human development	30	32	30	14
Established democracies	55	72	58	54
Consolidating democracies	31	43	33	26
Nondemocracies	24	29	25	18

Notes and Sources: Only countries with parliamentary websites in May 2000 (98 of 178 nations worldwide) are included here. All measures have been standardized to 0 – 100 point scales. See text for description.

The **standardized information index** equals the sum of constitution plus history plus documents plus press releases plus legislation. The **standardized communication index** equals the sum of links and feedback and search and email. See Table 7.2 for the classification of countries. **Parliamentary websites**: These were identified using the list maintained by the Inter-Parliamentary Union, May 2000, *www.ipu.org/cntr-e/web.pdf.*

initial classification provides a broad map of parliaments online today around the globe that is open to further development in future research.

The results by region in Table 7.3 show that North American, Western European, and Scandinavian parliaments had the richest informational and communication facilities on their websites. For example, the New Zealand House of Representatives provided daily updated notices of parliamentary business such as bills before select

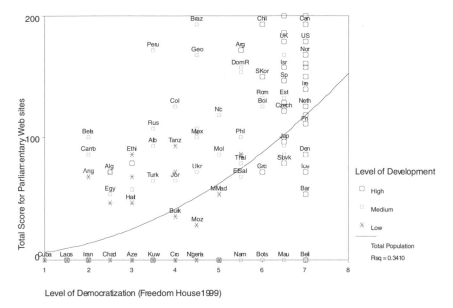

Figure 7.2. Online Parliaments and Democratization.

committee meetings, order papers, press releases and dates of sessions, searchable databases of all legislation and parliamentary questions including Hansard, electronic ordering of government reports and publications, and a highly professional and easily negotiated site. The Web pages in the French Assemblée Nationale and the Australian parliament proved imaginative and professionally designed (see Figure 7.2). In contrast, websites for the Yemeni Majlis al-Nuwaab, the Thai Ratha Sapha, and the Jordanian National Assembly proved the thinnest contents, providing basic information about the buildings and history but presenting far less information about current developments with news that was regularly updated for those wanting to follow legislative debates, government announcements, or the work of subcommittees. Scores on the information and communication indexes also varied substantially according to the country's level of socioeconomic development and level of democratization. A comparison of the quality of the legislative websites showed substantial contrasts around the globe. Compared with nondemocratic states, established democracies scored twice as well on the Information Index, and three times as well on the interactive Communication Index.

EXPLAINING THE DISTRIBUTION AND FUNCTION OF
ONLINE PARLIAMENTS

Can levels of democratic development explain the existence of online parliaments per se, or are broader trends in technological diffusion and human development influencing this pattern? As discussed earlier, the close interrelationship among all these factors makes this issue difficult to analyze, because most established democracies such as Norway, Canada, and Australia are also extremely affluent societies characterized by relatively high Internet penetration. To understand this further a series of regression models were run to predict the distribution of parliamentary websites and their levels of transparency and interactivity.

The detailed results are presented in Table 7.4. The most important finding is that, in contrast to the findings for e-governance, the distribution and information transparency of online parliaments are associated with levels of technological *and* democratic development, and all factors proved significant in predicting the level of communication interactivity of these sites. This suggests that democratic legislatures in societies where the digital revolution has advanced most fully are most likely to develop an online presence to supplement and reinforce traditional channels of dissemination and publicity such as lobby correspondents, televised proceedings, and the publication of official government documents. Established democracies ranging from the Norwegian Stortinget and Dutch Staten-Generaal to the Canadian House of Commons and U.S. Senate provide websites that are rich in information resources, giving multiple opportunities to follow the progress of pending legislation, to monitor current events such as debates and committee meetings, and to learn about elected representatives. Opportunities for the public to communicate via email, feedback forms, plus links with related parties and organizations were associated with developed societies with high levels of technological diffusion and democratization. This suggests that the factors driving public officials to develop e-governance may well be different from those influencing more representative bodies, which are open to greater political pressures from the electorate.

CONCLUSIONS: OLD INSTITUTIONS, NEW DEMANDS

The conclusions of this chapter are that parliaments are rapidly going online, providing new ways for concerned citizens to learn more about their structure, functions, and activities. People who want to find out

Table 7.4. *Explaining parliamentary websites*

	Distribution of parliamentary websites (i)		Information transparency scale (ii)		Communication interactivity scale (ii)	
	Beta	Sig.	Beta	Sig.	Beta	Sig.
Human development	1.354	.311	.109	.185	**.216**	**.007**
Technological development	**.179**	**.051**	**.323**	**.000**	**.250**	**.001**
Political development	**.250**	**.029**	**.310**	**.000**	**.312**	**.000**
Constant	−1.9		−14.5		−30.0	
Adjusted R²			.371		.401	
Nagelkerke R²	.301					
Number of nations	179		179		179	

Notes and sources: The coefficients for (i) represent the result of logistic regression model and for (ii) represent the standardized beta coefficients from OLS regression models predicting the functions of parliamentary websites measured by the contents analysis. Countries where a parliamentary website could not be located in May 2000 were coded as zero for the information and transparency scales.

Human Development is measured by the UNDP Human Development Index 1999. *Human Development Report 1999,* New York: UNDP/Oxford University Press; Percent Online from *www.nua.ie* (see Table 3.2 for details); **Level of democratization** is from Freedom House Annual Survey of Political Rights and Civil Liberties 1999–2000, *www.freedomhouse.org/survey/2000/;* **Total population 1997** is from the United Nations *U.N. Development Report, 1999,* New York: United Nations Press; **Parliamentary websites:** These were identified using the list maintained by the Inter-Parliamentary Union, May 2000, *http://www.ipu.org/cntr-e/web.pdf.*

about their elected representative can now track legislation in real time at Westminster, can watch live parliamentary debates in Denmark, Canada, and Australia, can email their elected representative on Capitol Hill, can experience a virtual tour of the U.S. Senate, and can link to learn more about international bodies in related sites for the European Parliament, Inter-Parliamentary Union, or United Nations. Potentially these websites can serve multiple constituencies: for voluntary associations, new social movements, party activists, and interest groups seeking to mobilize around particular pieces of pending legislation; for professional lobbyists and consulting companies trying to influence public affairs; for journalists needing to consult the record of ministerial speeches or government announcements; for schoolchildren and students learning about the workings of their government and constitution; as well as for the average citizen wanting to contact his or her member to complain about local roads or a housing problem. In general the availability of timely opportunities for information and communication can only help make the policymaking process more transparent and open. The most comprehensive websites – such as those for the Australian, South African, or Canadian governments – exemplify worthwhile innovations that help connect citizens to representative institutions.

Yet this positive potential needs to be tempered by more critical evaluations of current practices. Three have become common. Compared with the standards that have become commonplace today in the private sector, most parliamentary websites could adopt more professional designs. At minimal cost, most could easily become more user friendly by incorporating standard features for searching, a site map, a feedback page, and more imaginative graphics. In the British House of Commons, for example, when email has become ubiquitous in business and universities, only one-fourth of all MPs list an email contact address on the official parliamentary site, and only 12 percent provide a personal Web page. Even in the U.S. Congress, at the forefront of the technological revolution, many members are not using email to respond to constituents, in part because of the drain on staff resources this entails.[8] Official information is often presented on legislative websites in highly technical formats, assuming a familiarity with procedure that may be suitable for professional lobbyists or journalists, but may baffle much of the public. Printed papers are often published on the Web without redesign for a wider audience. Many weaker sites remain only a "shop window" façade with a few skeleton pages displaying the national flag, a picture of the building, and text about the formal constitution, more than any up-to-date practical guidance about parliamentary activities and members.

Moreover there is widespread criticism that parliaments could do more to develop opportunities for interactive communication through new technologies. Many advocates who favor strengthening direct democracy suggest that parliamentary websites should do more to facilitate and generate active citizenship, stimulating public deliberation and discussion, providing greater opportunities for feedback and popular participation, and giving the public new channels of influence.[9] Yet on balance this criticism seems to make certain questionable assumptions about the role and function of parliaments in representative democracy. The classical liberal view of parliaments stresses that the provision of information is essential for holding members individually and collectively accountable for their actions at periodic general elections and for transparency in government. If parliamentary websites provide comprehensive and detailed information about the legislative process, such as the voting records of members, the text of pending bills and White Papers, and the official record of parliamentary debates and committee discussions, then this function can be fulfilled. To expect parliamentary websites to generate new forums of public deliberation seems unreasonable, because this, after all, is the function of the multiple user groups, chat rooms, and listservs that proliferate online in civic society. Voter-member communications can also be strengthened more through private channels such as emails than by the public face of the Web. Of course it is important for democracy that the public has the opportunity to use the Internet as a virtual agora to discuss public affairs, to communicate about matters of mutual concern, and to mobilize support. But it is not at all clear that it should be the responsibility of parliamentary websites to fulfill this function.

Most important, the analysis of the contents of legislative websites says nothing about their actual use. It remains to be seen whether the development of virtual parliaments serves the needs of all citizens, or only those with the interest, knowledge, and motivation to follow current affairs. On the one hand, this development could produce what Bruce Bimber calls "accelerated pluralism" as more and more special interest groups and professional lobbyists use the informational resources available via the Internet to push particular causes, tracking specific pieces of legislation and flooding members with emails about these issues, fragmenting any broader sense of the national interest into incoherent pieces.[10] Or the process could widen the opportunities for many more diverse voices to be heard in the legislative process allowing the public to be in closer touch with their elected representative, opening wider the window on public affairs that has already been revealed with televised parliamentary debates. To explore this further, the next chapter goes on to examine the role of political parties on the Web, allowing us to see whether similar processes drive these organizations online.

CHAPTER 8

Virtual Parties

Parties have been adapting, by choice or necessity, to the new information and communication environment. More than 1,000 parties are now online, including over half of all major electoral parties, drawn from every political stripe and persuasion.[1] Cyberspace has become the virtual equivalent of Hyde Park corner. Depending on your inclination, you can see the platform of the Mongolian Communists, find the latest news about the South African ANC, read speeches by leaders of the Japanese LDP, sign the guest book for the Afghanistan Liberation Organization, watch campaign ads on the GOP site, consult the history of Sinn Fein, visit the "virtual" annual conference for the British Labour party, and join the German Greens. Major players like the Australian Labour Party and the U.S. Democrats are online, as are minor parties like Le Pen's National Front and the Scottish Nationalists, protest groups opposing the regime in China, Sudan, and Vietnam, and a plethora of fringe organizations publicizing single issues, including the New Zealand Aotearoa Legalize Cannabis party, the British Raving Loonies, and the Lithuanian Political Prisoners and Deportees party. The sign above Web portals should read: "(Almost) all forms of political life are here." The reasons for this phenomenon are not difficult to fathom: Potentially the Internet helps parties raise money, attract members, organize workers, gather feedback, and get out their message. What is not to like?

Cyber-optimists are hopeful that this development will contribute to revitalizing the role of parties in representative democracy, facilitating communications between citizen and the state, and strengthening support for these institutions. In contrast cyber-pessimists express doubts about the capacity of the Internet to function as more than "corporate wallpaper" – providing a vast electronic hording for party propaganda but providing few opportunities for genuine interaction. After reviewing theories about these issues, to examine the causes and consequences of digital politics this chapter focuses on four core questions surrounding the use of new technologies by political parties:

- To map the spread of digital politics, where and which type of parties are currently online? In particular, does use of digital politics vary systematically according to the size of parties and their position across the ideological spectrum, allowing more opportunities for insurgents and challengers to "level the playing field" of party competition?
- In terms of the consequences of this development for democracy, how far do party websites provide *comprehensive information* about their activities and opportunities for *interactive communication* between voters, members, and leaders?
- Finally, what explains this pattern and, in particular, how far does democratization, socioeconomic development, or technological diffusion drive the rise of digital parties?

THEORIES ABOUT THE DEMOCRATIC IMPACT OF PARTIES ONLINE

Cyber-optimists believe that the rapid proliferation of websites provides perhaps the best hope in modern times of reviving political parties, the core structure mediating between citizens and the state. As the renowned political scientist E. E. Scattschneider once concluded: "Modern democracy is unthinkable save in terms of political parties."[2] They differ from all other forms of political organization since only parties are capable of aggregating diverse interests, mobilizing activists, competing for elected office, and organizing government. Effective democratic parties should be accountable and responsive to their constituents while also generating mechanisms fostering party discipline and coherence in government.[3] Given these essential functions, there is widespread concern in Western democracies about weakening partisan identification in the electorate and waning membership rolls. Many interpret these trends as indicators of the decline and fall of political parties as mass organizations, although this process should not be exaggerated; it may represent a restructuring of mass-based party organizations rather than a simple demise.[4] Even more serious problems face parties in consolidating regimes such as Russia and the Ukraine, as well as Ecuador and Venezuela, where party systems are fragmented and polarized across the political spectrum, and parties contest elections based on transient leadership appeals rather than long-standing programmatic policies. Lacking a stable institutional structure, parliamentary representatives often splinter into unruly factions, based on clientalistic and personalistic local party organizations with a shallow electoral base. In many authoritarian regimes such as Burma, Libya, and Turkmenistan opposition parties are illegal organizations unable to contest elections. In these states, multiple websites by dissident parties ranging from the Afghan Hezb-e-Islami to the Zimbabwean Movement for Democratic Change may provide an invaluable channel of communication for mobilizing critical voices and challenging state propaganda.[5]

For all these reasons, cyber-optimists are enthusiastic about the democratic potential of this new technology. Yet such visions are tempered by more cautious voices stressing that it is naive to expect technology to transform existing disparities of power and wealth. Given the social and global inequalities of access that we have already observed, there are widespread fears that new technology will leave many behind in the digital race, serving to reinforce the voice of the more affluent and privileged sectors of society. Many observe that although major parties have developed websites to promote "top-down" publicity, and even state propaganda, there are few opportunities so far for genuine "bottom-up" feedback.[6] Some commentators conclude that digital parties represent politics as usual and nothing much has changed as a result of new technology.[7] But the key issues are whether the Internet provides a more level playing field facilitating party competition across the ideological spectrum, especially for challengers and insurgents, and an effective means of political communication and information supplementing traditional channels and strengthening internal party organizations. As in previous chapters, the appropriate question is not whether the Net suddenly manufactures a world of virtual Vermont town hall meetings or endless policy seminars where everyone spends their evenings earnestly discussing the latest proposals on community policing or the location of road crossings, but whether the proliferation of political resources available via the Web detracts from or enriches representative democracy. Ipso facto, more information is clearly better than less, but nevertheless the answer is not straightforward; clearly some trade-offs are involved. Are we staying at home surfing alone rather than attending face-to-face local party meetings and, if so, does this matter? Party websites provide materials for supporters and activists, but do these have the capacity to reach the disengaged and inattentive? In sum, in terms of the overall opportunities for political information and communication, are we better or worse off in the Internet age than say ten, twenty, or thirty years ago? To evaluate these issues we first need to establish where parties have moved ahead in the Internet age and then consider explanations for this distribution.

WHICH PARTIES ARE ONLINE WORLDWIDE?

Digital information and communication technologies may serve multiple internal administrative and organizational functions for parties, linking horizontally as well as vertically. Fax machines, beepers and cell phones, email, listservs, and Intranets can help integrate internal communications between branches, while computers and electoral databases help with campaigning, canvasing, and direct mail.[8] Electronic mail is particularly important for strengthening one-to-one communications and group networks within party organizations, as in the corporate world and local community, as well as linking citizens and parties.[9] Technologies such as fax machines and mobile phones serve to supplement or replace older machines without essentially changing the contents of communications. Detailed case studies provide insights into campaign communications within party organizations, such as targeted mailing and telephone canvasing, as well as email and electronic discussion groups or virtual conferences.[10] A growing body of research has described party websites in particular countries such as Denmark, Britain, and the Netherlands,[11] and many have analyzed the use of the Internet in election campaigns, particularly in the United States.[12]

DEFINING AND COMPARING ALL ONLINE PARTIES

Party websites are the primary focus of this chapter as the most important public face of the Internet. We can start by establishing where and which type of political parties were online in June 2000 using a comprehensive list of 1,371 political party websites provided by *Elections Around the World*.[13] The accuracy of this list was cross-checked and verified against two independent sources.[14] For a consistent overview, each political party with at least one official website was counted only once, excluding multiple entries such as separate websites for regional, state, or local branches, or for affiliated party organizations like youth or women's sections. The distribution of party websites was measured in 179 countries, excluding dependent territories. Given the pace of change, as with parliaments, the count of party websites in mid-2000 provides only a "snapshot" of contemporary developments during the emerging Internet era. The picture will inevitably change as more and more parties move online, but establishing benchmark data in the early stages of diffusion provides important information for monitoring subsequent developments.

The classification of websites raised some important definitional and measurement problems about what counts as a "party" that are common in the literature.[15] In some cases, it can be difficult to distinguish between a political party, conventionally defined as an organization that contests elections for government as well as advocating certain causes, and an interest group. Smaller ecology parties without any real chance of electoral success, such as Ralph Nader's bid for the U.S. presidency under the banner of the Greens, often run candidates for office primarily to raise issues on the policy agenda and promote public awareness of the environment. In similar vein, go online in America and you can discover the U.S. Taxpayers Party, the Family Values Party, the American Nazi Party, the Christian Coalition Party, the Pansexual Peace Party, and the Reasonable Party (what's not to vote for?). Should all these be counted as parties or as interest groups? Parties are also difficult to classify in parliaments such as the Russian Duma where there are frequent shifts in their nomenclature and membership, as well as the presence of many nonpartisans or independents. Closely allied parties that are in semipermanent coalition create other difficulties. For example, the Christian Democratic Union and Christian Social Union cooperate closely yet contest seats in different parts of Germany. Should they be counted as one or two separate parties? In such cases, all parties with a distinct name were counted separately in the analysis, on the grounds that each could have its own independent website as well as one that operated under any formal coalitional umbrella.

DEFINING AND COMPARING ELECTORAL PARTIES

Mapping all parties online provides a comprehensive overview but this process counts each equally, making no distinction between a minor protest group with just a Web presence and a few members, and major parties in government such as the German Social Democrats and the British Labour party. To refine the comparison, the study focused on *electoral parties,* based on the distribution of seats in the lower house of the national legislature following the most recent general election result prior to June 2000. Three main categories of electoral parties were then classified by size. *Major electoral parties* were defined as those with more than 20 percent of all seats in the lower house of parliament. *Minor electoral parties* were classified as those with more than 3 percent but fewer than 20 percent of seats in parliament. Finally, *fringe parties* were defined as those organizations that identified themselves as a political party and ran candidates to contest parliamentary elections, yet lacked at least 3 percent of the elected members of the lower house of the national parliament. This classification, while imprecise in the exact dividing lines, reflects the conventional distinctions made in the comparative literature; for example, the effective number of parliamentary parties commonly assumes a threshold of 3 percent of seats.[16] Electoral parties were also classified into party families or types, such as Social Democratic, Christian Democratic, or Green, based on the typology provided by *Elections Around the World*,[17] illustrated in Table 8.2. The complexity of identifying the ideological family of many parties proved most difficult with many religious, agrarian, and personalist parties, as well as with regional parties or those for certain social groups such as pensioners, without any other identification, which were simply categorized as "other." Finally, as with government departments and parliaments, content analysis was then carried out to measure and compare the information and communication functions of these sites.

THE DISTRIBUTION OF PARTY WEBSITES

Globally 1,250 party websites were found in the 179 nations under comparison, a remarkable phenomenon given that the Internet remains in its adolescence. On average about seven parties are online per country but, as with governments and parliaments, the regional and national disparities are marked with a patchwork quilt of websites displayed on the map (see also Table 8.1). North America has the greatest proliferation – about 41 parties online per country – Western Europe comes next, with just over two-dozen parties online per country, followed closely by Scandinavia. Multiple party websites are also common in Australia. Yet, reflecting the familiar pattern of Internet diffusion established in earlier chapters, party Webs were least common in the Middle East, parts of South America, and most of Sub-Saharan Africa, all with fewer than five parties online per country.

If we rank the distribution by country, the United States tops the list with 67 digital parties, a striking predominance given that America is one of the few remaining two-party systems in government.

Interestingly, other nations at the top of the ranking are Spain, Germany, Italy, Canada, and the United Kingdom, all with more than 45 parties online, a somewhat unexpected pattern for the Mediterranean countries given the relatively low diffusion of Internet access in this region. At the bottom of the ranking, no websites could be located for 45 nations, including some of the poorer democracies such as Vanuatu, Mali, and Benin, as well as authoritarian regimes that officially ban opposition movements. Reflecting the global inequalities observed in earlier maps showing the diffusion of Internet access, the regional contrasts were marked: more parties were online in Scandinavia alone than across all the continent of Sub-Saharan Africa. Outside of South Africa, where there were addresses for African party Webs, these often failed, and many of those that did exist tended to be updated sporadically, usually around the time of election, rather than providing a continuous service for members and supporters. The contrasts by type of political and economic system are also sharp: there were six times as many parties online in established democracies than in nondemocracies, and there are eighteen times as many in rich than poor societies. Not surprisingly, perhaps, this pattern seems at first glance to reflect the global inequalities already observed in general access to the Information Society. However, there are some clear exceptions to this pattern that need to be examined in more detail later, particularly poorer democracies with minimal public Internet access where party websites still proliferate, such as in Argentina (with 29 parties online), India (with 20), and South Africa (with 18).

WHICH TYPES OF PARTIES ARE ONLINE?

So far we have examined whether parties are online, but not which ones. The study therefore needs to compare patterns of party competition, referring to the number of parties and their spread across the ideological spectrum, whether in parliament, the electorate, or cyberspace. Cyber-optimists are hopeful that party competition will be maximized through the Internet, given the lower financial barriers smaller parties face when contemplating creating, hosting, and maintaining a website compared with the substantial costs necessary to reach the public via television, radio, or newspaper advertising, or even the less onerous costs of the mass distribution of conventional printed materials including pamphlets, bumper stickers, and posters. A few enthusiastic party supporters with know-how and technical skills can create a profes-

Table 8.1. *The world of party websites*

	All Party websites (i)		All Electoral Party websites (ii)
	Total number	Mean number per nation	Mean number per nation
All	1250	7.3	2.7
North America	124	41.3	5.0
Western Europe	374	24.9	8.9
Scandinavia	95	19.0	10.0
Central and Eastern Europe	185	7.4	3.9
Asia-Pacific	181	5.2	2.1
Middle East	69	4.9	1.2
South America	141	4.7	2.0
Sub-Saharan Africa	81	1.6	0.8
High human development	766	18.2	6.6
Medium human development	395	4.4	1.9
Low human development	46	1.3	0.5
Established democracies	913	12.3	5.0
Consolidating democracies	259	3.6	1.5
Nondemocracies	78	2.4	0.2

Notes and Sources: **All party websites:** Column (i) in the table summarizes the distribution of 1,250 official party websites in June 2000. Each party with at least one national-level official website was counted only once, excluding regional, state, or local branches or affiliated party organizations like youth sections with separate websites. Party websites were identified from *Elections Around the World, www.agora.stm.it/elections/alllinks.htm.*

Electoral Party websites: Column (ii) summarizes the distribution of the 488 websites identified for *electoral* parties, defined as all parties that contested seats for the lower house of parliament in the most recent election prior to June 2000. Electoral party websites were also identified from *Elections Around the World, www.agora.stm.it/elections/alllinks.htm.* **Level of human development** was derived from the UNDP Human Development Index 1999. UNDP, *Human Development Report 1999*, New York: UNDP/Oxford University Press. **Type of Democracy:** The level of democracy for each country was classified according to Freedom House seven-point scale of political rights and civil liberties. Countries were then classified as established democracies (1.0 to 2.5), consolidating democracies (3.0 to 4.5), and nondemocracies (5.0 to 7.0). Freedom House Survey of Political Rights and Civil Liberties 1999–2000, *www.freedomhouse.org.*

sional-looking site utilizing the free shareware and Web-hosting facilities that are available in many countries. Another feature that could potentially benefit minor and fringe parties is the relative lack of gatekeepers in cyberspace; search engines and portals such as Yahoo!, AOL, and InfoSeek are important ways for people to find sites but, conversely, the barriers to being listed are minimal compared with the difficulties of gaining sustained coverage in the mainstream news media. Standard addresses *(www.somethingparty.org)* also allow many party websites to be found with just a few guesses. Authoritarian regimes are attempting to silence dissident movements and critical opponents on the Internet in countries such as Cuba, China, and Vietnam, but this process remains more difficult than their ability to censor domestic TV stations.[18] For all these reasons, the Internet can be expected to maximize party competition, facilitating opportunities for many more insurgents and challengers to communicate their message, inform members, and gain visibility than via the traditional mass media.

Although there will be a more level playing field, this does not mean that absolute equality can be expected in cyber-space. In particular, major parties will probably have greater financial and personnel resources to create and maintain professionally designed websites complete with the latest multimedia bells and whistles like Java script and Macromedia, streaming audiovisuals, and opportunities for processing electronic commerce such as secure online payment of membership dues or campaign donations. In contrast minor or fringe parties are likely to have fewer financial and staff resources to maintain an extensive and professional website, although at the same time a basic online presence can be easily established at minimal cost using skilled volunteer labor.

The results in Table 8.2 show that the size of electoral parties was related to their Internet presence: about one-third (31 percent) of all fringe electoral parties had developed a website compared with 47 percent of minor parties, and just over one-half (52 percent) of all major parties. Nevertheless, the relatively similar development of minor and major parties online suggests that the Internet provides a more level playing field for party competition than the traditional mass media (e.g., the high costs of purchasing TV or newspaper advertisements), although it is still not a perfectly egalitarian battlefield.

Are there significant differences in the proportion of parties online by their ideological orientation; for example, have Social Democrats adapted faster to the Internet than Christian Democrats, and have Green parties adopted to digital politics faster than the far right nation-

Table 8.2. *Types of electoral parties online*

	Fringe parties (%)	Minor parties (%)	Major parties (%)	*All (%)*
Extreme left	35	65	44	*42*
Social Democrat	38	53	74	*52*
Greens	59	88	0	*71*
Center	33	45	28	*37*
Liberals	39	73	82	*57*
Christian Democrats	52	71	78	*62*
Conservative	36	55	66	*51*
Nationalist, far right	49	41	32	*41*
Others including religious, agrarian, and regional parties lacking another identification	18	22	19	*19*
All	*31*	*47*	*52*	*39*

Notes and Sources: The table lists the percentage of all electoral parties with an official national website in 179 nations in June 2000, and the ideological family for each party, according to *Elections Around the World, www.agora.stm.it/elections/alllinks.htm.* The total analysis examined 1,244 electoral parties in the countries under comparison of which 488 were found to have a website.

Electoral parties were defined as all those that contested seats for the lower house of parliament in the most recent election. Parties were classified by size according to the distribution of seats in the lower house of parliament in the latest election results. **Fringe parties** included those with fewer than 3 percent of seats in parliament. **Minor parties** have more than 3 percent and fewer than 20 percent of seats. **Major parties** have more than 20 percent of seats.

alists? Previous studies about political balance remain inconclusive. Hill and Hughes's study of interest groups on the Web in the United States found that, at least in the early years, those on the right of the political spectrum tended to have bigger and glitzier websites than their leftist counterparts.[19] Yet a comparison of Sweden and the Netherlands suggested that left-of-center parties put slightly more efforts into their websites.[20] The lack of barriers to minor players may produce more digital parties drawn from both the extreme left as well as right, in a potpourri ranging from the unreformed Cuban and Kyrgystan communist parties to the Austrian Freedom Party or the fascist Movimento Sociale Fiamma Tricolore in Italy. Multiple minor and fringe parties communicated online, from radical Marxist freedom fighters in Afghanistan to environmentalists, anarchists, and neofascist militia in America.

The distribution of websites by party family displayed in Table 8.2 suggests that there is no clear bias online toward either the "left" or "right"; instead a rough political balance exists on the Internet. Green parties are most likely to take advantage of the new opportunities, with 71 percent of all ecological parties online, perhaps because their membership is likely to be drawn from among the highly educated professional classes who, we have seen, are among highest users of the Internet, and Green parties are also strongest in advanced Information Societies. As discussed later, the predominant cyber-culture, at least in America, is also one that is broadly sympathetic to such causes as environmentalism. Among major mainstream parties, about half or more of all the Social Democrats, Christian Democrats, Liberal and Conservative parties are online. These parties are common in Scandinavia, Western Europe, and North America, all regions with high interconnectivity. About four of ten of the nationalist and extreme right parties were online, about the same level as the Communists and extreme right. Some fear (and others hope) that the Internet can provide a flourishing environment for groups that are currently marginalized in the traditional mass media, and the evidence suggests that although the mainstream parties are more commonly online, many minor and fringe parties on the extreme left and right have developed an online site for political expression, mobilization, and organization.

THE FUNCTIONS OF PARTY WEBS

The distribution of websites tells us nothing about their role and functions. The home pages shown in Figure 8.1 illustrate some of the differences and similarities in how parties choose to present themselves online and also the common functions of these sites, which range from the African National Congress and Afghanistan Liberation Organisation to the Bharatiya Janata Party in India and the British Labour Party, as well as the U.S. Democrats and Republicans. Some websites consist of a few pages about the history and principles of the party, updated at infrequent intervals, lacking sophisticated graphics and features, though often with hit counters suggesting few visitors over the years. In contrast other parties have developed detailed and rich sites commonly providing multiple features: many layers of archived information about the history, organization, and core principles, including the full text of

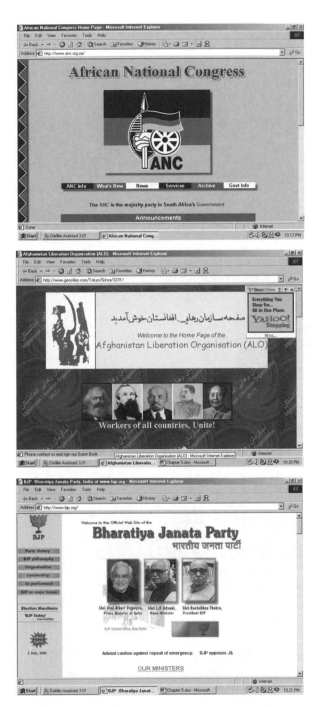

Figure 8.1. Examples of Party Websites in South
Africa, Afghanistan, India, Britain, and the United
States. (*Figure continues*)

Figure 8.1 Continued

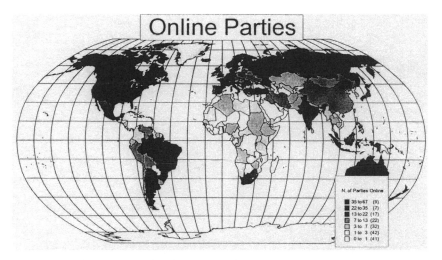

Figure 8.2. The Global Map of Parties Online.

party manifestos; biographical and contact information about the leadership of the party, parliamentary candidates, and elected members; regularly updated press releases and multimedia streaming audio video of events such as leadership speeches; a schedule of activities and events at branch, constituency, and regional levels plus links to local party websites; email addresses and telephone contact information, including how to join the party; links to related parties and affiliated groups at national and international levels; "virtual" live annual conference coverage; and professional keyword search facilities plus a site map. The major parties in the United States display some of the latest whiz-bang features, including facilities for multimedia presentations like streaming video, interactivity such as online polls, and the opportunity to make financial donations electronically using secure servers.

To explore this more systematically, the contents of the electoral party websites were analyzed. Websites were classified according to their *information transparency,* based on 19 criteria, listed in Table 8.3, such as whether online parties included information about their party history, constitution, organization, program, and schedule of events. In addition these websites were coded according to their *communication interactivity,* using 13 criteria such as whether people could join the party online, donate money, volunteer services, email officials, and join discussion groups. The items were summed into two scales that were then combined into a summary standardized 100-point digital party index.

Table 8.3. *The contents of electoral party websites*

	Communication function	Information function	Percent
Can email party officials	*		79
Party history		*	78
Program, manifesto, statement of principles		*	78
Press releases/media section		*	70
Party organization		*	63
Parliamentary candidate information (e.g., biographies)		*	60
Links to external websites		*	60
Email contact address for Web master	*		57
Join party	*		57
Leadership information or speeches		*	53
Party constitution and rules		*	52
Website in English		*	52
Submit message form	*		50
Parliamentary candidates contact details (e.g., mail address, fax, phone, or email)	*		50
Constituency information or election results by districts		*	45
What's new section/page		*	42
Party congress, conference, or convention		*	37
Schedule of events		*	37
Join discussion/listserv	*		35
Other affiliated organizational section		*	32
Can email party leader	*		32
Any multimedia video or audio		*	31
Youth section		*	31
Search facility	*		31
Volunteer services	*		28
Can sign up to receive a regular electronic newsletter	*		26
Can email elected members of parliament	*		26
Women's section		*	25

(continues)

Table 8.3 *Continued*

	Communication function	Information function	Percent
Website in other non-native language		*	24
Union section		*	20
Donate money	*		15
Buy party goods (e.g., publications)	*		7
Number	13	19	

Notes and Sources: The content analysis examined the websites for 339 electoral parties defined as the number of parties contesting the most recent election for the lower House of Parliament. Calculated from *Elections Around the World, www.agora.stm.it/elections/alllinks.htm.*

All the previous functions were coded as present (1) or absent (0) when the websites were content analyzed in November 2000. In total, 399 websites were analyzed worldwide, with 58 unable to be contacted from the listed Web address.

Table 8.3 shows the popularity of different types of activities. Websites most often provided basic information about the party history, program, organization, and press releases, as well as biographical information about parliamentary candidates and links to external websites. People were also often encouraged to join the party, with secure servers for electronic membership, and many provided opportunities to contact party officials by electronic mail. Yet parties proved reluctant to raise other sources of funds directly via the Internet, such as buying goods like publications or donating money, and there were also few opportunities to email members of parliament or party leaders via these sites. The contents of websites varied slightly among different types of parties, with major parties slightly richer in communication and information functions than minor parties, and the least developed facilities provided by the fringe parties, although overall competition on the Web proved fairly egalitarian. When compared by party families, (as shown in Table 8.4) again there is no clear bias online toward either the "left" or "right"; instead a rough political balance exists on the Internet, with greatest use by the moderate center. Green parties proved among the most successful in adapting to the multiple functions inherent in the new medium, especially those such as the Green Links in the Netherlands, les Verts in France, and Dei Greng in Luxembourg, although websites for Christian Democrat and Conservative parties were also well developed online; the

Table 8.4. *The function of electoral party websites*

	Number of parties	Fringe parties (%)	Minor parties (%)	Major parties (%)	*All (%)*
Extreme left	(28)	46	54	39	*47*
Social Democrat	(80)	35	46	54	*46*
Greens	(20)	52	67	–	*60*
Center	(27)	57	45	58	*50*
Liberals	(31)	43	56	60	*49*
Christian Democrats	(26)	48	71	66	*57*
Conservative	(51)	49	53	60	*53*
Nationalist, far right	(31)	55	51	40	*49*
Others including religious, agrarian, and regional parties lacking another identification.	(45)	40	40	32	*40*
All	*(339)*	*45*	*51*	*54*	*49*

Notes and Sources: The table lists the combined standardized (100-point) score on the Information Transparency and Communications Interactivity website scale. See Table 8.2 for the items used in constructing the scale, based on contents analysis of 339 electoral parties in 179 nations in November 2000.

The ideological family for each party was classified according to *Elections Around the World, www.agora.stm.it/elections/alllinks.htm.* **Electoral parties** were defined as all those that contested seats for the lower house of parliament in the most recent election. Parties were classified by size according to the distribution of seats in the lower house of parliament in the latest election results. **Fringe parties** included those with fewer than 3 percent of seats in parliament. **Minor parties** have more than 3 percent and fewer than 20 percent of seats. **Major parties** have more than 20 percent of seats.

highest scoring parties proved as diverse as the Social Democratic parties in Germany and Switzerland, the Liberal Democrats in the United Kingdom and the Communist party in Japan.

EXPLAINING THE DISTRIBUTION AND FUNCTION OF PARTY WEBS

What helps to explain the patterns we found? Based on the results from the previous chapter analyzing parliaments, it might be anticipated that the type of political system is one of the leading candidates, in particular that these websites would be more commonly available in older democratic states with a long tradition of well-established party organizations, such as Norway, Germany, and Australia, rather than in consolidating and transitional democratic societies such as Russia, Sri Lanka, and Tanzania. The contrasts are likely to be even stronger in one-party regimes and authoritarian states that legally ban opposition parties from mobilizing and contesting parliamentary elections, such as in Cuba, Bhutan, and Burma. The previous chapter demonstrated the influence of democratization in predicting the existence and quality of parliamentary websites. Yet there may also be many exceptions to this pattern because socioeconomic development, and in particular the broader technological diffusion of the Information Society, may also influence digital politics. If so, poorer democracies lagging behind the Internet revolution in Sub-Saharan Africa and South East Asia (e.g., Mali and Bangladesh) may have few wired parties, but in contrast far more may be online in affluent states such as Singapore and Saudi Arabia. As in previous chapters, levels of democratic, technological, and socioeconomic development can be examined to help explain the distribution of party websites worldwide.

The results in Table 8.5 show that the strongest and most significant indicator of the presence of all parties online is technological diffusion, measured by the proportion of the population online, followed by levels of socioeconomic development. As Chapter 3 demonstrated, more affluent industrialized economies characteristically have the richest access to multiple forms of communication and information technologies, including old media like telephones and televisions as well as new ones like computers and Internet hosts, and this environment is most conducive to the spread of online parties. These organizations respond to the opportunities within their broader economic and technological environment. Parties are most likely to have the necessary infrastructure for establishing and maintaining websites in countries that are rich in a wide range of digital technologies, and the incentive to compete for the attention of the electorate is also greatest where much of the population is wired. After controlling for socioeconomic and technological development, the level of democratization in a country proved unrelated to the density of parties online, or their information and communication functions, a pattern that requires further scrutiny.

To confirm this interpretation, the main patterns were further examined graphically with scatter plots that also help to identify any outlier nations. Figure 8.3 reveals additional reasons for the poor fit between

Table 8.5. *Explaining party websites*

	Distribution of party websites		Information transparency scale		Communications interactivity scale	
	Beta	Sig.	Beta	Sig.	Beta	Sig.
Human development	**.186**	**.016**	.103	.548	**.409**	**.007**
Technological development	**.502**	**.000**	**.425**	**.002**	**.437**	**.000**
Political development	.100	.168	.045	.777	−.123	.367
Constant	−6.4		6.09		−.438	
R²	.457		.238		.436	

Notes and sources: The beta coefficients represent the results of stepwise OLS regression models predicting the distribution and function of party websites.

Total Number of Parties: The number of online parties in June 2000 calculated from *Elections Around the World, www.agora.stm.it/elections/alllinks.htm.* For the items contained in the Communication and Information scales analyzed in November 2000, see Table 8.2. **Human Development** is measured by the UNDP Human Development Index 1999, *Human Development Report 1999,* New York: UNDP/Oxford University Press. **Total population 1997** is from the United Nations Development Report, 1999. **Percent Online** is from *www.nua.ie* (see Table 3.2 for details). **Level of democratization** is from the Freedom House Annual Survey of Political Rights and Civil Liberties 1999–2000, *www.freedomhouse.org/survey/2000/.*

the level of democratization and the density of online parties. Most authoritarian regimes such as China and Vietnam have few parties online, a pattern that was not unexpected given the concentration of powers in the state, and the restriction on opposition movements. Slightly more parties are found online in some of the transitional and consolidating democracies (e.g., Russia and Brazil), but many countries in this category also have few parties online (e.g., Bangladesh). Finally, there is tremendous variation in the density of online parties among the established democracies, ranging from the proliferation of party websites in the United States, Canada, and Spain at the top end of the spectrum down to many smaller democracies such as in Barbados, Trinidad, and Micronesia where there are few or none. This suggests that, once controls are introduced for socioeconomic and technological development, then democratization per se fails to explain to what extent parties have moved online. In contrast the scatter plots of the density of party websites by the penetration of the Information Society displays a closer fit. The most plausible reason is that, as with government departments,

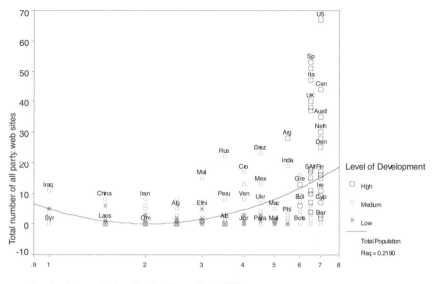

Figure 8.3. Online Parties and Democratization.

Sources: **Total number of all party websites** identified in June 2000 from Elections Around the World, *www.agora.stm/it/elections/alllinks.htm.* **Level of Democratization:** From Freedom House seven-point scale of political rights and civic liberties, 1999, *www.freedomhouse.org.*

in societies where few are online there is minimal incentive for parties to develop websites, and the infrastructure hinders their development. Countries that have supported the distribution of computers and Internet access are also the leading societies in which party organizations have adapted to the opportunities of digital technologies. This further suggests that the growth of the Information Society has influenced the political resources available on the Internet, and therefore the process of democratization, more than democracy, has affected the presence of parties on the Internet.

CONCLUSIONS: THE IMPACT OF DIGITAL PARTIES

Parties are among the most important institutions mediating between citizens and the state, providing an avenue for political activism and expression for members, an institutional structure for the recruitment and selection of parliamentary candidates, and a mechanism for the coordination and organization of electoral competition and govern-

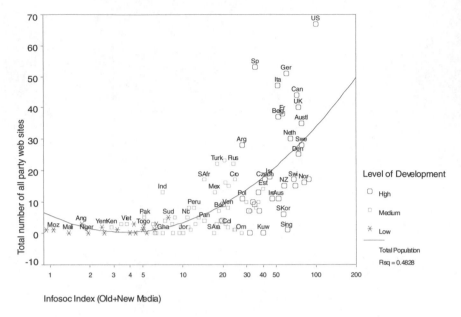

Figure 8.4. Online Parties and the Information Society.

Sources: **Total number of all party websites** identified in June 2000 from *Elections Around the World, www.agora.stm/it/elections/alllinks.htm.* **Infosoc Index:** Old media plus new media, see Table 3.2.

ment. All of these activities have taken place for centuries without the Internet, and digital technologies can only be expected to supplement rather than replace these functions, just as telephones, fax machines, and personal computers have gradually altered, without essentially revolutionizing, the nature of political campaigns. If parties are falling out of favor with the public, or becoming detached from their supporters, as some evidence suggests, then the effective use of new communication channels may potentially provide one way to revive public confidence.

Among digital technologies, the use of emails is likely to be most important for strengthening party organizations, because it is far more popular and widespread than use of alternative mechanisms such as party-run chat rooms, electronic party conferences, or their equivalent. Party sites on the Web represent the most important public face for connecting with the attentive public. What will be the consequences of these developments for representative democracy? As was emphasized in previous chapters, any evaluative judgments relate to broader visions of democracy and the appropriate functions of parties. Like governments and parliaments, party websites should be evaluated in terms of the quality and effectiveness of their informational and communication functions in representative democracy.

The criteria of transparent *information* is important because citizens can only make effective electoral decisions if they can evaluate the record, programs, and leadership of the alternative parties and candidates competing for office. People can thereby cast informed ballots that accurately match their political preferences. Information can and does come from multiple sources, more commonly the mass media such as television news, as well as unmediated channels of political communications such as political advertisements and personal discussions. The most extensive party websites supplement these sources for the attentive public, party members, and middle-level elites, not just with more of the same information, but with an easily accessible archived source of unmediated party information, such as the full official text of manifesto policies and detailed policy documents, updated press releases, information about the party organization and structure, as well as information about the biographical background and experience of the leadership team and parliamentary candidates. For those who are interested, more timely unmediated information about political parties is more easily available via the Internet than ever before. The ability to employ innovative multimedia for core activities such as annual conference party debates, or to drill down to research particular policy issues, holds considerable potential for strengthening representative democracy. Parties publicize the information and images that they believe are most positive for serving their own interests, but this should not necessarily be dismissed as "only propaganda." Insofar as much of this information is often not readily available from other sources, and as long as the public can compare information across competing party websites, this process can be seen to add to electoral competition in representative democracy. As we will see in subsequent chapters, party websites tend to reach sympathizers and the attentive more than the mass of the politically disengaged. But as with the classic functions of the partisan press, campaign rallies, or stump speeches, the "one-sided" nature of information provided by party websites can serve to crystallize wavering supporters and mobilize activists, essential in any get-out-the-vote drive.[21]

Representative democracy requires two-way *communication* as well as information, at regular intervals beyond elections, so that leaders receive feedback and maintain contact with the grassroots. Many advocates of "strong" or "direct" democracy commonly argue that these functions are not well served by digital parties. It is true that on balance slightly fewer opportunities existed for "bottom-up" interactivity in communicating with parties than for "top-down" information. Nevertheless more than three-quarters of the sites provided email addresses to contact party officials, one-half the websites provided submit-message forms, one-third of all party websites included discussion forums or listservs, while one-quarter provided ways to email elected MPs. Moreover, deliberation within parties may be more easily facilitated through more private electronic communications, such as emails circulated among members, rather than public message boards. All these forms of electronic communication may reinforce internal party democracy, facilitate political participation, mobilize around campaigns, and help the party leadership and officials to keep in touch with the concerns of their supporters and activists. This function may prove particularly important for parties that already have an established mass-branch organization, facilitating faster and easier communication about local meetings and events.

The evidence in this chapter suggests that many parties have taken advantage of digital technology – about one-half of all major parties currently have websites – and the momentum is likely to continue until it would be unusual if any party were not online. Moreover while the major parties were most commonly found online, and these sites tended to offer the richest information and communication functions, there were only modest differences among major, minor, and fringe electoral parties in these regards. Out of all party families, there was a broad overall left-right balance online, although the Green websites offered the most developed information and communications facilities, followed by the Christian Democrats. Compared with other channels of mass communications, the Internet therefore offers a relatively egalitarian battleground for party competition, allowing minor parties to present a website that is just as developed as those offered by many of the governing parties. Smaller opposition parties and minor challengers may often lag behind in campaign funds and traditional mass membership organizations, but they may be able to compensate via technical mastery of the digital technologies and greater flexibility to adapt to building support, networking, and mobilizing in the new environment. Are similar patterns found in other arenas of civic society? So far we have not considered the potential impact of the digital technologies for traditional interest groups, new social movements, and the news media. The next chapter considers these institutions.

CHAPTER 9

Civic Society

The networking potential of the Internet and its ability to link transnational advocacy networks, grassroots political organizations, and the independent media around the world has aroused hopes that civic society can be nurtured and mobilized through digital technologies. "Civic society" is understood to refer to the multiple organizations buffering between citizens and the state, including parties discussed in the previous chapter, as well as the news media, traditional interest groups such as trade unions and professional associations, in addition to such alternative social movements as environmentalist organizations, the women's movement, human rights groups, and peace activists. The news industry was one of the first organization to venture online, whereas transnational advocacy networks have been among the most active organizations taking advantage of the Web for mobilizing, publicity, and interaction. Stealth protest coalitions have formed like virtual guerrilla armies around issues such as world trade, fuel taxes, and genetically modified food, then subsequently dissipated, only to reappear in different guise at a later date. But what have been the political consequences of these developments? After reviewing debates in the literature theorizing about these issues, we examine evidence comparing civic society worldwide by focusing on three questions:

- Which news media, interest groups, and new social movements are online throughout the world?
- What is the potential impact of online civic society on political participation, community building, and democracy?
- What explains this distribution, in particular how far does democ-

ratization or technological diffusion foster the spread of civic societies on the Internet?

THEORIES ABOUT THE DEMOCRATIC
IMPACT ON CIVIC SOCIETY

As always, there are alternative interpretations about whether the virtual glass is half-empty or half-full, depending on the normative foundations of democratic theory underlying any evaluations. On the one hand, cyber-optimists hope that the Internet will prove the great equalizer.[1] Digital technologies may serve to strengthen the institutions of civic society, widening the opportunities for information, communication, and participation in the electronic public sphere, allowing well-organized and nimble David's to run circles around lumbering corporations and international bodies.[2] The characteristics of the Internet to shrink costs, maximize speed, broaden reach, and eradicate distance provide transnational advocacy networks with an effective tool for mobilization, organization, and expression that can potentially maximize their leverage in the global arena.[3] If what matters are openness in the marketplace of ideas and ways to link with like-minded advocates, then the Web delivers an equal opportunity soapbox. Protest movements have traditionally relied on activities such as street theater, public demonstrations, and direct action to challenge authorities.[4] The Internet has altered this dynamic by electronically promoting the diffusion of protest ideas and tactics efficiently and quickly across national borders.[5] The mobilization of transnational advocacy networks has caught policymakers off guard. The World Trade Organization meeting in Seattle in late November 1999 exemplified this process, bringing together an alliance between labor and environmental activists – the Turtle Teamster partnership – together with a network of consumer advocates, anticapitalists, and grassroots movements that attracted a firestorm of media attention. Websites, like that maintained by the International Civil Society (ICS), provided hourly updates about the major demonstrations in Seattle to a network of almost 700 NGOs in some 80 countries, including environmentalists, students, religious groups, human rights organizations, trade unions, and related movements.[6] Although the Seattle meeting was a particularly dramatic demonstration of the potential of this medium, there are other well-known examples including the anti–landmine campaign in the mid- to late-1990s, the anti-globalization protests against the World Bank and IMF in Prague in December 1999, and the widespread anti-

fuel tax protests that disrupted European politics and unsettled governments in October 2000.[7] In Chicago in 1968, protestors chanted "The
whole world is watching" as TV broadcast pictures of police beating
demonstrators outside the Democratic Convention. But such publicity
depends on journalistic gatekeepers, and today campaigners can do it
directly for themselves, bypassing the traditional news media by organizing a few inexpensive Web cams broadcasting live pictures, lending local
activities a worldwide platform. To learn about Burma, for example, you
can listen to the speeches of human rights activist, Aung San Suu Kyi, or
read reports by Human Rights Watch, Amnesty International, or Free
Burma Coalition (an activist network), although you can also learn
about the news from the government's perspective on their website.[8]
Many environmentalists have incorporated the multimedia capabilities
of the Internet into their direct action strategies. Global Forest Watch,
for example, is a transnational network of scientists and local groups
regularly monitoring, recording, and reporting the erosion of forests,
using digital maps and Web cams to publicize abuses by the timber
industry and agribusiness, providing a flexible kind of regulatory process
working outside of formal government structures.[9] The Internet also
facilitates a host of independent newspapers, magazines, and radio stations, at minimal cost compared with the investment required for a traditional printing plant and distribution networks, or broadcasting
transmission channels. Digital outlets can be particularly important
under authoritarian regimes, where protest activities and the independent news media are severely constrained or silenced, although cases such
as the Falun Gong in China and anti-state dissidents in Cuba illustrate
that the authorities can move effectively to block and suppress Internet
use by insurgent forces.[10]

Many communitarian theorists adhering to the values of direct or
"strong" democracy have also expressed hopes that at the most diffuse
level the Internet can strengthen virtual grassroots groups, moving
from traditional "communities of place" based on physical location and
ascribed identities toward "communities of choice" based on collabo-
rating on common interests.[11] Howard Rhinegold has presented one of
the strongest arguments that electronic bulletin boards, discussion
groups, and listservs can be used to exchange ideas, debate issues, and
mobilize opinion, building lasting relationships and social bonds.[12] The
sociologist Amatai Etzioni also believes that the Internet can foster virtual communities, as well as complementing, strengthening, and sus-
taining existing social ties in the nonvirtual world.[13] In similar vein,

Tsagarousianou hopes that new information technologies can revitalize civic networks in urban neighborhoods.[14]

Yet more pessimistic prognostications can also be heard. Ayres warns that cyber-diffusion among NGOs has a cautionary side: While significantly enhancing the potential for disparate individuals and groups to collectively pool resources and strategy, the Internet also has the power to turn unreliable and unverifiable information into global anarchy.[15] Bimber argues that the process may produce accelerated or hyper-pluralism, in which the Internet reinforces the fragmentation of the American political system moving from interest-based group politics toward a more fluid, issue-based group politics with less institutional coherence.[16] In contrast, others fear that instead of empowering new actors, digital technologies may function to reinforce the power of established interests and organizations. Taylor Boas warns that authoritarian regimes such as Cuba restrict the Internet for dissident forces, while allowing pro-state groups full access, as well as using the medium to boost inward investment, marketing of its products, tourism, and traditional areas of development including education and health. The Cuban government's official website serves to present an official face to the world.[17] McChesney fears that the commercialization of the Internet as a tool of mass entertainment, funded by advertising, will entrench the power of mega media conglomerates in the global marketplace, allowing international corporations like Disney, Time Warner, and Bertelsmann to "don a new set of clothing."[18] The commercial side of the Web threatens to overwhelm the public sector as the number of dot.coms has been expanding far faster than governmental and nonprofit organizations. The Internet Software Consortium estimate that in January 2000 out of 72 million domain hosts worldwide there were about 25 million dot.coms, compared with 0.9 million dot.orgs and 0.7 million dot.govs.[19] Nonretail corporate Web pages are often designed as another form of public relations wallpaper, promoting glossy images and favorable puff but providing minimal two-way interaction, even by email.[20] Moreover, as with parties, it is not clear whether there is a "balanced" or equal representation in civic society: Hill and Hughes examined a random sample of American interest groups on the Web and found that conservative websites were on average larger, glitzier, and more visible than their liberal counterparts, although the latter were better networked in terms of links.[21] There is also widespread concern that although the new political resources on the Web are potentially open to all with Internet access, in practice these will serve to reinforce the voices of those who are already most active and engaged, as well as those who are already among the most well informed from traditional news outlets, rather than reaching the inactive in society.[22] To explore the evidence underpinning these views, we first need to establish how the news media and transnational advocacy networks have exploited the potential of this new medium, then go on to assess the possible consequences of this development.

WHICH NEWS MEDIA ARE ONLINE?

The news industry has been one of the most active players in the online world. Journalists were among the first to jump on the Internet bandwagon although conflicted between fears of being left behind, like the quill pen and illustrated parchment in the age of the Gutenberg press, and fears about the economic consequences of "giving away the store."[23] In the 1970s, "online" meant costly investments using special Viewtron and videotex news accessed over phone lines. In the early 1980s, electronic versions of eleven U.S. newspapers such as the *L.A. Times* and the *Washington Post* were accessible (expensively and slowly) via proprietary services like CompuServe, Prodigy, and America Online. In the early 1990s newspapers like the *San Jose Mercury News* and the *Albuquerque Tribune* experimented with online textual retrieval of newspaper stories. By 1993, 20 daily newspapers had ventured online and by 1996 there were about 1,000.[24] Today *AJR Newslink* estimates that worldwide there are probably more than 5,400 online newspaper sites, broadly defined to include major metros, nondailies, the business press, the alternative press such as the *Village Voice,* specialty newspapers like DC's *Roll Call* or Seattle's *Gay News,* as well as promotional or limited content websites.[25] Yahoo lists even more news sites, although again not all providing daily updates, including 6,600 newspapers, 2,500 magazines, 8,500 radio stations, and 538 television stations, not counting the 14,000 general sites devoted to television. Surf the Internet café over breakfast and you can browse *Le Monde,* the *Jerusalem Post,* the *Washington Post,* or (my morning reading) the London *Times.* At first some newspapers provided only a shop window announcing their existence, but the content rapidly expanded until many provide all the daily news printed in the paper version and more, such as special archives, audio interviews, photomontages, rolling banner news headlines, readers polls, and links to related sites.

Radio and television ventured online shortly after the press. Twiddle the Internet dial and you can listen 24/7 to live streaming audio of samba from Rio, or perhaps, given your particular tastes, blues from

Chicago, Celtic gigs from Connemara, swing big bands from New York, or the BBC World Service in Arabic, Spanish, Russian, Chinese, and Welsh. Technologies morph into each other, with the Web becoming available through television sets, just as broadband television can be watched online via common software such as RealPlayer and Windows Media Player. The most extensive online news and current affairs services have been provided by public broadcasters, such as the British BBC, Canadian CBC, Australian ABC, the American PBS, as well as by some of the American commercial networks like ABC and CNN.[26] Figure 9.1 shows the typical formats commonly offered by these websites, including regularly updated headline news, sections for weather, sports, and kids, as well as search indexes, archives with in-depth programs, tickertape stock reports, and special features. Live coverage of parliament is also available. Nevertheless in many countries online television companies have often provided little streaming audiovisual contents. Many TV sites currently remain strictly promotional, containing little more than corporate advertising, providing daily TV schedules and information, as well as company reports about the organization, but minimal updated news contents or programming.

As discussed fully in subsequent chapters, this context is rapidly altering the typical profile of the news audience. Pew surveys in spring 2000 indicate that one in three Americans go online for news at least once a week, compared to 20 percent in 1998.[27] And 15 percent say they receive *daily* news from the Internet, up from 6 percent two years ago. At the same time, regular viewing of network news has fallen from 38 percent to 30 percent over this period, while local news viewing has declined from 64 percent to 56 percent. Internet users are also slightly less likely than nonusers to watch morning shows such as *Today* and *Good Morning America* and evening news magazines such as *60 Minutes, 20/20,* or *Dateline.* Regular use of Internet news is even higher among the younger generation, and there has also been a more moderate decline in newspaper and magazine readership. Although online news has probably penetrated less widely in countries with lower patterns of Internet access, there are many indicators of its potential market; for example, streaming financial news headlines are widely accessed via I-mobile phones in Japan, and the BBC is among the 10 most popular sites in the United Kingdom.[28] When asked about a range of activities available via the Internet, many Europeans expressed interest in reading news and magazines online, especially in Scandinavian countries where Internet use is among the highest in the world.[29]

Figure 9.1. Examples of Online Television News: Britain (BBC), Australia (ABC), United States (ABC), and Canada (CBC). Midday headlines July 19, 2000. *(Figure continues)*

Figure 9.1. Continued

WHICH NEWSPAPERS ARE ONLINE?

Given what we know about the global inequalities in Internet access, are similar geographic patterns also evident in the spread of the online news media? The distribution of newspapers and television stations across different countries is more difficult to establish than the classification of parliamentary, party, or government websites, in part because a simple keyword or indexed search using common engines reveals the multiplicity of organizations supplying digital "news" in one form or another, ranging from full text versions of national and regional daily papers down to local newspapers, electronic magazines and periodicals, as well as radio stations, TV sites, and news organizations. Portal sites such as Yahoo! and Lycos are content aggregators providing access to Associated Press, Reuters, and Bloomberg wire service news, and they run classified ads too. Microsoft owns the Microsoft Network, Sidewalk city guides and Slate, the high-profile Webzine. Many journalists also run their own personal websites, including phenomena like the *Drudge Report*. Like ants in the kitchen, "news," broadly defined, pops up all over the Web.

The best way to document the scope and reach of this phenomenon worldwide is to draw on established databases that regularly monitor online news media. The *AJRNewslink,* run by Newslink Associates and the *American Journalism Review,* provides the most comprehensive list that is currently available.[30] The one major limitation with relying on a single source such as the *AJRNewslink* is that this list is maintained by a U.S.-based organization, which may bias the results toward more comprehensive coverage of American newspapers and TV stations than those elsewhere, (e.g., in Africa or the Middle East). The information provided by this database was therefore cross-checked and verified against three other similar sites: one run by *Editor & Publisher,* which also provided details about the geographic spread of news outlets; the *World News Index* which indexes all daily news sources on the Internet, and Yahoo's more eclectic list of news media in each country. Even with multiple sources, another important limitation of this exercise is that each website is counted equally: whether a glitzy, continually updated, content-rich, all bells-and-whistles 24/7 news audio–video broadband TV station or a weekly online magazine or quarterly periodical containing the contents page and details about how to subscribe. Moreover the boundaries of "news," always permeable, have become even fuzzier. If defining what counts as a "party" creates headaches, then demarcating "the news media" generates an instant migraine. Because the process of calculating the number of online media outlets is not dissimilar to counting tadpoles wriggling in a jam jar, the data should be regarded as broadly indicative, a rough and ready tally, rather than a definitive global census. For comparison with the traditional news media, these

Table 9.1. *The world of online newspapers*

	Total number of online newspapers (2000)	Total number of daily newspapers (1966)	Proportion of all daily newspapers online	Total number of nations
All	2,494	8,145	40	161
Western Europe	388	1,134	63	15
North America	1,355	1,922	53	3
South America	165	981	52	26
Scandinavia	133	275	50	5
Middle East	55	198	45	14
Sub-Saharan Africa	67	212	39	47
Asia-Pacific	238	2,712	30	28
Central and Eastern Europe	93	711	24	23
High human development	1,982	3752	51	42
Medium human development	427	4171	36	80
Low human development	34	175	28	31
Established democracies	2,111	3,937	53	64
Consolidating democracies	298	1,739	35	67
Nondemocracies	50	469	20	30

Note: The table summarizes the distribution of online newspapers in 179 nations as of June 2000 according to *AJRNewslink. www.Ajr.newslink.org.* These data were cross-checked and verified against the lists of newspapers (media links) maintained by *Editor & Publisher, www.mediainfo.com;* the World News Index, *http://wni.Harold.nu;* and the list provided by Yahoo *www.Dir.yahoo.com/News and Media/Newspapers/By region/Countries.*

The total number of daily newspapers per nation: The latest year available, normally 1996, in 174 nations with data drawn from the *UNESCO Statistical Yearbook 1999,* Paris: UNESCO. **Level of human development** was derived from the UNDP Human Development Index 1999. UNDP, *Human Development Report 1999.* New York: UNDP/Oxford University Press. **Type of Democracy:** The level of democracy for each country was classified according to the Freedom House seven-point scale of political rights and civil liberties. Countries were then classified as established democracies (1.0 to 2.5), consolidating democracies (3.0 to 4.5), and nondemocracies (5.0 to 7.0). Freedom House Survey of Political Rights and Civil Liberties 1999–2000, *www.freedomhouse.org*

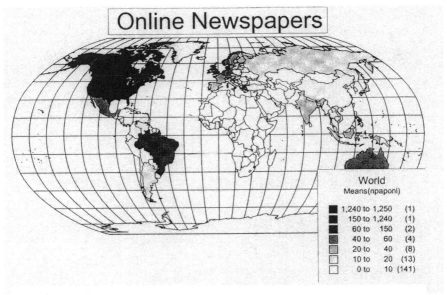

Figure 9.2 The World of Online Newspapers.

estimates can be compared with the number of daily newspapers published in each country, as monitored worldwide by UNESCO.[31]

The global distribution of online newspapers is displayed in Table 9.1 and mapped in Figure 9.2. The most important comparison for this study is less the *number* of online newspapers in each region – which often closely reflects the degree or concentration or dispersion in the newspaper market[32] – than the *proportion* of newspapers currently available online within each region or country. The latter – representing the density of online newspapers – provides the best gauge of the penetration of the Internet society per se. The results of the comparison suggest that about 2,500 or four out of ten daily newspapers are now online worldwide. This estimate is, more conservative than some others because this figure excludes nondailies and promotional newspapers and magazines sites. Newspapers in Western Europe have the highest online newspaper density, with almost two-thirds of all papers having a digital version on the Web. North America, South America, and Scandinavia are next, all with about half their papers online.

North America leads the world in terms of the sheer *number* of online daily newspapers, in part because of the penetration of Internet access in these countries as well as the fragmentation of traditional news outlets in the United States, Canada, and Mexico.[33] The physical size of the continent coupled with historically poor national distribution systems, together with the dispersal of power in the federal system of government, means that the U.S. and Canadian press largely serve local and regional communities, despite a few notable exceptions with a coast-to-coast readership such as *USA Today*, the *Wall Street Journal*, the *New York Times* and, north of the border, the *Toronto Globe and Mail*. With more than 1,000 online papers, the United States is a striking outlier across the world, and only the vast and diverse population of India has almost as many newspaper outlets.

In contrast Scandinavia has fewer printed or digital newspapers, but a far higher per capita newspaper readership. Sub-Saharan Africa, Asia Pacific, and Central and Eastern Europe all lag behind with a lower online newspaper density than average. There are 67 daily newspapers online in the whole of Sub-Saharan Africa, compared with twice as many in the United Kingdom alone, and 1,247 in the United States. The situation in the post-Communist societies is somewhat surprising given the distribution of Internet access observed in earlier chapters and relatively high levels of literacy and education in the population, suggesting that potentially the news media in these countries could catch up within the next few years. Inequalities in the distribution of online newspapers are also evident by levels of socioeconomic and democratic development: about half of all newspapers are online in the richest nations compared with just over one-fourth of all newspapers in the poorest. Yet it should be stressed that the contrasts by levels of development are evident in both new and old media, with Sub-Saharan Africa and the Middle East lagging behind in the total number of daily newspapers printed in these regions, as well as in per capita readership. The Internet is therefore largely reinforcing and exacerbating long-established global disparities in access to the press, although the technology is not necessarily causing the differences among rich and poor societies, which antecede the birth of the World Wide Web.

The worldwide distribution of all different types of media outlets – including almost 12,000 websites for newspapers, magazines, radio stations, TV sites, and news service organizations – is shown in Table 9.2. These data are drawn from an alternative source, the *Editor & Publisher* database. The regional classification of countries is slightly different (Mexico and Central America is categorized with South America, and Central, Eastern, and Western Europe are counted together) but the overall pattern largely confirms the geographic map already drawn from information in the *AJRNewslink* database. In terms of the number

Table 9.2. *The world of online news media*

	Newspapers	Magazines	Radio stations	TV sites	News services	All %	All N
United States	65.2	64.2	66.7	75.0	74.3	66.4	7,880
Europe	14.2	18.9	11.7	13.6	12.2	15.3	1,813
Asia	4.8	4.7	7.6	5.0	1.8	5.2	616
Canada	5.7	4.2	6.9	0.1	6.3	4.8	566
South America	6.7	2.3	1.5	2.5	1.4	3.8	452
Oceania	1.1	3.0	3.7	2.2	1.4	2.3	268
Africa	1.3	1.6	1.4	0.7	1.4	1.3	160
Middle East	1.1	1.2	0.4	0.8	1.4	1.0	117
Total	100.0	100.0	100.0	100.0	100.0	100.0	11,872

Source: Editor & Publisher, June 2000, www.mediainfo.com.

of websites, the United States dominates with almost 8,000 online media across all categories, representing two-thirds of all newspapers, magazines, and radio stations, and three-fourths of all TV sites and news services. As noted earlier, this predominance could be attributed to the use of databases compiled and monitored by an organization based in the United States, although roughly similar regional patterns are confirmed by analysis of other available media databases. This pattern probably reflects America's international dominance of the television production process and ownership of such entertainment conglomerates as Time-Warner and Disney Corp. – it is no coincidence that Silicon Valley is next door to Hollywood – along with the widespread penetration of the Internet access in American society. Europe ranks in second place across all categories, with almost 2,000 online news media sites, and at the bottom of the chart the fewest online media are located in Africa and the Middle East.

EXPLAINING THE DISTRIBUTION OF ONLINE NEWSPAPERS

What explains this global distribution? Figure 9.3 examines the simple correlations between the number of online newspapers and the number of printed newspapers in a country. The results show a strong correlation although a closer examination of the scatter plot of this relation-

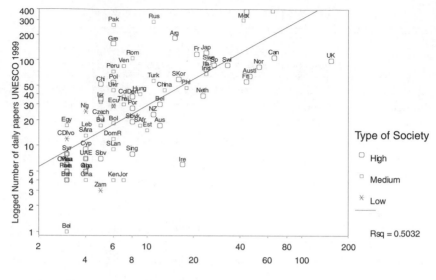

Figure 9.3. The Printed Press and Digital Newspapers.

Note: For ease of visual interpretation the United States and India are excluded as outliers, each with more than 1,000 printed newspapers, and the comparison of 174 nations also automatically excludes all countries with fewer than two online newspapers.

ship in Figure 9.3 reveals some important outliers to this pattern. Many of the Anglo-American English-speaking nations have more online newspapers than would be expected by the distribution of the printed press, including the United Kingdom, Canada, Australia, and Ireland, perhaps reflecting and also contributing to the predominance of the English language on the Internet. In contrast, some societies with minimal Internet access among the public, such as Pakistan, Russia, and Greece, have many more printed papers than digital versions.

To test these relationships further regression analysis was used, entering the usual indicators of socioeconomic, technological, and political development in the first model, for comparison with previous chapters, then adding the number of newspapers in the second with the number of online papers per country as the dependent variable. The results of the first model in Table 9.3 show that the proportion of the population that is online is a strong and significant predictor of online newspapers. This remains significant in the second model, although the number of printed newspapers is also important. Most strikingly, this provides fur-

Table 9.3. *Explaining the distribution of online newspapers*

	Model 1		Model 2	
	Beta	Sig.	Beta	Sig.
Human development	−.053	.585	−.031	
Technological development	**.422**	**.000**	**.294**	.000
Political development	−.021	.816	−.057	
Number of newspapers per nation			**.583**	.000
Constant	20.0		11.1	
R^2		.133		.456

Notes and Sources: The beta coefficients represent the results of stepwise OLS regression models predicting the number of online newspapers in 169 nations in June 2000.
Daily Newspapers: The number of daily newspapers per nation in 1996.
UNESCO Statistical Yearbook 2000, Paris: UNESCO. **Human Development** is measured by the UNDP Human Development Index 1999. *Human Development Report 1999,* New York: UNDP/Oxford University Press. **Total population 1997** is from the United Nations Development Report, 1999. **Percent Online** is from *www.nua.ie* (see Table 2.2 for details). **Level of democratization** is from the Freedom House Annual Survey of Political Rights and Civil Liberties 1999–2000, *www.freedomhouse.org/survey/2000/.*

ther independent corroboration that, just like the distribution of party and government websites, technological diffusion is a more important driver than the process of democratization per se. Digital newspapers are most widely available in those societies at the forefront of the Information Society where much of the population has moved online, whether established democracies, transitional and consolidating states, or authoritarian regimes. Democratization is not the driving force behind the move of the news media into the digital world, but in the longer-term it might well be the consequence, if independent journalists and a plurality of smaller news outlets flourish on the Web.

VIRTUAL CIVIC SOCIETY

The news media represents one part of civic society. The distinctions between traditional interest groups, alternative social movements, and transnational advocacy networks are fluid and imprecise, so that all these forms of association in civic society are compared in this chapter.[34] The term "interest group" conventionally refers to more formal organizations that are either focused on particular social groups and economic sectors, such as trade unions, business and professional associations, such as the NAACP or the American Medical Association, or on more specific issues such as abortion, gun control, or the environment. Often traditional interest groups have well-established organizational structures, formal membership rules, and their primary orientation is toward influencing government and the policy process and providing direct services for members, including trade union negotiations over pay levels in industry or the provision of informational networks for professional associations. Some develop an extensive mass membership base, whereas others are essentially lobbying organizations focusing on insider strategies, with little need for maintaining a larger constituency. New social movements, exemplified by the civil rights and antinuclear movements in the 1950s, and the counterculture environmental and women's movement of the 1970s, tend to have more fluid and decentralized organizational structures, more open membership criteria, and to focus on influencing lifestyles and achieving social change through direct action and community building as much as formal decision-making processes. Finally, transnational advocacy networks bring together loose coalitions of these organizations under a common umbrella organization that crosses national borders.

The Internet may serve multiple functions for all these organizations, similar to the utility of this medium for political parties, including lobbying elected representatives, public officials, and policy elites; networking with related associations and organizations; mobilizing organizers, activists, and members using action alerts, newsletters, and emails; raising funds and recruiting supporters; and communicating their message to the public via the traditional news media. The global reach and real-time speed of the Internet make it particularly useful for transnational advocacy networks, exemplified by diverse campaigns such as the movement against the production and sale of landmines, demonstrators critical of the World Trade Organization meeting in Seattle, environmentalists opposing genetically modified foods, and antisweatshop campaigners opposed to the manufacturing conditions of Nike shoes.[35] Go online and you can find thousands of networks devoted to bringing together like-minded souls ranging from Anarchists, Hippies, and Vegetarians to Skinheads, Survivalists, and Aryans, and a cornucopia of activist groups from the issues of abortion and Afrocentrism to welfare reform and xenotransplantation. You can monitor human rights with Amnesty International, the environment with Greenpeace, or the state of democracy with the National Democracy Institute. Or, should you be so inclined, you can learn how to make a homemade nitroglycerin bomb or join the Gay Nazis.[36] And you can visit hundreds of policy think tanks in DC, ranging from the Heritage Foundation and the Cato Institute to the Brookings Institution and the Twentieth Century Fund.

The potential activities for organization and mobilization involve far more than the passive reading of informational Web pages. Transnational advocacy networks represent "umbrella" websites aiming to amplify the impact of multiple smaller like-minded NGOs. As exemplified by the Institute for Global Communications progressive network (Figure 9.4), through the Internet you can subscribe to advocacy and lobbying groups, affiliate your organization, receive emailed policy newsletters and action alerts, send faxes or emails to decision makers, circulate electronic petitions, learn about forthcoming street demonstrations, protest events, job vacancies, and voluntary activities, as well as share effective strategies for activism, contribute short news items to the site, and participate in online discussions.[37] The IGC site, established in 1990, currently contains about 350,000 links contained in more than 8,000 pages. A similar networking function is fulfilled by One World.net, founded in 1995, a website containing 15,000 pages with almost 100,000 links to progressive organizations promoting human rights and sustainable development. The website available in four languages allows you to find news and press releases about trouble spots around the globe, to read in-depth policy reports, to listen to selected radio or watch TV reports, to locate volunteer jobs, to become active in a range of campaigns, to shop online; future developments for the site include a learning channel promoting education.

As illustrated by the Greenpeace site, social movements have taken advantage of many innovative features of the Internet; this website features breaking news, streaming audio and video clips, information resources, ways to join the organization, participate in a chat room, and subscribe to 20 to 30 cyber-activism listservs on topics such as biodiversity or nuclear power, and national and local branch addresses.[38] Daily counts show that *www.Greenpeace.org* received about 58,000 visitors in a typical week in mid-2000, up fourfold from four years earlier, with about half a million visitors in total since the launch of the current site in late 1997. Domain analysis indicates that users of the website come from all over the world including Europe (15 percent), North America (10 percent), Australia (4 percent), South America (3 percent), and Asia

Figure 9.4. Examples of Transnational Advocacy Networks Online.

(2 percent). If party and government websites are heavily "top-down," as traditional hierarchical institutions, the alternative philosophy of new social movements and NGOs may well provide a more congenial environment fostering "bottom-up" interactions in civic society. Nor is this a minor part of the virtual world. As we saw earlier (Table 5.2), a quick and simple search for the term "interest group" using Yahoo!, Alta Vista,

and InfoSeek produced almost five million hits across all engines, more than the combined total for "political parties," "elections," and "parliaments." In short, digital technologies facilitate the network of networks, which should be an environment where civic society and the public sphere flourish like summer gardens.

Establishing which groups and organizations have moved online, however, is not straightforward. Other studies have used search engines such as InfoSeek and Yahoo! to provide a sampling frame, analyzing a random selection of American groups listed in these indexes, including the American Civil Liberties Union, the National Association of Women, and the National Audubon Society.[39] This approach provides a representative selection of groups on the Internet, but unfortunately this process can tell us nothing about the broader universe of interest groups and social movements. For this we can turn to the Union of International Organizations (UIA) based in Brussels, which has published the *Yearbook of International Organizations* since 1908–09.[40] This source provides the most comprehensive list available of multifarious types of organizations worldwide, including nonprofit associations, societies, federations, institutes, bureaus and associations, as well as scientific and academic research centers, trade unions, business groups, and nonprofit foundations. The Yearbook is probably stronger on traditional interest associations with a formal organizational structure rather than more disparate alternative social movements, especially groups and coalitions that only exist online, but nevertheless its geographic scope and subject coverage are wideranging. The online UIA database lists details about 55,465 international governmental organizations (IGOs) and national nongovernmental organizations (NGOs) worldwide in November 1999, including their location, type, and whether they have established a website. A representative sample of 468 organizations was selected from this source by a process of random selection (picking the first organization on each page of the database listed alphabetically), and the websites were examined for those organizations that were found to be online.

The diverse and eclectic organizations under comparison ranged from the African Democratic League, the Anti-Slavery International, and the Association for Lesbian, Gay and Bi-Sexual Psychologies to the Woodworking Association of North America, the World Copyright Organization, and the Zoo Conservation Outreach Group. Overall from the random sample of 468 organizations the analysis suggests that about one-fourth (109) had a website identified by the UIA. This may seem like a relatively low proportion, but even if this is a conservative estimate (underestimating the recent proliferation of websites by new social movements), if we extrapolate more generally from this sample the results suggest that about 12,400 interest groups are online world-wide. A systematic analysis of these groups by type, organizational structure, and sector, as well as the contents of these websites, would require a much larger sample to prove reliable, but nevertheless a glance through the list of websites quickly confirmed the multiplicity and vari-ety of the groups found online: the Christian Jugglers Association and the B'nai B'rith Hillel Foundation mixed company in cyber-space along-side the European Metalworkers' Federation, the International Potato Center, the European Board of Urology, the International Naturist Federation, the Mammal Society, the Nordic Youth Committee, and the International Chamber of Shipping. Beyond geography, there was no discernible pattern to the groups found online: The sacred and the pro-fane coexisted together, as did business associations and trade unions, and the Christian right and the progressive liberals. The geographic spread confirmed the pattern already widely observed in previous chap-ters, including the predominance of sites for organizations headquar-tered in North America, Western Europe, Scandinavia, and Australia, even if their mission was broader; for example, Australian associations promoting international human rights and conflict resolution, Nordic academicians studying Middle Eastern cultures, or Virginian evangelists concerned about spreading the word in Africa. The initial impression of interest groups and transnational advocacy networks on the Web based on this comparison is one of tremendous diversity, a virtual Hyde Park Corner where a plurality of multiple actors can and do find opportuni-ties to network, organize, and express their viewpoints.

CONCLUSIONS: THE RISE OF THE VIRTUAL CIVIC SOCIETY

This examination of the presence of civic society on the Internet cannot answer deeper questions about the long-term consequences of digital technologies for deepening and broadening democracy. The process of technological diffusion remains in transition and, just like parties and governments, organizations are still learning how to use the potential of the Web to do more than act as a static form of electronic pamphlet or poster. Yet, the existence of "flash" movements triggered by particular issues or events, such as antiglobalization protests in the streets of

Seattle, Washington, DC, and Prague, and the anti-fuel tax coalition shutting down highways from London to Oslo, suggests that this digital information environment has the capacity to alter the structure of opportunities for communication and information in civic society. In this environment a culture is provided that is particularly conducive for alternative social movements, fringe parties from the libertarians to the Greens, and transnational advocacy networks seeking to organize and mobilize dispersed groups for collective action. Compared with the traditional channels of television and print journalism, the many-to-many and one-to-many characteristics of the Internet multiply manifold the access points for publicity and information in the political system. The global dimension of the Web facilitates transnational movements transcending the boundaries of the nation-state. The linkage capacity strengthens alliances and coalitions. Moreover, as discussed in the next chapter, the values that pervade many transnational advocacy networks – such as those seeking to promote such issues as women's rights, the environment, and conflict resolution – seem seem highly conducive to the irreverent, egalitarian, and libertarian character of the cyber-culture. The transition to the Internet seems to be altering and transposing certain common ways of doing things (e.g., lobbying, communication, and organizing), thereby subtly tipping the balance of power and resources among intermediary political actors, like the shift from network TV news to their wired cousins, or from traditional international organizations such as the WTO and IMF toward transnational networks. Traditional communication media do not disappear, but a new repertoire of communication and information strategies appear, which are used by the most flexible and adaptable organizations. The traditional resources of organizational structures, mass members, and money become less significant than know-how and technical skills that smaller and more flexible insurgents can use to organize, mobilize, and express themselves to challenge established authorities. Companies such as Amazon.com appear on the commercial scene to rival traditional bricks-and-mortar booksellers like Barnes and Noble; services like Napster threaten the core profits and way of doing business of music companies like Sony; and electronic magazines like *Wired* and *Slate* compete for readers with long-established outlets including the *New York Times* and the *Washington Post*. Traditional institutions may have the capacity, far-sightedness, flexibility, and resources to reinvent themselves in virtual form, like the venerable BBC winning multiple awards and critical kudos for its online news service, although others lose their strategic predominance, such as when Encarta challenged the *Encyclopedia Britannica*. The radical shake-up provided by the Internet revolution opens a window of opportunities for insurgents such as Yahoo! and Napster. To assess the full consequences of this process we need to examine how the public has responded to the virtual political system and, in particular, whether opportunities for political communication and information on the Internet are used mainly by those who are already the most active, or whether they have the capacity to reach out to more marginal sectors of society such as the younger generation who are otherwise disengaged from public life. Governments and civic society are providing a cornucopia of information on the World Wide Web – but who is paying attention? It is the public's use of digital technologies to which we now turn.

PART III

The Democratic Divide

Where is the wisdom we have lost in knowledge?
Where is the knowledge we have lost in information?
T. S. Eliot, *The Rock* (1934) pt. 1.

CHAPTER 10

Cyberculture

Previous chapters have examined the way that the political system has responded to the new structure of opportunities for information and communication that have become available via the Internet. To summarize developments, the evidence presented in earlier chapters demonstrates how far political websites have flourished and multiplied in cyberspace: In 179 countries around the globe, today almost 100 parliaments can be found online, along with 1,250 parliamentary parties, 14,500 governments departments, 2,500 newspapers, 12,000 news sites, and more than 12,000 groups and new social movements. This process can only be expected to continue, given the wider spread of Internet access and use among the public. To assess how much these developments will influence the democratic process we need to determine how ordinary citizens have responded to the new opportunities for civic engagement in the virtual world.

Digital technologies could influence mass public opinion in different ways, and this process can be understood using the fourfold schema illustrated in Figure 10.1. As discussed in the next chapter, the participation hypothesis holds that the opportunities for information, networking, and communication via digital technologies might affect patterns of civic engagement, either *reinforcing* those citizens who are already most active through traditional channels, or *mobilizing* new participants who are currently disengaged from the political process; for example, by energizing younger voters who pay little attention to newspapers and TV news, or by stimulating community activists. Alternatively the *cultural* hypothesis – examined in this chapter – holds that the rise of the Internet will influence the predominant values and attitudes within society, such as strengthening the values of individualism and cosmopolitanism, or heightening concerns about environmentalism or

195

Participation Thesis

		Traditional Groups	New Group
Mobilization Thesis	Traditional Values	*Reinforcement*	*Mobilization*
	New Values	*Cultural Change*	*Transformation*

Figure 10.1. The Potential Impact of the Internet on Public Opinion.

globalization. If politics on the Internet affects both new groups *and* new values, then this has the potential for the greatest transformation of public opinion, which is what commentators frequently assume when searching for the impact of cyber-democracy. But any of the four functions can be understood as important effects on the body politic. Representative democracy can still be strengthened through the reinforcement of traditional participants and traditional issue cleavages; for example, if digital technologies facilitate campaign organizing or get-out-the-vote drives by mainstream party activists and candidates, or if established news media such as the *New York Times* or *BBC News* gain the capacity to reach a broader audience when online, or if government websites provide official documents for lobbyists, or if interest groups such as the National Organization of Women or the National Rifle Association attract more supporters.

The cultural approach aims to understand the impact of the Internet by examining whether the predominant values, attitudes, and beliefs found within the online world are distinctive from the broader political culture. Many have speculated that the freewheeling, individualistic, and somewhat irreverent spirit that appears to be characteristic of the World Wide Web, captured by many of the quirkier dot.com ads and Webzines, may help shape a distinctive cyber-culture, as well as altering ascribed social identities such as those of gender and race.[1] The theory of postmaterialism and postmodernization associated with the work of Ronald Inglehart provides perhaps the most developed theoretical argument for value change. If this theory is applied to the online community it suggests that, given the typical age and educational profile of Internet users, we might expect to find a cyber-culture that is particularly sympathetic toward postmaterialist values of freedom of expression, and tolerance of diversity, social egalitarianism, secularism, internationalism, self-expression, and participatory democracy.

The argument developed in this chapter is not suggesting that the experience of going online is, by itself, altering the values and priorities of most individual users, because social and political values are understood as deep-rooted phenomena that are grounded in early patterns of socialization in the home, school, and workplace. Cybersociety is a place of choice par excellence so that where people go and what they do are likely to be strongly channeled by their prior preferences and interests: music lovers can be expected to gravitate toward Napster and its equivalent, financial analysts will download stock-market tickers, and political sites will primarily attract activists. In this sense, as many commentators have argued, in the short-term the experience of going online can be expected to reinforce rather than alter individual attitudes and values.

But could digital technologies still have a more diffuse and enduring impact on the political culture? The central hypothesis examined here is that the online community is likely to display an ideological orientation that is particularly sympathetic toward postmaterialist values. *If* we establish that a distinctive cyber-culture does predominate, this could affect the political system in many different ways. Earlier chapters have demonstrated how the Internet provides a public space that is particularly conducive for expression, organization, and mobilization, and thereby consolidating and reinforcement, of like-minded groups. If the cyber-culture reflects postmaterialist values this could provide a sympathetic environment for alternative social movements and transnational advocacy networks sympathetic to these values. Moreover in the longer term, the impact of the Internet culture may be expected to shape the values and attitudes of the youngest generation of users, including children who are growing up surrounded by this technology in their homes and schools, contributing to the process of value change in postindustrial societies. The transmission of this culture globally could also be expected to accelerate the process of value change in traditional societies.

After briefly outlining Inglehart's theory of postmaterial value change and considering how it could be applied to the Internet, this chapter examines American and European survey evidence concerning three issues:

- Do Internet users in America sympathize strongly with new social movements promoting postmaterialist values, such as the gay rights, civil rights, and feminist movements?
- Do these Internet users strongly favor secular rather than traditional moral values on issues such as marriage and the family, homosexuality, and censorship, and do they also favor economic freedom or government intervention on such issues as welfare and business regulation?
- And, where we have comparative evidence, are the patterns established in American surveys also evident in European societies?

THE THEORY OF POSTMATERIALISM

How might the cyber-culture prove distinctive? This chapter starts by briefly summarizing the well-known theory of societal modernization developed in a series of studies by Ronald Inglehart, to see whether this framework can be extended and applied to understand the digital world.[2] The theory suggests that economic and technological development produces profound transformations in the social and economic system and that these, in turn, lead to fundamental shifts in underlying social and political values. In the industrialized world, Inglehart suggests, the younger generation growing up in the postwar era experienced conditions of unprecedented affluence and security. Baby-boomers in Western Europe and the United States lived through decades of steady economic growth in their early years and could take for granted the existence of the basic welfare safety net to take care of problems of health, education, and unemployment. These formative experiences, the theory suggests, led to values among the postwar generation that differed in several significant ways from those held by their parents' generation. Based on analysis of the World Values survey, Inglehart demonstrates that important generational differences in basic priorities are evident across industrialized societies, with the younger generation giving greater emphasis to quality-of-life issues such as concern for environmental protection rather than economic growth, sexual equality rather than traditional roles within the family, secular rather than religious values, and the importance of individual freedom, self-expression, internationalism, and participatory democracy. The counterculture new social movement of the 1960s and 1970s exemplifies the political expression of these values, together with the development of new parties such as the Greens.

In contrast Inglehart shows that the older generation, whose formative youthful experiences occurred amid the insecurities caused by the era of the Great Depression, as well as the two world wars, prioritizes more traditional bread-and-butter issues such as basic economic growth, jobs, low inflation, and national security, the class politics of economic redistribution and the welfare state, as well as displaying more deferential attitudes toward bureaucratic and political authorities. Rather than support for cosmopolitanism, surveys show that the older generation remains nationalistic in orientation.[3] Postmaterialist theory suggests that the long-term process of value change through generational turnover and societal modernization has produced more secular cultures in postindustrial societies, with declining support for traditional moral values associated with respect for hierarchical institutions including government, the army, and the Church.

> In the Postmodern shift, values that played a key role in the emergence of industrial society – economic achievement motivation, economic growth, economic rationality – have faded in salience. At the societal level, there is a radical shift from the priorities of early industrialization, and a growing tendency for emphasis on economic growth to become subordinate to concern for its impact on the environment. At the individual level, maximizing economic gains is gradually fading from top priority: self-expression and the desire for meaningful work are becoming even more crucial for a growing segment of the population.[4]

Although remaining controversial, the evidence for this thesis has been examined in more than sixty countries through successive waves of the Eurobarometer survey since the early 1970s, and the World Values Study since the early 1980s. Inglehart's work provides a plausible account of the flowering of alternative social movements in postwar America and Western Europe, as well as providing insights into some of the major contrasts between traditional and secular moralities found among rich and poor countries worldwide.

POSTMATERIALISM AND THE INTERNET CULTURE

This theoretical framework poses many intriguing questions that could be applied to understand the ways in which the online community differs from the audience for the traditional mass media. A number of reasons would lead us to suspect that we should find a distinctive culture on the Web, particularly one sympathetic to postmaterialist values. First, we know that the online community is disproportionately young, affluent, and well educated, as already discussed in Chapter 4, as well as being clustered in wealthier societies, and therefore the population fits the exact profile that should prove most sympathetic to post-material values. The generational gap among Internet population has been established in hundreds of surveys; the 1999 Eurobarometer, for example, shows that about one-third of those under twenty-five use the Internet, ten times more than among the retired population. In contrast, as shown in Figure 10.2, in Europe the regular audience for television news and readers of the daily press are disproportionately found among older age groups, a well-established pattern that has been evident for decades, suggesting that this is largely a by-product of lifestyle choices and more sedentary leisure patterns as people age.[5] Similar generational divisions in the use of the traditional and digital media are also well established in the United States.[6] If the typical demographic profile of the online community is reflected in the contents and activities on the Web, then an egalitarian and secular culture should flourish on the Web.

Moreover Chapter 9 has already demonstrated that the Internet provides an environment where many alternative social movements and transnational networks can and do flourish. As illustrated by websites established by Peace.net, IGC.org, One World.net, and Greenpeace, the online community contains literally thousands of groups able to organize, mobilize, and express themselves at local, national, and international levels about liberal and progressive issues such as environmentalism, human rights, and conflict resolution. The process should not be exaggerated; after all, the comparison presented in Chapter 8 found a broad ideological balance among the range of parties that are online, including far-right nationalist and neofascist organizations, as well as communists and social democrats. Nevertheless out of all parties, environmentalists have moved online with the greatest enthusiasm, since almost three-quarters of all Green parties have a website. The limited comparison of interest groups, alternative social movements, and transnational networks presented in Chapter 9 could establish no discernible ideological pattern, because multiple conservative and religious groups coexisted alongside liberal ones. Yet the impression of surfing the network of organizations on the Web, as well as dramatic events like the WTO "battle for Seattle," the anti-landmine campaign, and the anti-globalization protests against the World Bank, suggests that the Internet provides an environment that diverse new social

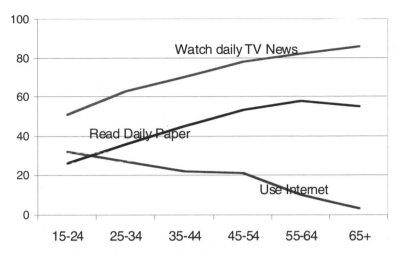

Figure 10.2. Use of the Mass Media by Generation.
Source: Eurobarometer EU-15, 1999.

movements sympathetic to postmaterial values find broadly conducive to their ethos, aims, and objectives.

Moreover, the available survey research in America does provide some limited support for the claim that a distinctive culture can be found online, although the previous evidence remains scattered. Davis and Owen found that in the mid-1990s the online U.S. population (defined as those who went online at least once every few weeks) tended to be slightly more liberal toward equal rights, less supportive of traditional lifestyles and families, more interested in government and public affairs, with stronger than average levels of political efficacy, although Internet users proved indistinguishable from the general public in terms of their partisan identification and trust in government.[7] Another study of the American online community in the mid-1990s by Hill and Hughes also reported that Internet political activists were consistently more liberal than the general public on issues such as censorship and homosexuality, as well as being slightly more antigovernment in orientation than the rest of society, although the survey results were somewhat mixed and inconsistent.[8] These studies are suggestive but these attitudes may reflect the early profile of the Internet population rather than today's typical user, as the pioneering and cooperative spirit of alternative politics characteristic of the chat rooms, bulletin boards, and MUDs found in the university community of online users in the early

1990s may have been overtaken by a more commercially dominant corporate-interest shopping-mall Web of eBay and Amazon.com today. It also remains unclear to what extent it is possible to generalize more widely from the American cyberculture to other countries, and more systematic cross-national evidence is needed to support the claim of a distinctive cyberculture around the world.

The limitations of the sources of existing survey data mean that it is not yet possible to compare the political attitudes of the Internet population across a wide range of developing societies and consolidating democracies, an issue that will have to await further research. Systematic social surveys or official census measures monitoring the Internet community have not yet become widely available in most poor countries, and the evidence that is available from market research is often based on unrepresentative samples, biased by respondent self-selection. Where the Internet population is limited, surveys representative of the general population usually provide too few users to allow analysis of the attitudes and behavior of this group. Nevertheless we can examine the Internet culture in more depth using representative surveys of the American public conducted in late-1999 by the Pew Research Center for the People and the Press.[9] Although not containing identical items, some of the results can be compared with Eurobarometer surveys conducted in the 15 member states of the European Union in spring 1999.[10] This context allows us to analyze a range of postindustrial societies that vary substantially in Internet use: as shown earlier, the United States and the Nordic states have record levels of Internet penetration while other societies in Mediterranean Europe have minimal access. Chapter 3 showed that if the proportion of the online population is compared, Portugal and Greece ranked far behind many poorer societies elsewhere such as Latvia and Slovenia (see Figure 3.3). Previous chapters have also demonstrated how the virtual political system reflects these differences in public access, with far more government departments, parties, and news media online in countries at the forefront of the information revolution. Therefore the comparison, while narrower than ideal, allows us to analyze cultural differences found in the American and European context.

THE INTERNET POLITICAL CULTURE IN AMERICA

What are the predominant social and political identities of Internet users in America? What values do they hold for society and government? And what is their political orientation? The Pew Political

Typology survey conducted in late-1999 was selected for analysis because it contained many suitable items monitoring use of the Internet and the traditional news media, as well as an exceptionally rich range of items tapping identities, attitudes, and values.

To what extent is the Internet culture one that is particularly sympathetic toward "liberal," "new left," or progressive alternative social movements? The Pew Survey asked people to describe themselves using twenty different identity scales, such as being "an environmentalist," "a supporter of the women's movement," "a supporter of the pro-life movement," as well as being an "Internet enthusiast." People were asked to indicate their appropriate position on the ten-point scales, ranging from a totally wrong description (1) to a perfect description (10).[11] Based on this measure we can analyze the political characteristics and orientation of those who described themselves as *Internet enthusiasts*, defined as those scoring highly (from 6–10) on the scale. The survey found that 43 percent of the population classified themselves as Internet enthusiasts, and this measure was significantly related to indicators of online behavior; for example, this group proved to be regular readers of Internet news. To examine the characteristics of the cyber-culture, the first model in Table 10.1 compares the difference between Internet enthusiasts and nonenthusiasts on the identity scales without any social controls. To explore the reasons behind this phenomenon, the second model then uses regression analysis to see whether these differences remain significant even after entering the standard demographic controls of age, gender, education, and income.

The evidence confirms that, as suspected, there is a distinctive cyber-culture found among the most enthusiastic members of the online community in the United States (see Figure 10.3). American Internet enthusiasts are far more supportive of progressive new social movements, such as the gay rights movement, the pro-choice movement favoring reproductive rights, the women's movement, and the environmental movement. American Internet enthusiasts were also more likely to be self-described liberals. Internet enthusiasts also proved slightly less supportive of "new right" causes like the National Rifle Association and the pro-Life abortion lobby. Moreover, this pattern is not simply a by-product of the younger and well-educated population found online, since the difference between groups remains significant in regression models even with the introduction of prior social controls. The defining feature is less whether someone is online per se than how they feel about digital technologies: Those who see themselves most strongly as Internet enthusiasts are also most likely to sympathize with the alterna-

Table 10.1. *Internet identities, United States, 1999*

| | Model 1 | | | | Model 2 | |
| | Internet enthusiasts (mean) | Internet nonenthusiasts (mean) | Mean diff. | | | |
Identity scales	(i)	(ii)	(i)–(ii)	Sig.	Beta	Sig.
Support gay rights	4.62	3.66	.96	**	.148	**
Financially well-off	5.68	4.82	.86	**	.101	**
Support pro-choice	6.27	5.46	.81	**	.105	**
Support civil rights	7.49	6.79	.70	**	.132	**
Support women's movement	6.84	6.19	.65	**	.103	**
Pro-business	6.65	6.01	.64	**	.184	**
A liberal	5.13	4.51	.62	**	.124	**
An environmentalist	6.94	6.51	.43	**	.086	**
A Republican	4.95	4.69	.26	*	.030	
A patriot	7.78	7.65	.13		.050	*
A union supporter	5.35	5.24	.11		.044	*
A Democrat	5.17	5.14	.03		.030	
Antigovernment	3.28	3.25	.03		.010	
A conservative	5.76	5.83	−.07		.013	
A religious person	7.01	7.25	−.24	*	.003	
NRA supporter	4.37	4.62	−.25	*	−.023	
Working class	7.70	7.96	−.26	**	−.016	
Support pro-life	5.52	5.95	−.43	**	−.047	*

Note: Q: *"Next I'm going to read you some words or phrases and ask you to rate how well each describes you. Ten represents a description that is perfect for you, and one represents a description that is totally wrong for you… On this scale of 1 to 10, how well does … describe you?"*

Internet Enthusiasts: Those who say the term "Internet enthusiasts" describes them well.

Model 1: The figures represent the mean scores of self-identified Internet enthusiasts and nonenthusiasts on the political identity scales without any controls. The significance of the difference between group means is measured by ANOVA.

Model 2: The figures represent standardized beta coefficient in OLS regression models measuring the impact the Internet enthusiasm scale on the political identity scales after controlling for age, gender, income, and education. Sig. ** = .01, * = .05.

Source: The Political Typology Survey conducted July 14 to September 9, 1999 among a representative nationwide sample of 3,973 American adults by Princeton Survey Research Associates on behalf of the Pew Research Center for the People and the Press.

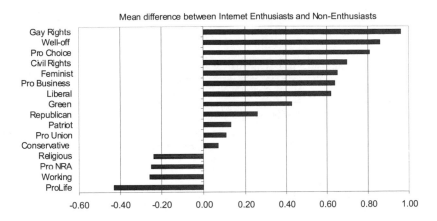

Figure 10.3. Identities on the Internet, 1999.
Source: Pew Survey, 1999.

tive social movements. Regarding the economy, however, there is a different pattern, because Internet enthusiasts are also more likely to be pro-business, as well as describing themselves as being personally well off. They are also slightly more likely to be self-identified Republicans, although this difference fades in significance once social controls are introduced. Clearly rather than a single left–right dimension, Internet enthusiasts display a more complex set of identities, suggesting an orientation sympathetic toward a range of alternative movements on the social agenda but also a free-market perspective toward the economy.

CULTURAL VALUES ON THE INTERNET

Does other evidence, such as the attitudes, values, and beliefs of the online population, confirm the existence of a distinctive cyber-culture? To explore this in more detail the Pew Survey included four-point Likert-type scales where respondents were invited to express agreement or disagreement with a series of value statements. These items covered multiple cultural dimensions, and principle components factor analysis was employed to identify the underlying dimensions. Sixteen items were eventually selected as falling into two distinct scales: support for traditional religious or secular *moral values,* such as the belief in God, the importance of prayer, and traditional attitudes toward marriage and the family; support for left–right *economic values* including attitudes toward corporations, labor unions, and the government's role in welfare

Table 10.2. *Moral and economic values, United States, 1999*

Agreement with the following statements:	Religious or secular	Left–right
Moral values		
We all will be called before God at the Judgment Day to answer for our sins	.794	
Even today miracles are performed by the power of God	.752	
Prayer is an important part of my daily life	.732	
I never doubt the existence of God	.699	
Books that contain dangerous ideas should be banned from public school libraries	.603	
I have old-fashioned values about family and marriage	.567	
There are clear guidelines about what's good or evil that apply to everyone regardless of their situation	.558	
AIDS might be God's punishment for immoral sexual behavior	.525	
School boards ought to have the right to fire teachers who are known homosexuals	.501	
Economic equality values		
Today it's really true that the rich just get richer while the poor get poorer		.631
There is too much power concentrated in the hands of a few big companies		.614
Business corporations make too much profit		.569
There need to be stricter laws and regulations to protect the environment		.563
The government should guarantee every citizen enough to eat and a place to sleep		.550
Labor unions are necessary to protect the working person		.421
It is the responsibility of the government to take care of people who cannot take care of themselves		.404
Percent of variance	21.6	12.8

Note: The coefficients represent the results of principal component factor analysis. The questions asked respondents whether they strongly agreed, agreed, disagreed, or strongly disagreed with each of the statements.

Source: The Values Update Survey conducted from September 28 to October 10, 1999 among a representative nationwide sample of 985 American adults by Princeton Survey Research Associates on behalf of the Pew Research Center for the People and the Press.

(see Table 10.2). Each of these proved highly intercorrelated dimensions in public opinion and they formed consistent value scales. Although lacking the classic Inglehart measure of support for postmaterialist values, these represent some of the traditional ideological cleavages that have long divided public opinion and party politics in Western democracies, and a post-materialist orientation should be indicated in support for secular morality. The analysis compared the proportion agreeing with these statements among Internet users and nonusers.[12] As before, the first model shows the simple correlation between use of the Internet and support for these values. To help explain this pattern, the second model presents the results of the regression coefficients after introducing the standard demographic controls for age, sex, race, education, and income.

The findings confirm the existence of a distinctive cyber-culture in America, even after controlling for social characteristics. Moreover the results broadly reflect the pattern already observed concerning the identities of Internet enthusiasts, lending greater confidence to the conclusions. Table 10.3 shows that Internet users are significantly more secular toward traditional morality, such as fundamentalist Christian beliefs; for example, almost two-thirds of nonusers believe in the importance of prayer compared with fewer than half of those online. Internet users are also more tolerant toward alternative lifestyles such as homosexuality, less supportive of traditional ideas about marriage and the family, and less approving of censorship.[13] Most important, these contrasts are not simply the by-product of the younger age and higher education of the online population, because the difference in moral values remains significant across all items even after introducing demographic controls. This evidence supports the idea that there is an alternative cyber-culture, and one that is more secular in orientation than nonvirtual Americans. Many of the core components underlying the theory of a postmaterialist culture are reflected in these values of social tolerance and rationalism.

At the same time this is not just a simple matter of a more liberal or "new left" cyber-culture across the board, since Internet users proved significantly more right wing than nonusers concerning the role of the welfare state and government regulation of business and the economy (see Table 10.4). The online community displays a more free-market orientation toward these issues; for example twice as many Internet nonusers than users agreed with the value statements that "business corporations make too much profit" and "it is the responsibility of government to take

Table 10.3. *Moral values by Internet use, United States, 1999*

	Percent "Strongly agree"		Model 1		Model 2	
	Net users	Non-users	R.	Sig.	Beta	Sig.
We all will be called before God at the Judgment Day to answer for our sins	55	70	.17	**	.10	**
Even today miracles are performed by the power of God	56	67	.11	**	.07	**
Prayer is an important part of my daily life	47	65	.15	**	.10	**
I never doubt the existence of God	63	78	.15	**	.06	*
Books that contain dangerous ideas should be banned from public school libraries	24	50	.30	**	.22	**
I have old-fashioned values about family and marriage	43	66	.19	**	.09	**
There are clear guidelines about what's good or evil that apply to everyone regardless of their situation	43	54	.15	**	.06	*
AIDS might be God's punishment for immoral sexual behavior	10	18	.17	**	.15	**
School boards ought to have the right to fire teachers who are known homosexuals	15	29	.15	**	.08	*
Traditional moral values scale			*.34*	**	*.17*	*

Notes: **Net Users:** Those who go online to access the Internet or World Wide Web or to send and receive email.

Model 1: The figures represent simple correlation coefficients between use of the Internet and agreement with the statement without any controls.

Model 2: The figures represent standardized beta coefficient in OLS regression models measuring the impact the Internet use on the value scales after controlling for age, gender, race, income, and education. Sig. **= .01, *= .05.

Source: The Values Update Survey conducted from September 28 to October 10, 1999 among a representative nationwide sample of 985 American adults by Princeton Survey Research Associates on behalf of the Pew Research Center for the People and the Press.

Table 10.4. *Support for economic values by Internet use,
United States, 1999*

	Percent "Strongly agree"		Model 1		Model 2	
	Net users	Non-users	R.	Sig.	Beta	Sig.
Today it's really true that the rich just get richer while the poor get poorer	24	44	.14	**	.08	*
There is too much power concentrated in the hands of a few big companies	25	40	.11	**	.08	*
Business corporations make too much profit	14	35	.13	**	.19	**
There need to be stricter laws and regulations to protect the environment	38	47	.03		.07	*
The government should guarantee every citizen enough to eat and a place to sleep	24	36	.07	*	.12	**
Labor unions are necessary to protect the working person	22	36	.08	*	.15	**
It is the responsibility of the government to take care of people who can	15	28	.10	**	.08	*
Economic laissez-faire scale			.28	**	.18	**

Notes: **Net Users:** Those who go online to access the Internet or World Wide Web or to send and receive email.

Model 1: The figures represent simple correlation coefficients between use of the Internet and agreement with the statement without any controls.

Model 2: The figures represent standardized beta coefficient in OLS regression models measuring the impact the Internet use on the value scales after controlling for age, gender, race, income, and education. Sig. ** = .01, * = .05.

Source: The Values Update Survey conducted from September 28 to October 10, 1999 among a representative nationwide sample of 985 American adults by Princeton Survey Research Associates on behalf of the Pew Research Center for the People and the Press.

care of people who can't help themselves," a pattern broadly consistent with that already observed concerning economic identities. The online community proves more laissez-faire toward the role of state, expressing lower support for government intervention to alleviate poverty. Interestingly on the issue of the environment, in contrast to the expectations of the postmaterialism thesis, Internet users are less supportive of

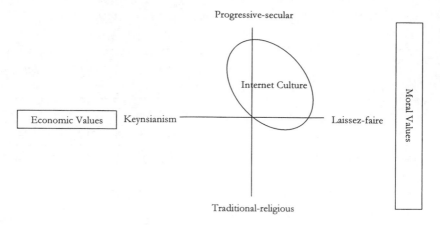

Figure 10.4. Map of Political Cyber-culture, United States 2000.

government regulation. Again these findings about economic values hold even after introducing the standard demographic controls, so this is not just a result of the age, income, race, gender, or education of Internet users.

Therefore on balance the evidence examined here suggests that the cyber-culture sympathizes with the values of openness, freedom, and tolerance, on both the social and economic agenda, perhaps reflecting the broader ethos of individualism and alternative lifestyles that seems to flourish online. The typical ideological profile of Internet users in America (illustrated in Figure 10.4) reflects a culture that favors secular values on the traditional moral issues such as marriage and the family, sexual choice and fundamentalist Christian beliefs, as well as laissez-faire values with a minimal role of the state toward business and the economy. The evidence does not simply reflect a pure "postmaterialist" culture, as expected by Inglehart's thesis, but it does contain multiple elements that are sympathetic toward these values. The typical ideological profile crosscuts many of the conventional cleavages in traditional American party politics, but Table 10.5 examines how far these value priorities were reflected in party preferences and electoral behavior. Compared with non-Internet users, the evidence shows a slight tendency for American online users to vote Republican in successive elections, to identify more strongly with the GOP, and to express disapproval of President Clinton and stronger support for the House Republicans.[14] The difference between the

Table 10.5. *Partisan sympathies by Internet use, United States 1999*

	Percent		Model 1		Model 2	
	Net users	Non-users	R.	Sig.	Beta	Sig.
Approve of the way Clinton is handling the presidency	56	61	−.07	*	−.04	*
Approve of the Republican leaders of Congress	37	31	.09	*	.06	*
Recalled House vote in 1998: % Republican	54	48	.07	*	.04	*
Recalled vote in the 1996 presidential election: % Republican	24	19	.04	*	.01	
Recalled vote in the 1992 presidential election: % Republican	30	27	.01		.01	
Party identification: % Republican	27	20	.08	*	.05	*

Notes: Internet users are those who go online to access the Internet or World Wide Web or to send and receive email.

Model 1: The figures represent Gamma coefficients without any controls.

Model 2: The figures represent standardized beta coefficient in logistic regression models measuring the impact of Internet use on the items after controlling for age, gender, race, income, and education. Sig. **= .01, *= .05.

Source: The Values Update Survey conducted from September 28 to October 10, 1999 among a representative nationwide sample of 985 American adults by Princeton Survey Research Associates on behalf of the Pew Research Center for the People and the Press.

online community and the ordinary public was not large but it was significant and consistent across all items.

THE CYBER-CULTURE IN EUROPE

Are similar patterns evident elsewhere? The 1999 Eurobarometer allows us to monitor some comparable indicators within the 15 member states of the European Union. One way to tap values is to compare a range of policy priorities for the EU, to see whether the online community is distinctive from the general public. The survey asked people to express their priorities for European Union policy initiatives using a dozen items ranging from "fighting unemployment," "fighting poverty and social exclusion," and "fighting organized crime" (which reflect classic materialist concerns about economic and personal security) to "protecting the environment" and "guaranteeing individual rights and respect for democracy" (which can be understood as indicators of classic post-materialist quality-of-life values). Following the previous approach, the first models show the simple associations and the second shows the coefficient after introducing the standard demographic controls.

The results in Table 10.6 show that compared with the general public, the online community in Europe does lean more strongly toward a more postmaterialist agenda, reflecting the values of cosmopolitanism and participatory democracy. This includes favoring expansion of the European Union and its reform, giving citizens more information, and guaranteeing individual rights and respect for democracy. Internet users were also more supportive of the introduction of the euro and of environmental protection, while the general public gave slightly higher priority to consumer protection and asserting the importance of the EU around the world. In all cases the differences between the online community and the general public were modest, but they remained statistically significant.

The Eurobarometer does not allow us to examine all types of social and political identities in Europe, as in the American Pew survey, but a related area where the cyber-culture may prove distinctive concerns support for globalization and internationalism. Post-materialist theory suggests that the younger generation of well-educated Europeans, who are most commonly found online, brought up in postwar conditions of peace and prosperity, are more likely to display an internationalist or cosmopolitan orientation and support for removing the old borders within the European Union. In contrast, their parents' generation can be expected to remain more supportive of maintaining distinct national identities.[15] In the longer term, the experience of the Internet can be expected to reinforce globalization, breaking down the physical barriers of space and national boundaries in communication, as well as fostering transnational networks linking social movements and parties in different countries. This issue can be examined by monitoring the strength of cosmopolitan, national, and local identities, measured by how far people express a strong attachment to different places such as their town or village, their region, their country, and to Europe. The results in Table 10.7 confirm that, compared with the general public, the online community in Europe proved more cosmopolitan in their

Table 10.6. *Policy priorities by Internet use, EU-15 1999*

Percent "It should be a priority for the European Union"	Model 1				Model 2	
	Online	Not online	Diff.	Sig.	Beta	Sig.
Welcoming new member countries	39	29	+10	**		
Reforming EU institutions	63	54	+9	**		
Giving citizens more information about the EU	80	72	+8	**		
Guaranteeing individual rights and respect for democracy	88	82	+6	**		
Implementing the single European currency, the euro	71	66	+5	**		
Protecting the environment	90	85	+5	**		
Maintaining peace and security in Europe	93	91	+2	**		
Fighting poverty and social exclusion	90	89	+1			
Fighting organized crime	91	89	+1	*		
Fighting unemployment	90	91	−1	*		
Protecting consumers	78	81	−3	*		
Asserting the political importance of the EU around the world	50	53	−3			

Note: Q: *"I am going to read out a list of actions that the European Union could under-take. For each one, please tell me if in your opinion it should be a priority or not."*

Model 1 includes no controls and the significance of the difference between groups is measured by gamma coefficients.

Model 2 is based on standardized regression coefficients using logistic regression models predicting knowledge by Internet use controlling for age, gender, income, and education. Sig. **=.01, *=.05.

Percent Online: Q: *"Do you have access to, or do you use … the Internet or the World Wide Web?"*

Source: Eurobarometer 51.0, spring 1999.

orientation, identifying more weakly with their local town, village, or region, and displaying slightly stronger support for Europe. This provides important evidence that in the long term the rise of the Internet may affect the globalization process, at least in more affluent societies, as well as reinforcing and strengthening cultural linkages within the European Union.

Table 10.7. *Cosmopolitan, national and local identities by Internet use, EU-15, 1999*

Percent "Very attached to…"	Model 1				Model 2	
	Online	Not online	Diff.	Sig.	Beta	Sig.
Your town/village	39	57	−18	**		
Your region	37	53	−15	**		
[Our country]	51	57	−6	**		
Europe	23	20	+3	**		

Note: Q: *"People feel different degrees of attachment to their town or village, to their region, to their country or to Europe. Please tell me how attached you feel to…"*

Model 1 includes no controls and the significance of the difference between groups is measured by gamma coefficients.

Model 2 is based on standardized regression coefficients using logistic regression models predicting knowledge by Internet use controlling for age, gender, income, and education. Sig. **=.01, *=.05.

Percent Online: Q: *"Do you have access to, or do you use … The Internet or the World Wide Web?"*

Source: Eurobarometer 51.0, spring 1999.

CONCLUSIONS

The comparison within this chapter is limited by the availability of survey data monitoring both cultural values and Internet use across a wide range of nations, and future research will be able to examine these issues in much greater depth. Nevertheless, the initial results from this analysis present some interesting findings about the cyberculture that, if confirmed in subsequent studies, promise to have important implications for understanding how the Internet may affect society in the longer term. The issue at the heart of this chapter is whether a distinctive culture predominates among the online communities in the United States and Europe, in particular whether the social backgrounds of Internet enthusiasts and users mean that they are more likely to display a more sympathetic orientation toward postmaterialist values such as individualism, cosmopolitanism, and environmentalism, as well as supporting alternative social movements such as those favoring gay rights or sexual equality. Although the evidence remains limited, the results demonstrate that those online in America can be characterized as located somewhere between the secular or progressive pole on moral values and the laissez-faire pole on economic values, favoring freedom on both dimensions. Internet enthusiasts favor the private sector more than government intervention to produce economic equality, but they are also strong supporters of the alternative social movements that arose in the counterculture 1960s, such as those seeking to promote gay rights, pro-choice, civil rights, feminism, and environmentalism. American users also tended to be more secular rather than religious, although also supporting a limited role for the state in terms of welfare, business, and the economy, with a slight pro-Republican leaning. Nor is this simply an American phenomenon: the European evidence suggests a postmaterialist orientation among Internet users, who support the values of expanding and reforming the EU, as well as favoring more cosmopolitan rather than local identities.

What are the implications of this distinctive cyberculture? As suggested in the introduction, this chapter is not suggesting that the experience of going online has *changed* the attitudes and values of most adult users. In line with traditional socialization theories, social and political values are understood as deep-rooted phenomena that are grounded in early experiences in the home, school, and workplace. Children may indeed be affected by the experience of going online if immersed for long periods of time, just as they are shaped by what they read or watch in the mass media, what they learn from their family, and what they hear in the classroom, but adults come to the Internet community with preexisting cultural dispositions. Given the multiple choices available on the Internet, even more than with the experience of watching television news or reading newspapers, there is a strong self-selection process at work. Despite the role of popular search engines such as Yahoo or services like AOL, users select and filter their own bookmarks, not editors or journalists or broadcasters. People determine which emails they respond to, which online chat rooms (if any) they join, which listservs they subscribe to, which engines they search, and which websites they prefer. As a result of this self-selection process, in the short-term the experience of the Internet is unlikely to convert pro-life advocates to pro-choice, to remake traditionalists into feminists, or to turn nationalists into cosmopolitans. As many commentators have emphasized, and as advocates of direct democracy fear, at individual level, the impact of the Internet is far more likely to produce reinforcement rather than conversion.

But can digital technologies still exert a more diffuse collective impact on the broader social and political culture? The evidence examined here, while admittedly limited, suggests that the online community in Europe and the United States is broadly sympathetic to postmaterialist values like freedom and tolerance, although also more free-market in the economic sphere. The cyberculture provides a public space particularly conducive to progressive networks and alternative social movements, the insurgents challenging the authorities. In the longer-term, socialization theory suggests that the cyber-culture will help shape the values of the children surrounded by this technology in their homes and schools, as well as accelerating cultural changes by transmitting these values to developing and traditional societies worldwide. But will the rise of the Internet mobilize people who are currently disengaged from the political process? The next chapter goes on to consider this issue.

CHAPTER 11

Civic Engagement

In many democracies there is widespread concern that the public has become more and more disenchanted with the core institutions of representative democracy and disillusioned with the traditional channels of political participation. The substantial literature on cyber-democracy commonly claims that the Internet provides a distinctive structure of opportunities that has the potential to revive civic engagement, especially for many peripheral groups currently marginalized from mainstream politics. "Civic engagement" can be understood to include three distinct dimensions: *political knowledge* (what people learn about public affairs), *political trust* (the public's orientation of support for the political system and its actors), and *political participation* (conventional and conventional activities designed to influence government and the decision-making process).[1] But will hopes for a virtual democratic revival be realized? There remains concern that given the pattern of unequal technological access demonstrated in earlier chapters, political resources available via the Internet will empower those with the resources and motivation to take advantage of them, stranding the disengaged farther behind. After outlining theories around this issue, this chapter goes on to analyze survey evidence to examine political participation within the online community in the United States and Western Europe.

MOBILIZATION AND REINFORCEMENT THEORIES

The previous chapter demonstrated the influence of the Internet on changing cultural values. The focus here is the participation hypothesis, which suggests that digital politics will affect public affairs either through the mobilization of new groups or the reinforcement of those

217

who would participate through traditional channels, as illustrated in the typology in Figure 10.1. The *mobilization* hypothesis holds that the Internet may serve to inform, organize, and engage those who are currently marginalized from the existing political system – such as the younger generation, people living in isolated peripheral communities, or fringe political minorities disaffected by the traditional system – so that these groups will gradually become drawn into public life and civic communities. The rich structure of political opportunities becoming available on the Internet may encourage users to become more engaged, whether through traditional channels of representative government as voters, group members, and party supporters, or alternatively through direct participation as community organizers and protest activists. The reduced costs of information and communication could potentially remove some of disincentives to political participation, such as the ability to network about local issues, to learn where parties or candidates stand on issues during election campaigns, or to contact government officials. Cyber-optimists hope that the almost limitless information available via the Internet has the potential to allow the public to become more knowledgeable about public affairs, more articulate in expressing their views via e-mail, online discussion lists, or chat rooms, and more active in mobilizing around community affairs. As a new channel of two-way communication, the Internet can function to strengthen and enrich the connections between citizens and intermediary organizations in the virtual political system, including political parties, social movements, and interest groups, and the news media, as well as with public officials and agencies of local, national, and global governance.

In contrast, the more skeptical perspective suggests that online resources will be used primarily for *reinforcement* by those citizens who are already active and well connected via traditional channels, such as by middle-level actors including journalists and lobbyists, party members, and grassroots activists.[2] Studies of the social and political characteristics of Internet activists in the 1996 and 1998 American elections, based on Pew Surveys of online users and the general public, reported an overall pattern of reinforcement rather than mobilization: People who used the political resources available on the Internet were drawn from the population that was already among the most motivated, informed, and interested in the American electorate.[3] In this sense, during these campaigns, politics on the Internet was essentially preaching to the converted, displacing and supplementing existing channels. Digital technologies still provided a valuable service in widening the range of information that was easily available to the online community during the campaign. But the Web was used more often as a means to access traditional news sources, including the *New York Times* and *CNN*, rather than as a radical new source of unmediated information and communication between citizens and their elected representatives. Reinforcement can still be understood as an invaluable function in representative democracy, akin to the older channels of the partisan press or the campaign rally, but this function continues to dash the hopes of those who believe that the Internet should facilitate a more deliberative or direct form of democracy.

Although the reinforcement pattern does seem to characterize Internet users in past American elections, it remains to be seen whether this pattern is maintained in subsequent elections as access broadens and as digital politics develop new formats and functions. The measures commonly used to gauge civic engagement have often been restricted, and more extensive analysis of different forms of activism is needed, as well as an examination of the role of the Internet in different types of virtual political systems. It is well established that on matters such as voting turnout and associational membership the United States is atypical of most established democracies.[4] Surveys monitoring Internet political participation in developing societies are not yet available but in this chapter we can examine the European and American evidence, comparing the political knowledge, interest, and participation of the online community with the general population.

THE INTERNET ENGAGEMENT MODEL

How can we best conceptualize the many factors that might help to explain political uses of the new information technologies and then theorize about which factors might prove most significant in explaining online civic engagement, meaning levels of knowledge, trust, and participation in the political process? This question raises complex theoretical issues about the direction of causality in any media "effects," and systematic evidence remains scarce. We are only starting to understand the functions of the traditional news media in the process of civic engagement, so it is hardly surprising that our understanding of the role of new technologies remains sketchy and underdeveloped.[5] The Internet engagement model developed in this book suggests that the political use of new technologies can best be conceptualized as the product of the *technological, social,* and *economic environment* discussed in Part I, and the *virtual political system* providing a structure of opportunities for activism within each society covered in detail in Part II, combined with the individual-level *resources* and *motivation* people bring to new information technologies (as illustrated schematically in Figure 1.1). This understanding cannot claim to be novel as it is grounded in the broader normative and empirical literature on democratic theory, social movements, and political participation. The concept of the institutional structure of opportunities builds on the work on collective action and new social movements developed by Charles Tilly, Doug McAdam, and Sidney Tarrow, among others.[6] Differences in resources, such as those of socioeconomic status, income and education, and motivational factors such as political efficacy and interest have long been part of the standard repertoire of variables commonly used by political scientist Sidney Verba and colleagues to explain differences in conventional forms of political participation through voting, party campaigning, and contact activity, in the United States and elsewhere.[7] The theory also expands further on the idea of a "virtuous circle" developed in my earlier work on political communication to explain the pattern of civic engagement associated with use of traditional media such as newspapers and television news.[8]

The context of the *virtual political system* varies substantially across representative democracies, both new and old. As we have seen, in countries such as the United States, Australia, and Sweden, multiple parties are now on the Web along with hundreds of interest groups, social movements, and news media, and thousands of listservs, chat rooms, and discussion groups flourish. In many developing societies, in sharp contrast, such opportunities are sharply constrained since few political institutions have moved online, even in democratic states. The institutional environment provides collective goods: Many individuals living within such information-rich societies as the United States, Sweden, and Australia can take advantage of these opportunities, even if they have few personal resources.

Motivation can also be expected to prove important in determining Internet access and use, including the interest, knowledge, and confidence that people bring to the process of political participation, as well as broader cultural attitudes such as trust in government and satisfaction with the democratic process. Owing to the self-selection mechanism already discussed, motivation seems likely to be particularly important in determining whether people are interested in seeking out political resources once online. Within the Internet community, as a medium of choice, some people seek electronic information about stocks and banking, others opt for music or entertainment, and still others devote more time and energies to political sites.[9] By filtering the contents, personalizing browsers to visit favorite websites, and subscribing to selected listservs and particular user-groups, the Net is becoming similar to Negroponte's "Daily Me" newspaper.[10] There are a million places to go and sites to see on the Internet. Unless they stumble across political contents accidentally (e.g., if reading an online paper or glancing through the headline on a generic search engine like Yahoo!), those who choose to visit political sites will probably have far higher than average civic interest.

Resources refer to the attributes and capacities that individuals bring to public life. As demonstrated in Chapter 4, income, education, and occupation directly affect access to digital technologies. The key issue in this chapter is whether, among those who are online, resources exert an additional indirect effect on political participation via the Internet, such as who follows campaign news, contacts politicians by email, or engages in chat room discussions about current affairs. Previous studies commonly suggest that resources are some of the most important factors influencing whether people are active in conventional politics, such as voting or joining parties.[11] The interesting question is whether this is equally true of the digital world or whether the new environment alters the costs and benefits of civic engagement, such as perhaps lowering the time required to learn about particular referendum issues or to email an elected representative. *Economic* resources include personal or household income, which influences the ability to afford home computers, as well as the service and telecommunication charges for Internet access,[12] and the availability of leisure time or financial resources that facilitate civic engagement such as attending local meetings, volunteering in a campaign, or donating to worthy causes. *Educational* resources provide the capacity to use digital technology including technological and keyboard skills, as well as basic literacy, numeracy, and language skills. In multiple studies education has also proved one of the strongest predictors of conventional forms of participation such as electoral turnout or party membership. Attending high school and college provides analytical and cognitive skills that help make sense of the complexities of the political process, as well as contributing to greater confidence, efficacy, and awareness. *Occupational* resources include access to the type of jobs in management and the professions where computer hardware, software, and training are easily available. The work environment may also provide social networks of colleagues, professional associations, and trade union organizations that may engage in political discussion and mobilization. The basic demographic factors of *age, race,* and *gender* can also be classified in this category, all factors that we have established are important in predicting levels of Internet access and which multiple studies have found relate strongly to civic engagement. First we can describe the political interest, knowledge, political trust, and conventional participation characteristics of the online community in Europe and the United States, and then consider the more complex interaction of resources, motivation, and context.

POLITICAL MOTIVATION AND THE INTERNET

How far is the public motivated to pursue politics via the Internet? The 1997 Eurobarometer asked people whether they would be interested in using the Internet for a variety of online services. Groups can be classified into *actual users* (who already accessed the Internet), *potential users* (who did not currently use the Internet but who remained interested in doing so), and *nonusers* (who did not use and were not interested in using the Net). The results in Figure 11.1 show that education and email generated greatest interest in using the Internet across all groups. One-third or fewer Europeans expressed interest in using the Internet to consult a local town or council services for information from home, whereas only one in ten of the online community expressed an interest in the more demanding forms of civic engagement, such as using digital technologies to contact politicians or to participate in political debates. The results suggest that there will be a sizable minority of Europeans who are drawn to the Internet for its political functions such as news and the delivery of online services but, as in the nonvirtual world, fewer are interested in the more difficult types of participation. The pattern varied slightly in different EU member states. Some variations probably reflected different national experiences; for example, many Scandinavians expressed interest in accessing online newspapers, in a region characterized by relatively high readership of the traditional print sector. Yet potential interest did not necessarily reflect the actual experience of Internet use; for example, about one-third of those living in Portugal, Spain, and Greece would like to consult their local council through these channels, far more than in Scandinavia, despite extremely low levels of online access in the Mediterranean region.

To monitor behavior more closely, the spring 2000 Eurobarometer asked people accessing the Internet from home about their activities during the prior three months, in particular whether they had used the

Table 11.1. *European interest in uses of the Internet, EU-15, 1999*

Percent of each group interested in using Internet to...	Use Internet	Does not use Internet but interested	Does not use Internet and not interested
Follow a training program from home	59	56	46
Send and receive email	41	34	16
Read newspapers and magazines	*36*	*27*	*17*
Get a doctor's advice on a health problem	35	38	38
Manage banking and financial services	35	36	25
Consult local town or council services from home	*28*	*31*	*28*
Get travel information	28	28	25
Consult employment offices	22	28	25
Go on a museum tour	21	20	15
Get product consumer information	20	21	14
Take part in group discussion about work-related and personal subjects	16	15	9
Contact a politician and take part in political debates	*10*	*10*	*8*

Note: Q: "*I am going to name several examples of services you could have access to by using one of these communication networks, for example, the Internet. For each of these services could you please tell me if it interests you or not?*"
Source: Eurobarometer 47.0, Jan–Feb 1997, No. 16,362.

Internet for a number of common functions such as playing computer games, searching for information about job opportunities, education and health, and using e-commerce functions, as well as visiting different types of political websites. The results in Table 11.2 confirm that email among family, friends, and colleagues remains the most popular "killer app" in Europe, as in the United States. Informational needs are also widely popular on the Internet, such as for education, product details, or leisure and travel activities. But the comparison also confirms that reading articles from newspapers is a widespread activity, experienced by about one-third of those on the Internet. Visiting a local authority website was also done by one-fifth of the online population in Europe (19

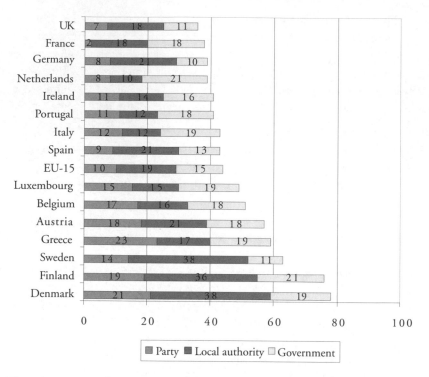

Figure 11.1. Use of Political Websites, EU-15, 2000.
Note: The proportion of home Internet users visiting political websites within the previous three months.
Source: Eurobarometer 53.0, spring 2000.

percent), while visiting a government website was done by 15 percent, and finally, using a party website was done by one in ten. The overall results suggest that "political" activity, broadly defined, while clearly less popular than many leisure uses, was still experienced by a sizable minority of Internet users in Europe. Moreover consultation of party, local authority, and government websites showed considerable variations across the EU member states, with the greatest use in Scandinavian nations and least activity in the UK, France, and Germany.

Across many other dimensions, the attitudinal profile of the online community in Europe showed that Internet users were drawn from the groups who were among the most knowledgeable and the most predisposed toward participation through conventional channels, such as voting or party membership. Reflecting their educational background,

Table 11.2. *The popularity of online activities, EU-15, 2000*

Emailed family, friends, or colleagues	69
Searched for educational materials	47
Searched for product information	47
Downloaded free software	43
Searched for information about sports or leisure activity	42
Searched for holiday and travel information	38
Read articles on a national newspaper website	**31**
Played computer games	28
Carried out operations on bank account	25
Searched for information about health	23
Searched for job opportunities	23
Listened to radio or music online	21
Visited a local authority website	**19**
Visited a museum website	18
Visited a government website	**15**
Bought a CD	14
Bought a book	14
Built own website	11
Visited a political party website	**10**
Bought software	9
Make telephone call using the Internet	9
Answered public opinion survey	8
Bought stocks or shares	7
Watched TV channels online	6
Make a bid in online auctions	4
Held video conference over the Internet	3

Note: Asked of those using the Internet from home. Q: *"Which of the following, if any, have you done online in the last three months?"*
Source: Eurobarometer 53, spring 2000. No. 16,078. EU-15.

Internet users proved consistently more knowledgeable about EU institutions, with a sizable gap in awareness of the European Parliament, Commission, and Court of Justice (Table 11.3). Many advocates of direct democracy have speculated that the Internet might provide a home for those who were currently disaffected with the tra-

Table 11.3. *Knowledge of EU institutions, EU-15, 1999*

Percent Aware of...	Online	Not online	Diff.	Sig.
European Parliament	21	6	+15	**
European Commission	22	7	+15	**
Council of Ministers of the EU	23	13	+10	**
Court of Justice of the EU	24	10	+14	**
European Ombudsman	24	17	+7	**
European Central Bank	23	11	+12	**
European Court of Auditors	19	20	−1	
EU Committee of the Regions	22	19	+3	**
EU Social and Economic Committee	23	18	+5	**

Note: Q: *"Have you heard of...?"*
Percent Online: Q: *"Do you have access to, or do you use ... The Internet or the World Wide Web?"*
Source: Eurobarometer 51.0, spring 1999.

ditional political system but in fact those online were consistently more trusting toward a wide range of social and political institutions, ranging from the traditional news media such as radio and the press to the core institutions of representative government such as parliament, the national government, parties, the civil service, and the legal system (see Table 11.4). The only exception was the church, which perhaps reflects the greater adherence to secular values among the online community, documented in the previous chapter. Internet users were also more satisfied with how democracy worked in their own countries, not less, and they did not differ significantly from the general public in their evaluations of the way democracy worked within the European Union (see Table 11.5).

Finally, Internet users proved more positive than average across all the indicators of conventional political participation and news consumption, as shown in Table 11.6. Compared with the general public, Internet users more commonly discussed politics, felt that they knew more about the EU, voted in EU elections, and regularly read printed newspapers or listened to the radio news every day. The only exception to this pattern was a slight tendency for online users to be less frequent TV news viewers, which can probably best be explained by

Table 11.4. *Trust in political institutions, EU-15, 1999*

Percent "Tend to trust"	Online	Not online	Diff.	Sig.
Radio	78	68	+10	**
The police	72	62	+10	**
The United Nations	63	48	+15	**
Justice/the [national] legal system	62	46	+16	**
Television	72	70	+2	
The army	67	64	+3	**
Trade unions	43	40	+3	*
The European Union	41	38	+3	**
Political parties	22	19	+4	*
Non-governmental organizations	44	40	+4	*
Charitable or voluntary organizations	63	59	+4	**
Civil service	50	45	+5	**
Big companies	41	36	+5	**
The [national] government	47	41	+6	**
The press	59	51	+8	**
The national parliament	53	42	+9	**
The Church	49	53	−4	**

Note: Q: *"I would like to ask you a question about how much trust you have in certain institutions. For each of the following could you tell me if you tend to trust it or tend not to trust it?"*
    Percent Online: Q: *"Do you have access to, or do you use … The Internet or the World Wide Web?"*
Source: Eurobarometer 51.0, spring 1999.

Table 11.5. *Satisfaction with democracy, EU-15 1999*

Percent "Very" or "fairly" satisfied	Online	Not online	Diff.	Sig.
Satisfaction with the way that democracy works in own country	73	61	+12	**
Satisfaction with the way that democracy works in the European Union	42	42	0	

Note: Q: *"On the whole, are you very satisfied, fairly satisfied, not very satisfied, or not at all satisfied with the way democracy works in [our country]? And what about the way democracy works in the European Union?"*
    Percent Online: Q: *"Do you have access to, or do you use … The Internet or the World Wide Web?"*
Source: Eurobarometer 51.0, spring 1999.

Table 11.6. *Indicators of political participation and news consumption,*
EU-15, 1999

	Online	Not online	Diff.	Sig.
Political participation				
Frequently discuss politics with friends	18	13	+5	**
Often persuade friends to share views	18	10	+8	**
Voting record in EU elections	65	61	+4	**
News media consumption				
Watch television news every day	67	72	–5	**
Read newspaper every day	53	43	+10	**
Listen to radio news every day	53	45	+8	**

Note: **Percent Online:** Q: *"Do you have access to, or do you use … (The Internet or the World Wide Web?"*
Source: Eurobarometer 51.0, spring 1999.

the younger age profile typical among the online community. Table 11.7 shows that the differences in political knowledge and trust between Internet users and nonusers were modest, but these differences remained significant even after controlling for the standard demographic variables of education, age, gender, and income. That is to say, according to a range of indicators European Internet users expressed greater support for the political system; this is not simply explained by their social background. As was found in the United States, the structure of opportunities for participation and engagement available on the Internet is therefore likely to be available for the population that is most likely to want to use these resources.[13] In this regard, the rise of the virtual political system seems most likely to facilitate further knowledge, interest, and activism of those who are already most predisposed toward civic engagement, reinforcing patterns of political participation. This process is important for strengthening representative democracy, especially if the costs of activism are reduced further, for example, with the introduction of electronic registration and voting in local and general elections, and with more governmental services online. Whether the virtual political system can ever reach those who tune out from public affairs, however, is a different matter, because this group is underrepresented within the online community.

Table 11.7. *The political characteristics of online users, EU-15, 1999*

Attitudinal scales	Online users (M)	Non-users (M)	Zero order correlations (R)	Sig.	Standardized beta coefficients (B)	Sig.
	(i)		(ii)		(iii)	
Knowledge of EU institutions	6.03	5.14	.136	**	.033	*
Political efficacy	5.07	4.29	.138	**	.086	**
Trust in government institutions	2.76	2.33	.085	**	.049	**
Trust in EU institutions	3.74	3.20	.066	**	−.025	*
Trust in news media	2.08	1.89	.064	**	.026	*
Satisfaction with democracy in EU	2.43	2.48	−.029	**	−.075	**
Satisfaction with democracy in own country	2.83	2.67	.079	**	.051	**
EU voting participation	3.09	2.96	.036	*	.002	

Notes: (i) Mean score on the scales of online users and nonusers. (ii) Zero-order coefficients between online use and dependent variables without any controls (iii). Standard regression coefficients (betas) with prior controls for education, age, gender, and household income. Sig. P.** > .01, *> .05.

Satisfaction with democracy scales: See Table 11.3. Knowledge of the EU: See Table 11.4 (nine-point scale). **Trust in government**: See Table 11.4 (six-point scale) – The national government, the national parliament, the EU, political parties, the United Nations, and the civil service. **Trust in media**: See Table 11.4 (three-point scale) – the press, radio, and television. **EU voting participation**: *"Did you vote in the last elections to the European parliament in June 1994?"* plus *"Do you intend to vote in the next European elections this June?"*

Sources: Eurobarometer 51.0, spring 1999.

CONCLUSIONS: ACTIVATING THE ACTIVE

Why should there be a consistent relationship between civic engagement and use of the political resources on the Internet? This general pattern could be explained in any one of three ways. This association could be the result of "selection effects," if the chain of causality runs from prior civic engagement to use of the Net, that is, if people who are most politically interested and involved turn to news and public affairs on the Web to keep themselves well informed and networked. This perspective, which echoes the "uses and gratifications" theory of TV view-ing,[14] emphasizes the motivational basis of civic participation, and the need for prior predispositions before people use the political resources available on the Internet.

Alternatively, the association could be accounted for by "media effects," if the causal direction runs from use of the Internet to subse-quent civic activism; for example, if people who happen to go online (for whatever reason) discover resources such as chat rooms or issue campaigns that help them become more involved in public affairs. This view emphasizes that the Internet can engage many groups (e.g., the younger generation), those in isolated communities, or political minorities who might otherwise be unlikely to become involved through such conventional organizations as parties or community groups. Users may go online for many diverse reasons (e.g., because home shopping, entertainment, or financial services attract them), but when surfing they may stumble on political resources that stimulate further interest in public affairs. Both the "selection effects" and the "media effects" explanations may be true; however, both require strong assumptions that the effects are purely one-way.

In contrast, the theory of a *virtuous circle* suggests that there is a process of mutually reinforcing interaction in digital politics, similar to that found as a result of attention to newspapers or television news. In this account, the most motivated citizens could be expected to prove most likely to use the political opportunities on the Internet – such as reading political news, checking party Web pages, or coordinating com-munity activities online – driven by their prior interests, attitudes, and resources. In the longer term, however, as a result of accumulated expe-rience, this process can be expected to positively reinforce civic engage-ment: the more political information acquired, the more networks contacted, the greater the awareness of current affairs, the lower the costs of becoming further involved in the democratic process. This the-ory predicts that if the Internet is similar to the effects of the traditional news media, then through repeated use the most politically engaged will be reinforced in their civic activism. In contrast, this theory sug-gests that the most politically disengaged will be largely immunized from political messages on the Net because of three conditions: (1) this group will be least likely to seek political information on the Web; (2) lacking interest, they will pay minimal attention to any political mes-sages they do encounter; and finally, (3) if they do pay attention to political websites, they will be unlikely to trust the information provided. If this interpretation is correct, and if this situation persists as Internet use spreads and normalizes, it suggests that there will be a growing "democratic divide" in civic involvement. Far from mobilizing the general public, the Internet may thereby function to increase divisions between the actives and apathetics within societies. This pattern exists in the traditional news media as well, but this tendency may be exacerbated on the Internet because of its distinctive characteristics, namely the fragmentation of sources and à la carte choices about what to see and do, rather than the predetermined schedule and front-page headlines of the traditional mass media. True, there is a silver lining, because digital politics function to reduce the costs for the actives becoming more active. But as the media of choice par excellence it is difficult to know how the Internet per se can ever reach the civically disengaged.

CHAPTER 12

Conclusions: Promoting e-Democracy

Previous technological breakthroughs have commonly generated exaggerated hopes that machines can transform society and democracy. Luddites fear for the worse, but technophiles hope for the better. In its more utopian manifestations, this view has been dubbed "technoromanticism,"[1] expressed in earlier eras in response to Samuel Morse's electric telegraph, Alexander Graham Bell's telephone, and Guglielmo Marconi's wireless radio.[2] The more utopian visions of the Internet suggest a future society in which virtually unlimited qualities of information become available, civic society flourishes, government decision making becomes more open and transparent, and nation-state borders are eroded as people build virtual communities for work, learning, and leisure, spanning traditional boundaries of time and place. Although still in its adolescence, the core transformative capacities of the Internet include its potential for radically shrinking communications and information costs, maximizing speed, broadening reach, and eradicating distance. Compared with radio, television, and newspapers, controlled by editors and broadcasters, the World Wide Web facilitates a virtually unlimited choice of information and communication one-to-one (e.g., via email), one-to-many (e.g., via a personal home page or electronic conference), many-to-one (e.g., via an electronic poll) and, perhaps most important, many-to-many (e.g., an online chat room), with a minimal role for gatekeepers or government censors.[3] Internet messages have the capacity to flow farther, faster, and with fewer intermediaries.

Cyber-optimists are common in the United States where the Internet reflects certain deeply-held values in American culture; for libertarians the Web symbolizes the rewards of entrepreneurial risk-taking individualism and the benefits of the unfettered marketplace, while for communitarians the digital world mirrors the values of egalitarian forms of direct democracy and grassroots networking.[4] America's love affair with the latest, the smallest, the fastest electronic gizmos and gadgets is often expressed with an irrational gee-whiz exuberance similar to faith in the Nasdaq. Yet there are many reasons to temper the rosy scenarios with a more cautious vision stressing the substantial inequalities that may arise from technological development. Deep down many want to believe that the Internet represents the best of scientific progress, with a devil on our right shoulder whispering promises of technological quick fixes for civic engagement in democracy, akin to one-week wonder diets or surgical tummy tucks to save us from slothful selves without the need for painful exercise. Yet it remains difficult to silence the voice of the skeptical devil on our left, muttering warnings to mistrust glib promises of easy shortcuts for solving intractable social inequalities and civic ills. People marvel at the magical powers of newfangled mechanical inventions, yet simultaneously mistrust dependence on technology. So how do we strike an appropriate balance between these alternative visions and determine the most perspicacious assessment of future scenarios?

THE GLOBAL DIVIDE IN INTERNET ACCESS

The issue of widening technological disparities around the world has generated considerable concern by international agencies and national governments. The evidence considered in this book confirms that the global divide in access to digital technologies is substantial and that it has been growing during the first decade of the Internet age. While some postindustrial societies have experienced a remarkably fast transformation to all Internet, all-the-time, at present about one in twenty of the world's population is connected. Vast swathes of the population are excluded in Sub-Saharan Africa, Latin America, the Middle East, and Southeast Asia. There are reasons to hope that computer software and manufacturing will prove an important source of revenue in high-tech areas of development in Taiwan, Malaysia, India, and Brazil, but at present for most of the poorest nations the Internet represents one more area in which they lag behind the industrialized world.

The analysis demonstrates that the root cause of unequal global diffusion of digital technologies is lack of economic development, the same as the reasons for the uneven spread of old mass media like radio and television. Within about a decade of its launch, professionals and managers in America, Sweden, and Britain have come to take for granted access to Internet resources, surrounded by desktop microcomputers wired to high-speed LAN networks and technical advisers at work, with the paraphernalia of mobile phones, digital pagers, personal digital assistants, and laptop computers for road warriors when traveling, and electronic shopping catalogs, library databases, electronic banking, and email easily available from home. In contrast multiple barriers face many developing societies where access to household telephones and television remains uncommon, as well as a reliable supply of electricity, let alone computers. Cyber-cafés, wired village schools, and mobile cellular phone schemes may eventually help to connect more peripheral areas in poorer regions in Sub-Saharan Africa, Latin America, or Southeast Asia, but such initiatives are only starting to be introduced. As international agencies including the UNDP, World Bank, and G-8 have emphasized, wiring the world matters, not just in itself, but also because access to digital technologies is likely to reinforce the economic growth and productivity of richer nations while leaving the poorest ones farther behind.

THE SOCIAL DIVIDE WITHIN NATIONS

In postindustrial societies, as the Internet becomes increasingly common in the home, school, and workplace, it becomes even more important if certain groups are excluded from this resource, whether poorer neighborhoods and peripheral rural areas, of the older generation, girls and women, ethnic minorities, and those lacking college education. Many countries have recognized this issue and developed initiatives designed to tackle social access, often involving a combination of state, nonprofit, and market initiatives. Many assume that the digital divide is caused by certain characteristics associated with proximate access to this technology, such as the need for computing skills and affordable ISP connections. The policy solutions designed to ameliorate the digital divide commonly focus on specific fixes, such as wiring schools and classrooms, training teachers, and providing community access in poorer neighborhoods.

But will these initiatives work in terms of diversifying the online population? What the analysis in this book demonstrates is that the heart of the problem of the social divide in Internet access lies in broader patterns of socioeconomic stratification that influence the distribution of household consumer durables and participation in other common forms of information and communication technologies, as well as in the digital world. Moreover, it is not necessarily true that all dimensions of the social divide will automatically close as Internet access becomes more ubiquitous – the evidence from nations where use of new technologies has become widespread (e.g., Sweden and the Netherlands) is that the gaps by education, income, and occupation remain substantial and show no signs of closure during the first decade. It remains to be seen how this pattern changes in subsequent years. The process of generational turnover can be expected to gradually close some of these divisions, given the investments in school access and training. A combination of further technological developments, falling costs, and the appeal of mass entertainment delivered over the Internet all promise to widen access. But the continuing social inequalities in the distribution of older technologies such as cable and satellite TV, and even household telephones, suggests that some residual inequalities are unlikely to disappear completely in access to personal home computers and Internet connections.

THE DEMOCRATIC DIVIDE

Many have expressed hopes that cyber-democracy can revitalize public interest and participation. Political institutions have adapted to the new opportunities: chapters have demonstrated that thousands of sites have been established by political parties, interest groups and new social movements, government departments, and parliaments. Cyber-optimists have faith that these innovations will revitalize social networks and civic engagement. Digital technologies promise to provide new forms of horizontal and vertical communication that can facilitate social engagement and enrich deliberative democracy. Cyber-optimists hope that the Internet provides a distinctive structure of opportunities for political mobilization that differs, in several important ways, from such conventional activities as joining political parties, organizing grassroots community movements, or lobbying elected officials. Many believe that the Internet will diminish inequalities in public life by sharply reducing (although not wholly eliminating) certain barriers to civic engagement, leveling some of the financial hurdles, and widening the opportunities for political debate, the dissemination of information, and networks of new social movements. Given the lower information and communication costs via the Internet, it is hoped that new technology will allow people to be far more knowledgeable about public policy issues, articulate in expressing their opinions, and active in casting their votes. Enthusiasts often see information technology as a way to bypass the limitations of representative democracy, allowing fuller participation in direct democracy and public deliberation through electronic town hall meetings, online discussion lists, bulletin boards, newsgroups, and community networks, as well as protest activities, direct action campaigns, and civil disobedience coordinated via the Internet.

As we have seen, numerous websites have sprung up to encouraging participation and deliberation, particularly in the United States, as well as multiple nonprofit sites linking transnational advocacy networks concerned about issues such as the environment, human rights, and international development.[5] In the early to mid-1990s, enthusiasts expressed hopes that many features of digital technologies had the capacity to transform politics as we know it, stressing the interactive many-to-many and one-to-many features of Internet communications, its networking and organizational role, its global reach across national boundaries, and the almost unlimited supply of information available on the Internet. Many hoped that the combination of the World Wide Web, online discussion-groups, email, and bulletin boards had the Midas capacity to transform worthy but dull civic dross into democratic gold – generating a more participatory, egalitarian, and deliberative form of public affairs.

Yet, in contrast cyber-pessimists suggest that the new opportunities on the Internet will serve to reinforce the grip of established political actors and interests, such as the traditional news media, incumbent officeholders, and inside-the-beltway lobbyists. After just a few years the conventional mood among commentators became cautious and skeptical, stressing that despite the potential of new technologies, in practice the virtual world tended to reflect "politics as usual," with much the same dominant players, activities, and routines. In this view, far from generating new opportunities for deliberative and participatory politics, established interests predominate. Parties and candidates use the Web to hawk their electoral wares, boost their support, and raise their dollars. Parliaments and government departments put official documents online, saving ink and postage, but they rarely facilitate public discussions or develop interactive "bottom-up" formats. Newspapers and magazines give away electronic versions, usually hemorrhaging money in the process, but rather than widening the plurality of the news media, as in life, people tend to surf those sources they trust in the nonvirtual world – the *New York Times,* the BBC, CNN, and so on. Most people participating in online politics – contributing electronically to campaigns, surfing for news, or emailing their representatives – are those most likely to participate in traditional forms of face-to-face civic engagement.

One reason why the Internet arouses such fiercely contested visions of the future is that plausibly the new technology may act both as a "great leveler" restructuring communication and information resources among intermediary institutions and empowering the class of wired political activists, while also simultaneously reinforcing inequality for those nations, groups, and individuals lacking the resources and motivation to take advantage of the new structure of opportunities. Like the blind men of Indostan, by describing different parts of the elephant, depending on where we focus, as partial truths, "each was partly in the right ~ And all were in the wrong."[6] Government Web pages may serve as a new channel for transparency and accountability, and also as a form of state propaganda. Established interested parties can use the Internet to boost their fund raising, strengthen their organization, and communicate their message, but so can minor opposition parties and grass-roots groups of human rights or environmental activists.

Rejecting both the utopian revolutionary visions that everything will change (with technology driving politics), and the equally misplaced skeptical claims that nothing has changed in the virtual political world (with technology subordinate to its social uses), this study draws three main conclusions.

First, it is true, as many cyber-pessimists argue, that so far established political institutions usually remain relatively conservative in how far they have adapted to the potential of digital technologies. Many official agencies have established an online website and, as with firms in the commercial sector, within just a few years it will be unusual to find any major political institution that has not ventured online. Nevertheless, at least during the first decade, political uses of digital technologies have often proved relatively staid and unimaginative. Most mainstream political organizations have sought to communicate via digital channels much as they would through the conventional mass media, changing the channel but not the nature of communications, rather than radically rethinking their strategic information and communications functions in the light of the interactive capacities in digital technologies. Government departments, for example, often publish official documents and downloadable forms online, saving paper, postage, and ink, but they rarely launch deliberative consultation exercises through unmoderated chat rooms. Major party websites commonly publicize leadership speeches, press releases, and official policy statements, but they less often facilitate feedback mechanisms for public comments from supporters or critics. Interest groups often use the Web as a form of corporate wallpaper, publicizing their messages, but not utilizing the two-way capacities of digital media.

Moreover it is also true, as pessimists emphasize, that at mass level the Internet has difficulty in mobilizing the disengaged. In this regard, the Internet will largely serve to reinforce the activism of the activists, facilitating participation for those who are already interested in politics by reducing some of the opportunity costs of communicating, mobilizing, and organizing. The choice of where to go and what to do online means that a growing gap can be expected to develop between the politically engaged and disengaged. However, this conclusion needs one important modification: Although the Internet is not necessarily reaching new groups of citizens, the analysis suggests that the culture of the Internet in Europe and the United States is distinctive in certain important regards, and may therefore contribute to a diffuse process of changing values in society and politics. The evidence suggests that the online community in America is more tolerant of alternative lifestyles, more sympathetic toward new social movements, more secular toward moral values, more liberal in general on the social issues although also more pro-business on the economic agenda. This analysis needs to be extended further, but at present the available evidence points toward an Internet culture that will accelerate the process of value change associated with societal modernization.

Finally, and most important, despite these grounds for caution, the study suggests that "politics as usual" may be altered by digital technologies primarily by altering the balance of resources among the political institutions, reducing the costs of gathering information and communicating messages, with consequences that will mainly serve to benefit minor parties, smaller groups, and fringe movement activists. There are parallel developments in the knowledge economy, where information technology has shifted the balance of resources away from the investment in land and capital, and toward skills, expertise, and know-how. The process has mainly benefited small businesses in the service sector, with the organizational flexibility and aggressive entrepreneurship to adapt innovative ways of connecting directly with customers. The capacity of the Internet in the economic sphere lies in reducing the transaction costs for companies, thereby downsizing the optimal size of firms, and supplementing the importance of the traditional resources of land and capital by those of know-how and technical expertise. In less than a decade, innovative companies with the flexibility and imagination to take advantage of digital technologies, such as Amazon.com and eBay, have challenged the market share held by established companies. Utilizing niche markets, small businesses with the necessary skills and flexibility in manufacturing, sales, or services can supply customers directly, challenging large multinational corporations. Although thousands of dot.coms have failed, some succeeded.

In the same way, digital politics has shifted the balance of resources away from large-scale professional bureaucracies, mass-branch membership organizations, and financial resources, and toward technical knowledge and skills. This process should not be exaggerated; digital politics does not level the playing field for political actors – traditional resources remain important, and indeed they may be translated into ready-made know-how. Nevertheless the Internet provides an arena that facilitates more open and egalitarian competition in civic society. Digital politics therefore has the potential to amplify the voice of smaller and less well-resourced insurgents and challengers, whether parties, groups, or agencies, which have difficulty being heard through the conventional channels of the traditional mass media but which have the flexibility, skills, and innovative capacity to produce new coalitions capable of sudden "flash" protests around specific events. In the public sphere, the most dramatic exemplification of digital politics has come from transnational advocacy networks and alternative social movements that have adapted the resources of new technologies to communicate, organize, and mobilize global coalitions around issues, including world trade, globalization, and human rights, to challenge the legitimacy of established international organizations and national governments. As shown by the systematic comparison of fringe, minor, and major parties, the wired world cannot eliminate the power of traditional organizational, financial, or authoritative resources, but it provides a more egalitarian environment where technical expertise counts in gathering information and communicating messages. As the Internet spreads worldwide, the capacity for digital politics has particularly important implications for consolidating, and transitional democracies struggling to institutionalize their political systems. Many countries are characterized by free and fair elections yet they continue to lack stable party organizations and strong opposition movements, effective parliamentary checks on the abuse of power, a flourishing civil society and respect for the rule of law. Where the Internet spreads among civic society in these countries, it can be expected to contribute to the democratization process through strengthening the mechanisms for information and communication, and the influence for middle-level actors of representative governance.

More than a century ago the French sociologist Gabriel Tarde described the diffusion process as analogous to a stone dropping into a pond triggering rippling waves that spread in concentric circles, advancing slowly among core elites in the beginning, followed by rapid acceleration spreading through advanced urban societies, with progress gradually slackening until it finally stops.[7] This surge remains in process and the limitations of our ability to peer into the future of the Internet is self-evident: Few can predict with much confidence which of the multiple dot.coms stocks will rise or fall tomorrow, so it is hazardous to provide more than, at best, an educated guess about the long-term consequences of new technology for democracy. Historical analogies are commonly drawn with previous technologies like the electronic telegraph, telephone, or television but, like generals fighting the last war, there are many plausible reasons why, despite these lessons, digital technology may prove distinctive. Projections of future developments remain uncertain and hazardous, surrounded by health warnings, yet at the same time it is even more important that we seek to understand the underlying reasons for patterns of Internet access and use at this stage in the diffusion process, even imperfectly, before the initial inequalities rigidify into a virtual Berlin Wall dividing the information-rich and poor, within and between societies.

Nations in the Study and Abbreviated Names Used in Figures

	Nation	Abbreviation
1	Afghanistan	Afg
2	Albania	Alb
3	Algeria	Alg
4	Angola	Ang
5	Antigua and Barbuda	Ant
6	Argentina	Arg
7	Armenia	Arm
8	Australia	Austl
9	Austria	Aus
10	Azerbaijan	Aze
11	Bahrain	Bah
12	Bangladesh	Bng
13	Barbados	Bar
14	Belarus	Bela
15	Belgium	Belg
16	Belize	Beli
17	Benin	Ben
18	Bhutan	Bhu
19	Bolivia	Bol
20	Bosnia and Herzegovina	Bos
21	Botswana	Bots
22	Brazil	Braz
23	Brunei Darussalam	Bru
24	Bulgaria	Bul
25	Burkina Faso	Burk
26	Burundi	Bur
27	Cambodia	Camb

	Nation	Abbreviation
28	Cameroon	Came
29	Canada	Can
30	Cape Verde	CVerd
31	Central African Republic	CAR
32	Chad	Chad
33	Chile	Chil
34	China	China
35	Colombia	Col
36	Comoros	Comor
37	Congo	Cong
38	Costa Rica	CRica
39	Cote D'Ivoire	CD'Ivo
40	Croatia	Cro
41	Cuba	Cuba
42	Cyprus	Cyp
43	Czech Republic	Czech
44	Denmark	Den
45	Djibouti	Dji
46	Dominica	Dom
47	Dominican Republic	DomR
48	Ecuador	Ecu
49	Egypt	Egy
50	El Salvador	ElSal
51	Equatorial Guinea	Equ
52	Eritrea	Erit
53	Estonia	Est
54	Ethiopia	Ethi
55	Fiji	Fiji
56	Finland	Fin
57	France	Fr
58	Gabon	Gab
59	Gambia	Gam
60	Georgia	Geo
61	Germany	Ger
62	Ghana	Gha
63	Greece	Gre
64	Grenada	Gren
65	Guatemala	Gue
66	Guinea-Bissau	G-Biss

	Nation	Abbreviation
67	Guinea	Guin
68	Haiti	Hait
69	Hondurus	Hon
70	Hungary	Hung
71	Iceland	Ice
72	India	India
73	Indonesia	Ind
74	Iran	Iran
75	Iraq	Iraq
76	Ireland	Ire
77	Israel	Isr
78	Italy	Ita
79	Jamaica	Jam
80	Japan	Jap
81	Jordon	Jor
82	Kazakhstan	Kaz
83	Kenya	Ken
84	Kiribati	Kiri
85	Korea, Republic of	SKor
86	Kuwait	Kuw
87	Kyrgyzstan	Kyr
88	Laos	Laos
89	Latvia	Lat
90	Lebanon	Leb
91	Lesotho	Les
92	Liberia	Lib
93	Libya Arab Jamahiriy	Liby
94	Lithuania	Lith
95	Luxembourg	Lux
96	Macedonia	Mac
97	Madagascar	Mada
98	Malawi	Mala
99	Malaysia	Malay
100	Maldives	Mald
101	Mali	Mali
102	Malta	Malta
103	Marshall Islands	Mar
104	Mauritania	Maur
105	Mauritius	Mau

	Nation	Abbreviation
106	Mexico	Mex
107	Micronesia, Fed Stat	Mic
108	Moldova, Republic of	Mol
109	Mongolia	Mong
110	Morocco	Mor
111	Mozambique	Moz
112	Myanmar	Bur
113	Namibia	Nam
114	Nepal	Nep
115	Netherlands	Neth
116	New Zealand	NZ
117	Nicaragua	Nic
118	Niger	Niger
119	Nigeria	Nigeria
120	Norway	Nor
121	Oman	Om
122	Pakistan	Pak
123	Panama Canal Zone	Pan
124	Papua New Guinea	Pap
125	Paraguay	Para
126	Peru	Peru
127	Philippines	Phil
128	Poland	Pol
129	Portugal	Por
130	Quatar	Qua
131	Romania	Rom
132	Russian Federation	Rus
133	Rwanda	Rwan
134	Saint Lucia	StL
135	Sao Tome and Principe	STom
136	Saudi Arabia	SAra
137	Senegal	Sene
138	Seychelles	Sey
139	Sierra Leone	SLeo
140	Singapore	Sing
141	Slovakia	Slovk
142	Slovenia	Slov
143	Solomon Islands	Sol
144	Somalia	Som

	Nation	Abbreviation
145	South Africa	SAfr
146	Spain	Sp
147	Sri Lanka	SLan
148	St. Kitts and Nevis	StK
149	St. Vincent and Grenadine	StV
150	Sudan	Sud
151	Suriname	Sur
152	Swaziland	Swazi
153	Sweden	Swe
154	Switzerland	Swi
155	Syrian Arab Rep.	Syr
156	Taiwan	Tai
157	Tajikstan	Taj
158	Tanzania	Tanz
159	Thailand	Thai
160	Togo	Togo
161	Trinidad and Tobago	Tri
162	Tunisia	Tun
163	Turkey	Turk
164	Turkmenistan	Turkm
165	Uganda	Uga
166	Ukraine	Ukr
167	United Arab Emirates	UAE
168	United Kingdom	UK
169	United States	US
170	Uruguay	Uru
171	Uzbekistan	Uzb
172	Vanuatu	Van
173	Venezuela	Ven
174	Viet Nam	Viet
175	Western Samoa	Sam
176	Yemen	Yem
177	Yugoslavia	Yug
178	Zambia	Zam
179	Zimbabwe	Zim

Notes

Chapter 1. The Digital Divide

1. U.S. Department of Commerce. 1999. *The Emerging Digital Economy II.* Washington, D.C., U.S. Department of Commerce. *www.ecommerce.gov/ede* For estimates of productivity gains in other postindustrial societies see OECD. 2000. *Information and Technology Outlook.* Paris: OECD. Annex 1.

2. See Philip Evans and Thomas S. Wurster. 1999. *Blown to Bits: How the New Economics of Information Transforms Strategy.* Cambridge, MA: Harvard Business School; Don Tapscott, David Ticoll, and Alex Lowy. 2000. *Digital Capital: Harnessing the Power of Business Webs.* Cambridge, MA: Harvard Business School; Carl Shapiro and Hal R. Varian. 1998. *Information Rules: A Strategic Guide to the Network Economy.* Cambridge, MA: Harvard Business School; Clayton M. Christensen. 2000. *The Innovator's Dilemma: When New Technologies Cause Great Firms to Fall.* New York: HarperCollins.

3. See, for example, Steve Jones. Ed. 1998. *Cybersociety 2.0: Revisiting Computer-Mediated Communication and Community.* Thousand Oaks, CA: Sage. The estimate of the number of American users of Napster in August 2000 is from Media Metrix. *www.mediametrix.com*

4. The estimate of 2.1 billion unique Web pages publicly available on the Internet in July 2000 is provided by Cyveillance, a company based in Arlington, Virginia, in a report "Sizing the Internet," which suggests that 7.3 million unique pages are added daily to the total. *www.cyveillance.com/newsroom/3012.asp* Also reported in Janet Kornblum. 2000. "The News behind the Net." *USA Today.* July 2000. *www.usatoday.com/life/cyber/tech/jk071100.htm*

5. On the United States, see regular estimates from surveys conducted by the Pew Center for the People and the Press. *www.peoplepress.org* For a 20-nation study including Sweden and Australia see IriS/MORI Internet Survey Jan–March 1999.

6. See Chapter 3 for more details. *www.NUA.ie;* The estimate of approximately 407 million users worldwide is for November 2000.

7. Metcalf's law is named after Robert Metcalf, founder of 3Com Corporation. See Larry Downes and Chunka Mui. 2000. *Unleashing the Killer Apps.* Cambridge, MA: Harvard Business School Press. Pp. 24–5.

8. Tim Hayward. 1995. *Info-Rich, Info-Poor: Access and Exchange in the Global Information Society.* K. G. Saur; William Wresch. 1996. *Disconnected: Haves and Have-Nots in the Information Age.* New Brunswick, NJ: Rutgers University Press.

9. Francisco Rodriguez and Ernest J. Wilson III. 2000. "Are poor countries losing the Information Revolution?" *The World Bank infoDev Working Paper Series.* May. *www.infoDev.org/library/wilsonrodriguez.doc*

10. OECD. 1999. *Communications Outlook 1999.* Paris: OECD. Pp. 85–98. Also *www.oecd.org*

11. UNDP. 1999. *Human Development Report 1999.* New York: UNDP/Oxford University Press. P. 63.

12. UNESCO. 1998. *World Communication Report: The Media and Challenges of the New Technologies.* Paris: UNESCO.

13. See, for example, the G-8 *Okinawa Charter on Global Information Society.* July 23, 2000. *www.g8kyushu-okinawa.go.jp/w/documents/it1.html*

14. J. Galtung and M. Ruge. 1965. "The Structure of Foreign News." *Journal of Peace Research* 1: 64–90; Hamid Mowlana. 1997. *Global Information and World Communication.* 2d ed. London: Sage.

15. For a comprehensive overview see Surendra J. Patel. General editor. 1993–5. *Technological Transformation in the Third World.* 5 vols. Aldershot: Avebury. See also case studies in David J. Jeremy. 1992. *The Transfer of International Technology: Europe, Japan and the USA in the Twentieth Century.* Aldershot: Edward Elgar; Nathan Rosenberg and Claudio Frischtak. Eds. 1985. *International Technology Transfer: Concepts, Methods and Comparisons.* New York: Praeger; David Charles and Jeremy Howells. 1992. *Technology Transfer in Europe.* London: Belhaven Press; Manas Chatterji. 1990. *Technology Transfer in the Developing Countries.* New York: St. Martin's Press; S. R. Melkote. 1991. *Communication for Development in the Third World: Theory and Practice.* Newbury Park, CA: Sage; Wilbur Schramm. 1964. *Mass Media and National Development.* Stanford, CA: Stanford University Press.

16. G-8 *Okinawa Charter on Global Information Society.* July 23, 2000. *www.g8kyushu-okinawa. go.jp/w/documents/it1.html*

17. International Telecommunications Union. 1999. *Challenges to the Network: Internet for Development.* Geneva: ITU. P. 7; Celia W. Dugger. 2000. "Connecting Rural India to the World." *New York Times* 28 May. *www.nytimes.com/library/tech/yr/mo /biztech/articles/28india.html*

18. Tim Hayward. 1995. *Info-Rich, Info-Poor: Access and Exchange in the Global Information Society.* K. G. Saur; William Wresch. 1996. *Disconnected: Haves and Have-Nots in the Information Age.* New Brunswick, NJ: Rutgers University Press.

19. S. Arunachalam. 1999. "Information and Knowledge in the Age of Electronic Communication: A Developing Country Perspective." *Journal of Information Science* 25(6): 465–76.

20. M. Rao, S. R. Bhandari, S. M. Iqbal, A. Sinha, and W. U. Siraj. 1999. "Struggling with the Digital Divide: Internet Infrastructure, Policies and Regulations." *Economic and Political Weekly* 34(46–47): 3317–20.

21. On the deregulation and market liberalization of telecommunications see ITU. 1999. *Trends in Telecommunication Reform 1999.* Geneva: ITU. *www.itu.org* On the falling costs of ICT goods and services see OECD, 2000. *Information and Technology Outlook.* Paris: OECD. Chapter 2 "Information Technology Markets."

22. See the discussion in Jerry Everard. 2000. *Virtual States: The Internet and the Boundaries of the Nation-State.* London: Routledge.

23. Howard Frederick. 1992. "Computer Communications in Cross-Border Coalition-Building: North American NGO Networking against NAFTA." *Gazette* 50: 217–42.

24. See Sylvia Ostry. 2000. "Making Sense of It All: A Post-Mortem on the Meaning of Seattle." In *Seattle, the WTO, and the Future of the Multilateral Trading System*. Eds. Roger B. Porter and Pierre Sauve. Cambridge, MA: The Center for Business and Government, John F. Kennedy School of Government; Margaret E. Keck and Kathryn Sikkink, 1998. *Activists beyond Borders – Advocacy Networks in International Politics*. Ithaca, NY: Cornell University Press; Maxwell A. Cameron Ed. 1998. *To Walk Without Fear: The Global Movement to Ban Landmines*. Oxford: Oxford University Press; J. Zelwietro. 1998. "The Politicization of Environmental Organizations through the Internet." *Information Society* 14(1): 45–55.

25. J. M. Ayres. 1999. "From the Streets to the Internet: The Cyber-Diffusion of Contention." *Annals of the American Academy of Political and Social Science* 566: 132–43.

26. Leonard R. Sussman. 2000. "Censor Dot Gov: The Internet and Press Freedom 2000." *Freedom House Press Freedom Survey 2000*. *www.freedomhouse.org/ pfs2000/sussman.html*; Kevin A. Hill and John E. Hughes. 1998. *Cyberpolitics: Citizen Activism in the Age of the Internet*. Lanham, MD: Rowman & Littlefield; Mamoun Fandy. 1999. "Cyberresistance: Saudi Opposition between Globalization and Localization." *Comparative Studies in Society and History* 41(1): 124–47; William Drake, Shanthi Kalathil, and Taylor C. Boas, 2000. "Dictatorships in the Digital Age: Some Considerations on the Internet in China and Cuba." *IMP: Information Impacts Magazine*. October; Jon B. Alterman. 1998. *New Media, New Politics? From Satellite Television to the Internet in the Arab World*. Washington, DC: Washington Institute for Near East Policy.

27. The Lisbon European Council. 2000. *An Agenda of Economic and Social Renewal for Europe*. European Commission. 23–24 March. *www.europa.eu.int*

28. NTIA. 1999. *Falling Through the Net*. Washington, DC: Department of Commerce. *www.ntia.doc.gov.ntiahome/fttn99*; See also Anthony G. Wilheim. 2000. *Democracy in the Digital Age: Challenges to Political Life in Cyberspace*. New York: Routledge.

29. Yet considerable controversy continues to surround interpretations of the extent and causes of the digital divide, such as the relative importance of race and income in determining computer access. See, for example, different claims in the following: NTIA. 1999. *Falling Through the Net*. Washington, DC: Department of Commerce. *www.ntia.doc.gov.ntiahome/fttn99*; Norman Nie and Lutz Erbring. 2000. *Internet and Society: A Preliminary Report*. Stanford, CA; Stanford Institute for the Quantative Study of Society. Stanford University; and Ekaterina O. Walsh. 2000. "The Truth about the Digital Divide." *The Forrester Report*. Forrester Research Inc.

30. For details of initiatives by the U.S. government see *www.digitaldivide.gov*

31. David Bolt and Ray Crawford. 2000. *Digital Divide: Computers and Our Children's Future*. New York: TV Books.

32. NTIA. 2000. *Falling Through the Net*. Washington, DC: Department of Commerce. *www.digitaldivide.gov/reports.htm*

33. See, for example, the Benton Foundation's network, *www.digitaldividenetwork.gov* See also Bill Gates. 2000. "Statement at the White House Conference on the New Economy." 5 April. *www.microsoft.com/billgates/speeches/04–05wh.htm*; Steve Case. 1998. *Community Update: Election 98. www.aol.com*, keyword Steve Case. 6 October.

34. Department of Trade and Industry. 2000. *Closing the Digital Divide: Information and Communication Technologies in Deprived Areas.* www.dti.gov.uk See also www.open.gov.uk

35. Robert Wright. 2000. "Our Gang: TRB from Washington." *New Republic Online.* February 14.

36. For example, K-Mart's Bluelight in the United States and Dixons' Freeserve in the UK, although it should be noted that subscribers to the latter still have to pay for local telephone calls.

37. This argument is expressed by Robert Putnam. 2000. *Bowling Alone: The Collapse and Revival of American Community.* New York: Simon & Schuster. P. 175.

38. Pippa Norris. 2000. *A Virtuous Circle: Political Communications in Post-Industrial Democracies.* Cambridge: Cambridge University Press. Table 5.2. The figure represents the average percentage of households in 29 OECD nations with cable or satellite TV in 1997.

39. See Benjamin R. Barber. 1998. "Three Scenarios for the Future of Technology and Strong Democracy." *Political Science Quarterly* 113(4): 573–89.

40. George Gilder. 2000. *Telecosm: How Infinite Bandwidth will Revolutionize Our World.* New York: Free Press. For earlier discussions see, for example, Edward Schwartz. 1996. *Netactivism: How Citizens Use the Internet.* Sebastapol, CA: Songline Studios; Wayne Rash, Jr. 1997. *Politics on the Net: Wiring the Political Process.* New York: Freeman; Howard Rheingold. 1993. *The Virtual Community: Homesteading on the Electronic Frontier.* Reading, MA: Addison-Wesley.

41. See, for example, Peter Golding. 1996. "World Wide Wedge: Division and Contradiction in the Global Information Infrastructure." *Monthly Review* 48(3): 70–85; Peter Golding. 1998. "Global Village or Cultural Pillage? The Unequal Inheritance of the Communication Revolution." In *Capitalism and the Information Age: The Political Economy of the Global Communication Revolution.* Eds. R. W. McChesney, E. Meiksins Wood, and J. B. Foster. New York: Monthly Review Press; Peter Golding. 2000. "Information and Communications Technologies and the Sociology of the Future." *Sociology* 34(1): 165–84.

42. See, for example, Robert W. McChesney. 1999. *Rich Media, Poor Democracy: Communication Policy in Dubious Times.* Urbana, IL: University of Illinois Press. Pp. 182–85.

43. Michael Margolis and David Resnick. 2000. *Politics as Usual: The Cyberspace "Revolution."* Thousand Oaks, CA: Sage.

44. Media Metrix. October 2000. *Campaign 2000: Party Politics on the World Wide Web.* www.mediametrix.com

45. The reference is to the Hindu fable described in John Godfrey Saxe's poem "The Blind Man and the Elephant."

46. See Table 3.1 for details.

47. As at the time of writing, in fall 2000.

48. International Telecommunications Union. 1999. *Challenges to the Network: Internet for Development.* Geneva: ITU.

49. See Table 3.2.

50. See Richard Davis. 1999. *The Web of Politics.* New York: Oxford University Press Chapters 2 & 3; Anthony G. Wilhelm. *Democracy in the Digital Age: Challenges to Political Life in Cyberspace.* New York: Routledge. Chapter 5.

51. For the argument that the Internet is an intervening rather than driving variable in the rise of transnational advocacy networks see Margaret E. Keck and Kathryn Sikkink, 1998. *Activists beyond Borders – Advocacy Networks in International Politics.* Ithaca, NY: Cornell University Press.

52. For example, if 5 percent of the total generic top-level domains are from a particular country, then 5 percent of the total number of hosts surveyed under generic top-level domains are reallocated to that country. For details, see OECD. 1999. *Communications Outlook 1999.* Paris: OECD. P. 87.

53. Michael Margolis and David Resnick. 2000. *Politics as Usual: The Cyberspace "Revolution."* Thousand Oaks, CA: Sage.

54. Pippa Norris. 2000. *A Virtuous Circle: Political Communication in Post-Industrial Democracies.* New York: Cambridge University Press.

CHAPTER 2. UNDERSTANDING THE DIGITAL DIVIDE

1. For the brief popular history of the Internet see Katie Hafner and Matthew Lyon. 1998. *Where Wizards Stay Up Late: The Origins of the Internet.* New York: Touchstone/Simon & Schuster; Tim Berners-Lee. 1999. *Weaving the Web.* San Francisco: Marocrsanfrancisco.

2. Estimates are derived from NUA *How Many Online? www.NUA.ie* Latest is November 2000.

3. The first opinion polls referring to the term "Internet" found in a search of the Roper Center's archive were those conducted by Harris polls on June 30, 1994 and July 25, 1994.

4. The Pew Research Center for the People and the Press. *www.people-press.org*

5. For projections see eTForecast. June 12, 2000. "By 2005 55% of U.S. Internet Users Will Use Web Appliances." *www.etforecasts.com/pr/pr600.htm*

6. Larry Downes and Chunka Mui. 2000. *Unleashing the Killer App.* Cambridge, MA: Harvard Business School Press. *www.killer-apps.com*

7. Elaine Ciulla Kamarck. 1999. "Campaigning on the Internet in the Election of 1998." In *democracy.com? Governance in a Networked World.* Eds. Elaine Ciulla Kamarck and Joseph S. Nye, Jr. Hollis, NH: Hollis Publishing.

8. See *www.McCain2000.com*

9. Everett Rogers. 1995. *Diffusion of Innovations.* New York: Routledge. See also the review essay by Elihu Katz. 1999. "Theorizing Diffusion: Tarde and Sorokin Revisited." *Annals of the American Academy of the Political and Social Sciences* 566 (3): 144–55.

10. Everett Rogers. 1995. *Diffusion of Innovations.* New York: Routledge.

11. International Telecommunications Union. 1999. *Challenges to the Network: Internet for Development.* Geneva: ITU. It should be noted of course, that the population has risen during this period making this a somewhat misleading comparison.

12. For a broader discussion of the characteristics of American exceptionalism, see Graeme Wilson. 1998. *Only in America? The Politics of the United States in Comparative Perspective.* Chatham, NJ: Chatham House.

13. OECD. 1999. *Communications Outlook 1999.* Paris: OECD.

14. See, for example, Arend Lijphart. 1999. *Patterns of Democracy.* New Haven, CT: Yale University Press; Sidney Verba, Norman Nie, and Jae-on Kim. 1978. *Participation and Political Equality: A Seven-Nation Comparison.* New York: Cambridge University Press;

Richard Katz and Peter Mair. Eds. 1992. *How Parties Organize.* London: Sage; IDEA. *Voter Turnout from 1945 to 1999.* Stockholm: IDEA. *www.int-idea.se*

15. For a discussion of alternative methodologies see Steve Jones. Ed. 1999. *Doing Internet Research: Critical Issues and Methods for Examining the Net.* Thousand Oaks, CA: Sage.

16. For a discussion see Sandra Davidson. 1999. "Cyber-Cookies: How Much Should the Public Swallow?" In *Advertising and the World Wide Web.* Ed. David W. Schumann and Esther Thorson. Mahwah, NJ: Lawrence Erlbaum.

17. See Robert W. Buchanan, Jr. and Charles Lukaszewski. 1997. *Measuring the Impact of Your website.* New York: John Wiley.

18. For full details of the methodology and the latest figures see *www.NUA.ie*

19. Population figures for 1997 are drawn from the UNDP. 1999. *Human Development Report 1999.* New York: UNDP/Oxford University Press.

Chapter 3. Wired World

1. See Surendra J. Patel. General editor. 1993–5. *Technological Transformation in the Third World.* 5 vols. Aldershot: Avebury. See also case studies in David J. Jeremy. 1992. *The Transfer of International Technology: Europe, Japan and the USA in the Twentieth Century.* Aldershot: Edward Elgar; Nathan Rosenberg and Claudio Frischtak. Eds. 1985. *International Technology Transfer: Concepts, Methods and Comparisons.* New York: Praeger; David Charles and Jeremy Howells. 1992. *Technology Transfer in Europe.* London: Belhaven Press; Manas Chatterji. 1990. *Technology Transfer in the Developing Countries.* New York: St. Martin's Press; S. R. Melkote. 1991. *Communication for Development in the Third World: Theory and Practice.* Newbury Park, CA: Sage; Wilbur Schramm. 1964. *Mass Media and National Development.* Stanford, CA: Stanford University Press.

2. See, for example, Everett M. Rogers. 1995. *Diffusion of Innovations.* New York: Free Press; Jayati Sarkar. 1998. "Technological Diffusion: Alternative Theories and Historical Evidence." *Journal of Economic Surveys* 12(2): 131–76; Vijay Mahajan, Eitan Muller, and Frank M. Bass. 1999. "New Product Diffusion Models in Marketing: A Review and Direction for Research." *Journal of Marketing* 54: 1–16.

3. Tim Hayward. 1995. *Info-Rich, Info-Poor: Access and Exchange in the Global Information Society.* K. G. Saur; William Wresch. 1996. *Disconnected: Haves and Have-Nots in the Information Age.* New Brunswick, NJ: Rutgers University Press; S. Arunachalam. 1999. "Information and Knowledge in the Age of Electronic Communication: A Developing Country Perspective." *Journal of Information Science* 25(6): 465–76.

4. Celia W. Dugger. 2000. "Connecting Rural India to the World." *New York Times* 28 May. *www.nytimes.com/library/tech/yr/mo/biztech/articles/28india.html*

5. UNDP. 1999. *Human Development Report 1999.* New York: UNDP/Oxford University Press. P. 64.

6. OECD. 2000. *Information and Technology Outlook.* Paris: OECD.

7. Carlos Alberto Primo Braga. 1998. "Inclusion or Exclusion?" *www.unesco.org/ courier/1998 12*

8. World Economic Forum. 2000. *From the Global Digital Divide to the Global Digital Opportunity: Proposals submitted to the G-8 Kyushu-Okinawa Summit 2000. www.ceip.org*

9. OECD. 2000. *Information and Technology Outlook*. Paris: OECD. Table 2 p. 24.

10. OECD. 2000. *Information and Technology Outlook*. Paris: OECD.

11. For a discussion see Ed Yourdon. 1996. *The Rise and Resurrection of the American Programmer*. Englewood Cliffs, NJ: Prentice Hall.

12. By spring 2000, more than 1,000 phones had been provided, serving 65,000 people, and the eventual target is 40,000 phones. See Don Richardson. 2000. *Grameen's Telecom's Village Phone Programme in Rural Bangladesh*. Telecommons Development Group, Ontario. *www.telecommons.com* See also *www.grameenphone.com*

13. *www.SuliNet.hu*

14. UNDP. 1999. *Human Development Report 1999*. New York: UNDP/Oxford University Press. P. 64.

15. *Wired News*. June 5, 2000. "Africa One Project Targets 2002." For details see *www.AfricaOne.com*

16. OECD. 2000. *Information and Technology Outlook*. Paris: OECD. P. 81.

17. The World Bank. 2000. *World Development Indicators 2000*. P. 299. *www.worldbank.org/data*

18. International Telecommunications Union. 1999. *Challenges to the Network: Internet for Development*. Geneva: ITU.

19. Data from NUA. *www.nua.ie*

20. David C. Niece. 1998. "Measuring Participation in the Digital Techno-structure: Internet Access." *ACTS/FAIR Working Paper 44*. Brighton: SPRU.

21. Human Development is measured using the UNDP index combining three factors: *longevity* as measured by life expectancy at birth; *educational attainment* as measured by adult literacy and school enrollment; and *standard of living* measured by real GDP per capita. See UNDP. 1999. *Human Development Report 1999*. New York: UNDP/Oxford University Press.

22. Data are drawn from the spring 1999 Eurobarometer. See Pippa Norris. 1999. "The Emergent Internet Age in Europe: A New North-South Divide?" *The Harvard International Journal of Press-Politics* 5(1).

23. For example, if 5 percent of the total generic top-level domains are from a particular country, then 5 percent of the total number of hosts surveyed under generic top-level domains are reallocated to that country. For details, see OECD 1999: *Communications Outlook 1999*. Paris: OECD. P. 88–89. Also *www.oecd.org*

24. International Telecommunications Union. 1999. *Challenges to the Network: Internet for Development*. Geneva: ITU. *www.itu.org*

25. The World Bank. 2000. *World Development Indicators 2000*. *www.worldbank.org/data*

26. The analysis was also confirmed by principle component factor analysis, with the results not reported here.

27. Eszter Hargittai. 1999. "Weaving the Western Web: Explaining Differences in Internet Connectivity Among OECD Countries." *Telecommunications Policy* 23(10–11): 701–18.

28. International Telecommunications Union. 1999. *Challenges to the Network: Internet for Development*. Geneva: ITU. *www.itu.org*

29. Francisco Rodriguez and Ernest Wilson III. 2000. "Are Poor Countries Losing the Information Revolution?" *The WorldBank InfoDev www.infodev/library/wilsonrodriguez.doc*

30. Leonard R. Sussman. 2000. "Censor Dot Gov: The Internet and Press Freedom 2000." *Freedom House Press Freedom Survey 2000.* *www.freedomhouse.org/ pfs2000/sussman.html*
31. OECD. 1999. *Communications Outlook 1999.* Paris: OECD. Also *www.oecd.org* OECD. 2000. *Information and Technology Outlook.* OECD: Paris. P. 52.
32. Eszter Hargittai. 1999. "Weaving the Western Web: Explaining Differences in Internet Connectivity Among OECD Countries." *Telecommunications Policy* 23(10–11): 701–18.
33. Everett Rogers. 1995. *Diffusion of Innovations.* New York: Free Press.
34. UNDP. 1999. *Human Development Report 1999.* New York: UNDP/Oxford University Press. P. 176.
35. William Wresch. 1996. *Disconnected: Haves and Have-Nots in the Information Age.* New Brunswick, NJ: Rutgers University Press. P. 130–32. See also George Barnett and Young Choi. 1995. "Physical Distance and Language as Determinants of the International Telecommunications Network." *International Political Science Review* 16(3): 249–65.
36. Inktomi. 18 January 2000. "Web Surpasses One Billion Documents." Press release. *www.Inkotomi.com/new/billion.html*
37. Internet Society. June 1997. "Web Languages Hit Parade." *www.isoc.org:8080/ palmares.en.html*
38. M. Rao, S. R. Bhandari, S. M. Iqbal, A. Sinha, and W. U. Siraj. 1999. "Struggling with the Digital Divide: Internet Infrastructure, Policies and Regulations." *Economic and Political Weekly* 34(46–47): 3317–20.
39. Although this seems plausible, unfortunately this proposition cannot be systematically tested in this study. Ethnologue provides the most comprehensive data monitoring of the proportion of native speakers in different languages worldwide, but no single source provides reliable information monitoring of the proportion of the population familiar with English as a primary *and* secondary language. This measure fails to take account of the high level of familiarity with English as a second language, for example in Sweden, the Netherlands, and Norway. For details see *www.ethnologue.org*
40. Leonard R. Sussman. 2000. "Censor Dot Gov: The Internet and Press Freedom 2000." *Freedom House Press Freedom Survey 2000.* *www.freedomhouse.org/ pfs2000/sussman.html*
41. Freedom House. 2000. *www.freedomhouse.org*
42. The simple correlations examine the relationship between the independent variables (economic development, human capital, and democratic development) and the dependent variable in each country without any prior controls or causal ordering. The Ordinary Least Squared Regression Analysis models use multivariate analysis, assuming that the independent variables are interrelated. Variables are entered into the model in the order shown in the table, based on the prior theoretical assumptions. The analytical models assume that economic and social development are causal prior to democratic development, an assumption that reflects the standard literature on the process of democratization, although, of course the causal relationship could be reversed. Many alternative models were examined and tested with the variables entered in different causal sequences, and with alternative measures for economic and social development, using a series of scatter plots to examine the relationships, before the final model was selected on

the basis of goodness of fit (indicated by the adjusted R squared), parsimony (simplicity), robustness (consistency across different indicators), and the prior theoretical assumptions.

43. For a discussion of the relationship between economic development and democratization see Seymour Martin Lipset. 1993. "A Comparative Analysis of the Social Requisites of Democracy." *International Social Science Journal* 136(2):155–75.

44. This pattern was further confirmed by the fact that the UNDP Human Development Index (combining literacy and education, longevity, and per capita GDP) proved to be more weakly associated with Internet access than the economic development measure used in this study.

45. Eszter Hargittai. 1999. "Weaving the Western Web: Explaining Differences in Internet Connectivity Among OECD Countries." *Telecommunications Policy* 23(10–11): 701–18.

46. The World Bank. 1999. *World Development Report.* Washington, DC. P. 9.

47. OECD. 2000. *Information and Technology Outlook.* Paris: OECD. Figure 22. P. 51.

48. At individual level ownership of home computers was strongly and significantly correlated ($R > .75$ sig. P.01) with possession of many other household consumer durables including a video camera, clock radio, electric drill, electric deep fat fryer, two or more cars, and a second home. The correlation analysis was based on data in Eurobarometer 44.0 fall 1995.

CHAPTER 4. SOCIAL INEQUALITIES

1. NTIA. 1999. *Falling through the Net.* Washington, DC: U.S. Department of Commerce. *www.ntia.doc.gov.ntiahome/fttn99* NTIA. 2000. *Falling through the Net.* Washington, DC: U.S. Department of Commerce. See also David Bolt and Ray Crawford. 2000. *Digital Divide: Computers and Our Children's Future.* New York: TV Books; also sources at: *www.digitaldivide.org*

2. OECD. 2000. *Information Technology Outlook.* Paris: OECD. P. 85–8. National studies summarized in this report have found variations in use of PCs by income, education, and age and household size in Canada, Australia, and Finland. See also the Australian Bureau of Statistics. *Household Use of Information Technology, Australia. www.abs.gov.au/ausstats* For a discussion, see also Brian D. Loader. Ed. 1998. *Cyberspace Divide: Equality, Agency and Policy in the Information Society.* London: Routledge.

3. European Commission. 2000. *E-Europe Draft Action Plan,* for the European Council at Feira 19–20 June 2000. *www.europa.eu.int/comm./information society/eeurope/actionplan* See also The Lisbon European Council. 2000. *An Agenda of Economic and Social Renewal for Europe.* European Commission. March 23–24. *www.europa.eu.int*

4. Department of Trade and Industry. 2000. *Closing the Digital Divide: Information and Communication Technologies in Deprived Areas. www.dti.gov.uk* See also: *www.open.gov.uk*

5. For a discussion see David Resnick. 1998. "Politics on the Internet: The Normalization of Cyberspace." In *The Politics of Cyberspace.* Eds. Chris Toulouse and Timothy W. Luke. New York: Routledge.

6. Robin Wright. 2000. "Our Gang: TRB from Washington." *New Republic Online.* February 14.
7. Everett M. Rogers. 1995. *Diffusion of Innovations.* 4th ed. New York: Free Press. P. 269, 435–42.
8. David Birdsell, Douglas Muzio, David Krane, and Amy Cottreau. 1998. "Web Users Are Looking More Like America." *The Public Perspective* 9(3): 33. *www.ropercenter.uconn.edu/pubpr/pp93.htm*
9. The Pew Research Center for the People and the Press. 1999 News Release. "The Internet News Audience Goes Ordinary." January 14. *www.people-press.org*
10. CyberAtlas. April 26, 1999. "As Internet Matures, So Do Its Users." *www.cyberatlas.com/big pictiure/democgraphics/inteco.html;* Nicki Maraganore and Shelley Morrisette. December 1998. "The On-Line Gender Gap Is Closing." *Forrester Research Reports* 1(18).
11. Norman Nie and Lutz Erbring. 2000. *Internet and Society: A Preliminary Report.* Stanford Institute for the Quantative Study of Society, Stanford, CA: Stanford University; Ekaterina O. Walsh. 2000. "The Truth about the Digital Divide." *The Forrester Report.* Forrester Research Inc.; Ekaterina O. Walsh, March 1999. "The Digital Melting Pot." *The Forrester Report.* Forrester Research Inc.; Jupiter Communications. June 15, 2000. "Income and Age, Not Ethnicity, to Remain Largest Gap for U.S. Digital Divide." *www.jup.com/company/pressrelease.jsp?doc=pr000615*
12. NTIA. 1999. *Falling through the Net.* Washington, DC: U.S. Department of Commerce. *www.ntia.doc.gov.ntiahome/fttn99.* See also Donna Hoffman and Thomas P. Novak. 1998. "Bridging the Digital Divide: The Impact of Race on Computer Access and Internet Use." *Science;* Cheskin Research. April 2000. "The Digital World of the US Hispanic." *www.cheskin.com*
13. It should be noted that Wilhelm's analysis was based on the 1994 U.S. Current Population Survey data, which may currently be out of date. See Anthony G. Wilhelm. 2000. *Democracy in the Digital Age: Challenges to Political Life in Cyberspace.* New York: Routledge. P. 56.
14. Donna L. Hoffman and Thomas P. Novak. 1999. "The Evolution of the Digital Divide: Examining the Relationship of Race to Internet Access and Usage over Time." Paper presented at the Understanding the Digital Economy: Data, Tools and Research conference. *www.elabweb.com*
15. In the last few years a number of market research companies have sought to monitor the potential of the Internet for e-commerce and advertising. Regular cross-national surveys of e-commerce have been conducted by IriS/MORI in 20 nations, by National Opinion Polls (NOP) in Britain, Germany, and France, and by AC Neilsen Netwatch in 16 nations. Wherever possible, these results are used to cross-check the analysis presented in this study. In addition GVU's WWW User Surveys include some geographic information about users from 1994–98, but this is not based on a random sampling method and surveys have not been published in the last two years.
16. The Eurobarometer series has been conducted among a representative sample of the population in all EU member states. I am most grateful to the European Commission's DG10 for Information, Communication, Culture and Audiovisual-Unit Public Opinion Monitoring (X.A.2) for release of these datasets, without which this book would not have been possible. More details are available at *www.europa.eu.int*

17. A. Przeworski and H. Teune. 1970. *The Logic of Comparative Social Inquiry.* New York: John Wiley.

18. The complexity of comparing ethnic divisions in Europe, and limited sample size of minority populations in standard surveys, hinders any direct examination of how far these differences drive any digital divide in Europe that might be comparable with the U.S. research.

19. NTIA. 1999. *Falling through the Net.* Washington, DC: U.S. Department of Commerce. *www.ntia.doc.gov.ntiahome/fttn99*

20. Robert Kominski and Eric Newburger. 1999. "Access Denied: Changes in Computer Ownership and Use 1984–1997." Paper presented at the annual meeting of the American Sociological Association, Chicago.

21. OECD. 2000. *Information Technology Outlook.* Paris: OECD. Figure 7. P. 86.

22. OECD. 2000. *Information Technology Outlook.* Paris: OECD. P. 82.

23. The statistical difference between groups was measured by ANOVA. In Greece, the difference by income group proved statistically insignificant, in large part because so few Greeks from any social sector were online.

24. The June 1995 Pew survey reported that the U.S. online population split almost evenly between those gaining access from home (19 percent) or work (15 percent). In contrast, the September 1999 Pew survey found that there was a greater edge for home access (37 percent) over work access (21 percent). See Pew Research Center for the People and the Press. June 2000. "Internet Sapping Broadcast News Audience." *www.people-press.org/media00rpt.htm;* Similar trends toward home access have been found elsewhere, see OECD. 2000. *Information Technology Outlook.* Paris: OECD.

25. Anthony G. Wilhelm. 2000. *Democracy in the Digital Age: Challenges to Political Life in Cyberspace.* New York: Routledge. P. 56.

26. The Pew Internet Project Report. 10 May 2000. "Tracking Online Life: How Women Use the Internet to Cultivate Family and Friends." *www.pewinternet.org/reports*

27. AC Nielsen. October 25, 1999. *Net Watch. www.acnielsen.com/products/reports/net-watch*

28. David Bolt and Ray Crawford. 2000. *Digital Divide: Computers and Our Children's Future.* New York: TV Books. Chapter 3.

29. It should be noted that OLS results are presented here and the analysis was confirmed by logistic regression analysis in Table 4.4, producing identical results.

30. IDC. June 8, 2000. "Western European Internet Access Industry Continues to Reinvent Itself." *www.idc.com/emea/press/PR/ECM060800PR.stm*

31. eTForecast. June 12 2000. "By 2005 55% of U.S. Internet Users Will Use Web Appliances." *www.etforecasts.com/pr/pr600.htm*

32. For example, dedicated email units currently cost about $100 in the United States, compared with $500 or more for an inexpensive basic PC.

CHAPTER 5. THEORIES OF DIGITAL DEMOCRACY

1. Michel Crozier, Samuel P. Huntington, and Joji Watanuki. 1975. *The Crisis of Democracy: Report on the Governability of Democracies to the Trilateral Commission.* New York: New York University Press; Seymour M. Lipset and William C. Schneider. 1987. *The Confidence Gap: Business, Labor, and Government in the Public Mind,* rev. ed. Baltimore: Johns Hopkins University Press; Joseph S. Nye, Philip D. Zelikow, and

David C. King. Eds. 1997. *Why People Don't Trust Government.* Cambridge, MA: Harvard University Press; Susan Pharr and Robert D. Putnam. 2000. *Disaffected Democracies.* Princeton, NJ: Princeton University Press. For a critical counterargument based on European evidence, however, see Hans-Dieter Klingemann and Dieter Fuchs. Eds. 1995. *Citizens and the State.* Oxford: Oxford University Press.

2. Robert D. Putnam. 2000. *Bowling Alone: The Collapse and Revival of American Community.* New York: Simon & Schuster.
3. Russell J. Dalton and Martin P. Wattenberg. Eds. 2000. *Parties without Partisans: Political Change in Advanced Industrialized Democracies.* Oxford: Oxford University Press.
4. Pippa Norris. Ed. 1999. *Critical Citizens: Global Support for Democratic Governance.* Oxford: Oxford University Press.
5. Benjamin R. Barber. 1984. *Strong Democracy.* Berkeley, CA: University of California Press; Benjamin R. Barber. 1999. "Three Scenarios for the Future of Technology and Strong Democracy." *Political Science Quarterly* 113: 573–90. See also Dieter Fuchs and Max Kaase. 2000. "Electronic Democracy." Paper presented at the International Political Science World Congress, Quebec, August.
6. Ian Budge. 1996. *The New Challenge of Direct Democracy.* Oxford: Polity Press.
7. Edward Schwartz. 1996. *Netactivism How Citizens Use the Internet.* Sebastapol, CA: Songline Studios; Wayne Rash, Jr. 1997. *Politics on the Nets: Wiring the Political Process.* New York: Freeman; Amatai Etzioni. 1993. *The Spirit of Community.* New York: Crown.
8. Howard Rheingold. 1993. *The Virtual Community: Homesteading on the Electronic Frontier.* Reading, MA: Addison-Wesley.
9. Ian Budge. 1996. *The New Challenge of Direct Democracy.* Oxford: Polity Press.
10. Barry N. Hague and Brian D. Loader. 1999. *Digital Democracy: Discourse and Decision-making in the Information Age.* London: Routledge. P. 8; Roza Tsagarousianou, Damian Tambini, and Cathy Bryan. 1998. *Cyberdemocracy.* London: Routledge; Lawrence Grossman. 1995. *The Electronic Commonwealth.* New York: Penguin.
11. Michael Margolis and David Resnick. 2000. *Politics as Usual: The Cyberspace "Revolution."* Thousand Oaks, CA: Sage.
12. Robert W. McChesney. 1999. *Rich Media, Poor Democracy: Communication Policy in Dubious Times.* Urbana, IL: University of Illinois Press, pp. 182–85.
13. Robert Putnam. 2000. *Bowling Alone: The Collapse and Revival of American Community.* New York: Simon & Schuster. Chapter 9.
14. Richard Davis and Diana Owen. 1998. *New Media and American Politics.* New York: Oxford University Press.
15. Peter Golding. 1996. "World Wide Wedge: Division and Contradiction in the Global Information Infrastructure." *Monthly Review* 48(3): 70–85; Peter Golding. 1998. "Global Village or Cultural Pillage? The Unequal Inheritance of the Communication Revolution." In *Capitalism and the Information Age: The Political Economy of the Global Communication Revolution.* Eds. R. W. McChesney, E. Meiksins Wood, and J. B. Foster. New York: Monthly Review Press; Peter Golding. 2000. "Information and Communications Technologies and the Sociology of the Future." *Sociology* 34(1): 165–84; Anthony G. Wilheim. 2000. *Democracy in the Digital Age: Challenges to Political Life in Cyberspace.* New York: Routledge.

16. See Richard Davis. 1999. *The Web of Politics: The Internet's Impact on the American Political System.* New York: Oxford University Press. Chapter 6; Kevin A. Hill and John E. Hughes. 1998. *Cyberpolitics: Citizen Activism in the Age of the Internet.* Lanham, MD: Rowman & Littlefield. Chapter 3.

17. Bruce Bimber. 1998. "The Internet and Political Transformation: Populism, Community and Accelerated Pluralism." *Polity* 31 (1): 133–60.

18. Jeffrey B. Abramson, Christopher Arterton, and Gary Orren. 1988. *The Electronic Commonwealth: The Impact of New Media Technologies on Democratic Politics.* New York: Basic Books.

19. David Shenk. 1997. *Data Smog: Surviving the Information Glut.* New York: Harper-Collins.

20. Dana Ott. 1998. "Power to the People: The Role of Electronic Media in Promoting Democracy in Africa." *First Monday* 3: April 6. *www.firstmonday.dk/issues/issue3 4/ott*

21. Freedom House. 2000. *www.freedomhouse.org*

22. For a discussion, see Larry J. Diamond, Juan J. Linz, and Seymour M. Lipset. 1995. *Politics in Developing Countries: Comparing Experiences with Democracy,* 2d ed. Boulder, CO: Lynne Rienner Publishers; Axel Hadenius. Ed. 1997. *Democracy's Victory and Crisis.* Cambridge: Cambridge University Press; Juan J. Linz and Alfred C. Stepan. 1996. *Problems of Democratic Transition and Consolidation: Southern Europe, South America and Post-Communist Europe.* Baltimore: Johns Hopkins University Press.

23. For the theory of cyclical waves and reverse waves see Samuel Huntington. 1991. *The Third Wave: Democratization in the Late Twentieth Century.* Norman: The University of Oklahoma Press.

24. Leonard R. Sussman. 2000. "Censor Dot Gov: The Internet and Press Freedom 2000." *Freedom House Press Freedom Survey 2000. www.freedomhouse.org/pfs2000/sussman.html*

25. Geoffry Taubman. 1998. "A not-so World Wide Web: The Internet, China, and the Challenges to Non-Democratic Rule." *Political Communication* 15: 255–72 Ap/Je; Taylor C. Boas. 2000. "The Dictator's Dilemma? The Internet and U.S. Policy toward Cuba." *The Washington Quarterly* 23(3): 57–67; William J. Drake, Shanthi Kalathil, and Taylor C. Boas. 2000. "Dictatorships in the Digital Age: Some Considerations on the Internet in China and Cuba." *IMP: Information Impacts Magazine.* October. *www.cisp.org/imp*

26. Spiro. 1994. "New Global Communities: Nongovernmental Organizations in International Decision-Making Institutions." *The Washington Quarterly* 18(1): 45–56; Drazen Pantic. 1997. "Internet in Serbia: From Dark side of the Moon to the Internet Revolution." *First Monday* 2: April 7; Erik S. Herron. 1999. "Democratization and the Development of Information Regimes: The Internet in Eurasia and the Baltics." *Problems of Post-Communism* 46(4):56–68.

27. Kevin A. Hill and John E. Hughes. 1998. *Cyberpolitics: Citizen Activism in the Age of the Internet.* Lanham, MD: Rowman & Littlefield. Chapter 4.

28. Maxwell A. Cameron. Ed. 1998. *To Walk Without Fear: The Global Movement to Ban Landmines.* Oxford: Oxford University Press; Margaret E. Keck and Kathryn Sikkink, 1998. *Activists beyond Borders: Advocacy Networks in International Politics.* Ithaca, NY: Cornell University Press; Howard Frederick. 1992. "Computer

Communications in Cross-Border Coalition-Building: North American NGO Networking against NAFTA." *Gazette* 50: 217–42.

29. P. Brophy and E. Halpin. 1999. "Through the Net to Freedom: Information, the Internet and Human Rights." *Journal of Information Science* 25(5): 351–64.

30. Christopher R. Kedzie. 1997. "Communication and Democracy: Coincident Revolutions and the Emergent Dictator's Dilemma." Washington, DC: RAND. *www.rand.org/publications/RGSD/RGSD127*

31. It should also be noted that another study by Dana Ott found no significant relationship between democratization in Africa and measures of Internet access, including the number of Internet Service Providers and the monthly fee for Internet access in 1997. See Dana Ott. 1998. "Power to the People: The Role of Electronic Media in Promoting Democracy in Africa." *First Monday* 3(4). *www.firstmonday.dk/issues/issue3 4/ott*

32. Trevor Hayward. 1995. *Info-Rich, Info-Poor: Access and Exchange in the Global Information Society.* London/New Jersey: K. G. Saur.

33. Joseph Schumpeter. 1952. (1943). *Capitalism, Socialism, and Democracy.* London: Allen & Unwin. See also Robert A. Dahl. 1956. *Preface to Democratic Theory.* Chicago: University of Chicago Press; Robert A. Dahl. 1971. *Polyarchy: Participation and Opposition.* New Haven, CT: Yale University Press; Robert A. Dahl. 1989. *Democracy and Its Critics.* New Haven, CT: Yale University Press. For a fuller discussion see Pippa Norris. 2000. *A Virtuous Circle: Political Communications in Post-Industrial Democracies.* Cambridge: Cambridge University Press. Chapter 2.

34. For an alternative view see Benjamin Barber. 1984. *Strong Democracy.* Berkeley: University of California Press. For a discussion of the conflict between "classical" and "realist" models of democracy, and their implications for theories of the mass media, see Michael Schudson. 1995. "The News Media and the Democratic Process." In Michael Schudson *The Power of News*, Cambridge, MA: Harvard University Press.

35. See Freedom House. 2000. "The Comparative Survey of Freedom, 2000." *Freedom Review. www.freedomhouse.org*; Davis Beetham. 1994. *Defining and Measuring Democracy.* London: Sage.

36. See Larry J. Diamond, Juan J. Linz, and Seymour M. Lipset. 1995. *Politics in Developing Countries: Comparing Experiences with Democracy,* 2d ed. Boulder, CO: Lynne Rienner Publishers; Juan J. Linz and Alfred C. Stepan. 1996. *Problems of Democratic Transition and Consolidation: Southern Europe, South America and Post-Communist Europe.* Baltimore: Johns Hopkins University Press.

37. Daniel Bell. 1973. *The Coming of Post-Industrial Society: A Venture in Social Forecasting.* New York: Basic Books.

38. See the discussion in M. R. Smith and L. Marx. 1994. Eds. *Does Technology Drive History? The Dilemma of Technological Determinism.* Cambridge, MA: The MIT Press; William H. Dutton. Ed. 1999. *Society on the Line: Information Politics in the Digital Age.* Oxford: Oxford University Press; Nicholas Negroponte. 1995. *Being Digital.* New York: Knopf.

39. See for example William H. Dutton and Malcolm Peltu. 1996. *Information and Communication Technologies – Visions and Realities.* Oxford: Oxford University Press.

40. See, however, excellent discussions of this issue in Dietrich Rueschemeyer. 1992. *Capitalist Development and Democracy.* Chicago: University of Chicago Press.

Larry Diamond, Juan J. Linz, and Seymour Martin Lipset. 1995. *Politics in Developing Countries*, Boulder, CO: Lynne Rienner Publishers; Juan Linz and Alfred Stephan. 1996. *Problems of Democratic Consolidation.* Baltimore: Johns Hopkins University Press; Stephen Haggard. 1995. *The Political Economy of Democratic Transitions,* Princeton, NJ: Princeton University Press.

41. Seymour Martin Lipset. 1993. "A Comparative Analysis of the Social Requisites of Democracy." *International Social Science Journal* 136(2): 155–75.
42. The Human Development Index is based on longevity, as measured by life expectancy at birth; educational attainment, as measured by a combination of adult literacy (two-thirds weight) and the combined gross primary, secondary, and tertiary enrollment ratio (one-third weight); and standard of living, as measured by real GDP per capita in purchasing parity power. The measure is standardized. See UNDP. 1999. *Human Development Report 1999.* Technical notes p. 159. New York: UNDP/Oxford University Press.
43. Freedom House. 2000. *www.freedomhouse.org.* Note the combined scale for political rights and civil liberties was reversed for ease of graphical interpretation so that 7 = most democratic and 1 = least democratic.
44. Kevin A. Hill and John E. Hughes. 1998. *Cyberpolitics: Citizen Activism in the Age of the Internet.* Lanham, MD: Rowman & Littlefield. Chapter 1.

CHAPTER 6. E-GOVERNANCE

1. For a discussion, see Christine Bellamy and John A. Taylor. 1998. *Governing in the Information Age.* Buckingham: Open University; G. N. L. Stowers. 1999. "Becoming Cyberactive: State and Local Governments on the World Wide Web." *Government Information Quarterly* 16(2): 111–27; GOL. *G-8 Government On-line Project.* April 1999. *www.open.gov.uk/govonline/isw2.doc;* The U.S. Office of Intergovermental Solutions. *www.Policyworks.gov/org/main/mg/intergov/home.htm;* OECD Public Management and Public Management Service. 1999. *Impact of the Emerging Information Society on the Policy Development Process and Democratic Quality. www.oecd.org/puma;* Chris C. Demchak, Christian Friis, and Todd M. La Porte. 1998. "Configuring Public Agencies in Cyberspace: Openness and Effectiveness." *www.cyprg.arizona.edu/Tilburg98F.htm;* Todd M. La Porte, Chris C. Demchak, Martin de Jong, and Christian Friis. 2000. "Democracy and Bureaucracy in the Age of the Web: Empirical Findings and Theoretical Speculations." Paper presented at the International Political Science Association World Congress, Quebec, August; G. D. Garson. 2000. *Handbook of Public Information Systems.* New York: Marcel Dekker.
2. See Stavros Zouridis and Victor Bekkers. 2000. "Electronic Service Delivery and the Democratic Relationships between Government and its Citizens." In *Democratic Governance and New Technology.* Jens Hoff, Ivan Horrocks, and Pieter Tops. Eds. London: Routledge; Rob Atkinson. 2000. "Creating a Digital Federal Government." *IMP: Information Impacts Magazine.* October. *www.cisp.org/imp*
3. See Elisabeth Richards. 1999. "Tools of Governance," and Eileen Milner. 1999. "Electronic Government: More than Just a Good Thing?" In *Digital Democracy: Discourse and Decision Making in the Information Age.* Eds. Barry N. Hague and Brian D. Loader. New York: Routledge; Christopher Weare, J. Musso, and M. L. Hale. 1999. "Electronic Democracy and the Diffusion of Municipal Web Pages in

California." *Administration & Society* 31(1): 3–27; Chris C. Demchak, Christian Friis, and Todd M. La Porte. 1998. "Configuring Public Agencies in Cyberspace: Openness and Effectiveness." *www.cyprg.arizona.edu/Tilburg98F.htm;* Jerry Mechling. 1994. "A Customer Service Manifesto: Using IT to Improve Government Services." *Government Technology* 1: S27–33; Dan Jellinek. 2000. "E-Government – Reality or Hype?" *IMP: Information Impacts Magazine.* October. *www.cisp.org/imp*

4. Pippa Norris. 1999. *Critical Citizens: Global Support for Democratic Governance.* Oxford: Oxford University Press; C. Thomas. 1998. "Maintaining and Restoring Public Trust in Government Agencies and Their Employees." *Administration and Society* 30: 166–93.

5. OECD Public Management and Public Management Service. 1999. *Impact of the Emerging Information Society on the Policy Development Process and Democratic Quality. www.oecd.org/puma*

6. This criticism is pervasive throughout the literature. See, for example, Paul Nixon and Hans Johansson. 1999. "Transparency through Technology: The Internet and Political Parties." In *Digital Democracy: Discourse and Decision Making in the Information Age.* Eds. Barry N. Hague and Brian D. Loader. New York: Routledge.

7. Michael Margolis and David Resnick. 2000. *Politics as Usual: The Cyberspace "Revolution."* Thousand Oaks, CA: Sage.

8. C. Richard Neu, Robert H. Anderson, and Tora K. Bikson. 1999. *Sending Your Government a Message.* RAND. *www.rand.org/publications/MR/MR1095*

9. See, for example, P. J. Jackson. 1999. *Virtual Working: Social and Organizational Dynamics.* London: Routledge; J. Hagel and A. G. Armstrong. Eds. 1997. *Net. Gain: Expanding Markets through Virtual Communities.* Cambridge, MA: Harvard Business School; T. McEachern and B. O'Keefe. 1998. *Re-Wiring Business: Uniting Management and the Web.* Chichester: Wiley.

10. GOL. *G 8 Government On-line Project.* April 1999. *www.open.gov.uk/govonline/isw2.doc;* The U.S. Office of Intergovermental Solutions. *www.Policyworks.gov/org/main/mg/intergov/home.htm;* OECD/Public Management Service (PUMA). 1999. *Impact of the Emerging Information Society on the Policy Development Process and Democratic Quality.* Paris: OECD. *www.oecd.org/puma*

11. *Governments on the WWW. www.gksoft.com/govt/*

12. I am most grateful to the CyPRG group, particularly Todd M. La Porte (George Mason University), Chris C. Demchak (University of Arizona), Martin de Jong (University of Amsterdam), and Christian Friis (University of Roskilde) for access to this database for secondary analysis. Full details about the methodology and coding are available from *www.cyprg.arizona.edu* For more details of the results see Todd M. La Porte, Chris C. Demchak, Martin de Jong, and Christian Friis. 2000. "Democracy and Bureaucracy in the Age of the Web: Empirical Findings and Theoretical Speculations." Paper presented at the International Political Science Association World Congress, Quebec, August; Chris C. Demchak, Christian Friis, and Todd M. La Porte. 1998. "Configuring Public Agencies in Cyberspace: Openness and Effectiveness." *www.cyprg.arizona.edu/Tilburg98F.htm*

13. UK Online. *www.Open.gov.uk*

14. Full details about the methodology and coding are available from *www.cyprg.arizona.edu.*

15. GOL. *G 8 Government On-line Project.* April 1999. *www.open.gov.uk/govonline/ isw2.doc;* The U.S. Office of Intergovermental Solutions. *Policyworks.gov/ org/main/mg/intergov/home.htm*

16. See, for example, the UK National Audit Office. 1999. *Governments On the Web. www.GovernmentsOntheWeb.org;* Australian National Audit Office. 1999. *Electronic Service Delivery, including Internet Use, by Commonwealth Government Agencies. www.anao.gov.au*

CHAPTER 7. ONLINE PARLIAMENTS

1. For an early study of the impact of this process in the United States, see Chris Casey. 1996. *The Hill on the Net: Congress Enters the Information Age.* Boston: AP Professional.

2. See, for example, the discussion in Stephen Coleman, John Taylor, and Wim van de Donk. 1999. *Parliament in the Age of the Internet.* Oxford: Oxford University Press.

3. Inter-Parliamentary Union. May 2000. "Guidelines for the Content and Structure of Parliamentary Websites." *www.ipu.org/cntr-e/web.pdf* Note that the presence of national parliaments where no site was listed by the IPU was cross-checked using common search engines like Yahoo! and InfoSeek and no further such sites could be identified, confirming the reliability of the data.

4. Inter-Parliamentary Union. May 2000. "Guidelines for the Content and Structure of Parliamentary Websites." *www.ipu.org/cntr-e/web.pdf*

5. John Stuart Mill. 1964. (1861). *Representative Government.* London: Dent. P. 239.

6. The concepts of information and communication are similar to those used by the Cyberspace Policy Research Group when evaluating the transparency and interactivity of government websites. See Chris C. Demchak, Christian Friis, and Todd M. La Porte. 1998. "Configuring Public Agencies in Cyberspace: Openness and Effectiveness." *www.cyprg.arizona.edu/Tilburg98F.htm;* Todd M. La Porte, Chris C. Demchak, Martin de Jong, and Christian Friis. 2000. "Democracy and Bureaucracy in the Age of the Web: Empirical Findings and Theoretical Speculations." Paper presented at the International Political Science Association World Congress, Quebec, August.

7. Inter-Parliamentary Union. May 2000. "Guidelines for the Content and Structure of Parliamentary Websites." *www.ipu.org/cntr-e/web.pdf*

8. Matt Carter. 1999. "Speaking Up in the Internet Age: Use and Value of Constituent E-mail and Congressional Websites." In *Parliament in the Age of the Internet.* Eds. Stephen Coleman, John Taylor, and Wim van de Donk. Oxford: Oxford University Press.

9. See, for example, J. A. Taylor and Eleanor Burt. 1999. "Parliaments on the Web: Learning through Innovation." In *Parliament in the Age of the Internet.* Eds. Stephen Coleman, John Taylor, and Wim van de Donk. Oxford: Oxford University Press; Thomas Zittel. 2000. "Electronic Democracy – A Blueprint for 21st Century Democracy?" Paper presented at the International Political Science Association World Congress, Quebec, August.

10. Bruce Bimber. 1998. "The Internet and Political Transformation: Populism, Community and Accelerated Pluralism." *Polity* 31(1): 133–60.

CHAPTER 8. VIRTUAL PARTIES

1. For the measurement and sources, definition of a "major party," and detailed figures, see Table 8.2.
2. E. E. Schattschneider. 1942. *Party Government.* New York: Rinehart. P. 1.
3. For a comparative overview of the structure, organization, and function of political parties, see Alan Ware. 1996. *Political Parties and Party Systems.* Oxford: Oxford University Press.
4. For a discussion see Russell Dalton and Martin Wattenberg. 2000. *Parties without Partisans: Political Change in Advanced Industrial Democracies.* New York: Oxford University Press, particularly Chapter 5; see also Richard Katz and Peter Mair. Eds. 1992. *How Parties Organize.* London: Sage.
5. P. Brophy and E. Halpin. 1999. "Through the Net to Freedom: Information, the Internet and Human Rights." *Journal of Information Science* 25(5): 351–64.
6. Paul Nixon and Hans Johansson. 1999. "Transparency through Technology: The Internet and Political Parties." In *Digital Democracy: Discourse and Decision Making in the Information Age.* Eds. Barry N. Hague and Brian Loader. New York: Routledge.
7. Michael Margolis and David Resnick. 2000. *Politics as Usual: The Cyberspace "Revolution."* Thousand Oaks, CA: Sage.
8. For a case study of the adoption of these forms of technology in British parties see Colin Smith. 2000. "British Political Parties." In *Democratic Governance and New Technology.* Jens Hoff, Ivan Horrocks, and Pieter Tops. Eds. London: Routledge.
9. C. Richard Neu, Robert H. Anderson, and Tora K. Bikson. 1999. *Sending Your Government a Message.* RAND. www.rand.org/publications/MR/MR1095
10. See, for example, P. J. Jackson. 1999. *Virtual Working: Social and Organizational Dynamics.* London: Routledge; J. Hagel and A. G. Armstrong. Eds. 1997. *Net. Gain: Expanding Markets through Virtual Communities.* Cambridge, MA: Harvard Business School; T. McEachern and B. O'Keefe. 1998. *Re-Wiring Business: Uniting Management and the Web.* Chichester: John Wiley.
11. For Sweden and Holland, see Paul Nixon and Hans Johansson. 1999. "Transparency through Technology: The Internet and Political Parties." In *Digital Democracy: Discourse and Decision Making in the Information Age.* Eds. Barry N. Hague and Brian Loader. New York: Routledge. For Britain, see Rachel Gibson and Stephen J. Ward. 1998. "U.K. Political Parties and the Internet: "Politics as Usual" in the New Media?" *Harvard International Journal of Press/Politics* 3(3): 14–38; Stephen Ward and Rachel Gibson. 1998. "The First Internet Election? UK Political Parties and Campaigning in Cyberspace." In *Political Communications: Why Labour Won the General Election of 1997.* Eds. Ivor Crewe, Brian Gosschalk, and John Bartle (pp. 93–112). London: Frank Cass. For the Netherlands, see Pieter W. Tops, Gerrit Voerman, and Marcel Boogers. 2000. "Political Websites during the 1998 Parliamentary Elections in the Netherlands." In *Democratic Governance and New Technology.* Jens Hoff, Ivan Horrocks, and Pieter Tops. Eds. London: Routledge. On Denmark, see Karl Lofgren. 2000. "Danish Political Parties and New Technology." In *Democratic Governance and New Technology.* Jens Hoff, Ivan Horrocks, and Pieter Tops. Eds. London: Routledge. On New Zealand, see J. Roper. 1997. "New Zealand Political Parties Online: The World Wide Web as a Tool for Democratization or Political Marketing?" *New Political Science* 41: 69–84.

12. See Elaine Ciulla Kamarck. 1999. "Campaigning on the Internet in the Election of 1998." In *democracy.com? Governance in a Networked World*. Eds. Elaine Ciulla Kamarck and Joseph S. Nye, Jr. Hollis, NH: Hollis Publishing; Gary W. Selnow. 1998. *Electronic Whistle-Stops: The Impact of the Internet on American Politics*. Westport, CT: Praeger; Richard Davis. 1999. *The Web of Politics*. New York: Oxford University Press; Kevin A. Hill and John E. Hughes. *Cyberpolitics: Citizen Activism in the Age of the Internet*. Lanham, MD: Rowman & Littlefield.

13. *Elections Around the World: Parties on the Web*. The classification was drawn from the list of 1,371 parties that had been last modified on June 11, 2000. *www.agora.stm.it/elections/alllinks.htm*

14. The list of identified links from *Elections around the World* was confirmed for accuracy by cross-checking against two other sources: *Governments on the WWW www.gksoft.com/govt/* and also *Political Science Resources* "Political Parties, Interest Groups and Other Movements" *www.psr.keele.ac.uk/parties.htm*

15. For an excellent discussion of these classification problems see Arend Lijphart. 1999. *Patterns of Democracy*. New Haven, CT: Yale University Press. Chapter 5.

16. Markku Laakso and Rein Taagepera. 1978. "Effective Number of Parties: A Measure with Application to West Europe." *Comparative Political Studies* 12: 3–27.

17. *Elections Around the World*. June 2000. *www.agora.stm.it/elections/alllinks.htm*

18. Leonard R. Sussman. 2000. "Censor Dot Gov: The Internet and Press Freedom 2000." *Freedom House Press Freedom Survey 2000*. *www.freedomhouse.org/pfs2000/sussman.html*

19. Kevin A. Hill and John E. Hughes. 1998. *Cyberpolitics: Citizen Activism in the Age of the Internet*. Lanham, MD: Rowman & Littlefield. P. 155.

20. Paul Nixon and Hans Johansson. 1999. "Transparency through Technology: The Internet and Political Parties." In *Digital Democracy: Discourse and Decision Making in the Information Age*. Eds. Barry N. Hague and Brian Loader. New York: Routledge. P. 145.

21. For a discussion of the persuasive effects of "one-sided" and "two-sided" information, see John Zaller. 1993. *The Nature and Origins of Public Opinion*. New York: Cambridge University Press.

CHAPTER 9. CIVIC SOCIETY

1. Lincoln Dahlberg. Spring 1998. "Cyberspace and the Public Sphere: Exploring the Democratic Potential of the Net," *Convergence* 4(1): 71–84.

2. Andrew L Shapiro. 1999. *The Control Revolution: How the Internet Is Putting Individuals in Charge and Changing the World We Know*. New York: Public Affairs; see also C. Mukerji and B. Simon. 1998. "Out of the Limelight: Discredited Communities and Informal Communication on the Internet." *Sociological Inquiry* 68(2): 258–73; J. Zelwietro. 1998. "The Politicization of Environmental Organizations through the Internet." *Information Society* 14(1): 45–55; Peter Schwartz and Blair Gibb. 1999. *When Good Companies Do Bad Things*. New York: John Wiley.

3. W. T. Coombs. 1998. "The Internet as Potential Equalizer: New Leverage for Confronting Social Irresponsibility." *Public Relations Review* 24(3): 289–303; Allen Hammond and Jonathan Lash. 2000. "Cyber-Activism: The Rise of Civil

Accountability and Its Consequences for Governance." *IMP: Information Impacts Magazine.* May. *www.cisp.org/imp/may 2000/05 00hammond.htm*

4. See Samuel Barnes and Max Kaase. 1979. *Political Action: Mass Participation in Five Western Democracies.* Beverly Hills, CA: Sage; Doug McAdam, John D. McCarthy, and Mayer N. Zald. Eds. 1996. *Comparative Perspectives on Social Movements.* New York: Cambridge University Press.

5. J. M. Ayres. 1999. "From the Streets to the Internet: The Cyber-Diffusion of Contention." *Annals of the American Academy of Political and Social Science* 566: 132–43; Jessica Matthews. 1997. "Power Shifts." *Foreign Affairs.* January/February.

6. Sylvia Ostry. 2000. "Making Sense of It All: A Post-Mortem on the Meaning of Seattle." In *Seattle, the WTO, and the Future of the Multilateral Trading System.* Eds. Roger B. Porter and Pierre Sauve. Cambridge, MA: The Center for Business and Government, John F. Kennedy School of Government; Steve Cisler. 1999. "Showdown in Seattle: Turtles, Teamsters and Tear Gas." *First Monday* 4(2). *www.firstmonday.dk/issues/issue4 12/cisler/index.html*

7. See Sylvia Ostry. 2000. "Making Sense of It All: A Post-Mortem on the Meaning of Seattle." In *Seattle, the WTO, and the Future of the Multilateral Trading System.* Eds. Roger B. Porter and Pierre Sauve. Cambridge, MA: The Center for Business and Government, John F. Kennedy School of Government; Margaret E. Keck and Kathryn Sikkink, 1998. *Activists beyond Borders – Advocacy Networks in International Politics.* Ithaca, NY: Cornell University Press; Maxwell A. Cameron. Ed. 1998. *To Walk Without Fear: The Global Movement to Ban Landmines.* Oxford: Oxford University Press; J. Zelwietro. 1998. "The Politicization of Environmental Organizations through the Internet." *Information Society* 14(1): 45–55.

8. For example see *www.dassk.com* for streaming audio of speeches by Aung San Suu Kyi as well as details about her life and the latest news bulletins. For the Human Rights Watch report see *www.hrw.org/worldreport99/asia/burma.html* The Free Burma Coalition can be found at *www.hrw.org/worldreport99/asia/burma.html* For the alternative official government website, including streaming media and a chat room, see *www.myanamar.com*

9. Allen Hammond and Jonathan Lash. 2000. "Cyber-Activism: The Rise of Civil Accountability and Its Consequences for Governance." *IMP: Information Impacts Magazine.* May. *www.cisp.org/imp/may 2000/05 00hammond.htm*

10. Mamoun Fandy. 1999. "Cyberresistance: Saudi Opposition between Globalization and Localization." *Comparative Studies in Society and History* 41(1): 124–47; William J. Drake, Shanthi Kalathil, and Taylor C. Boas. 2000. "Dictatorships in the Digital Age: Some Considerations on the Internet in China and Cuba." *IMP: Information Impacts Magazine.* October. *www.cisp.org/imp;* Taylor C. Boas. 2000. "The Dictator's Dilemma? The Internet and U.S. Policy toward Cuba." *The Washington Quarterly* 23(3): 57–67.

11. See, for example, cases discussed in Barry N. Hague and Brian Loader. 1999. *Digital Democracy: Discourse and Decision Making in the Information Age.* London: Routledge; Edward Schwartz. 1996. *Netactivism: How Citizens Use the Internet.* Sebastapol, CA: Songline Studios; Wayne Rash, Jr. 1997. *Politics on the Nets: Wiring the Political Process.* New York: Freeman; Steve Jones. Ed. 1998. *Cybersociety 2.0: Computer-Mediated Communication and Community.* Thousand Oaks, CA: Sage; Steve Jones. Ed. 1998. *Virtual Culture: Identity and Communication in Cybersociety.*

Thousand Oaks, CA: Sage; Stecen Doheny-Farina. 1996. *The Wired Neighborhood.* New Haven, CT: Yale University Press; Amy Jo Kim. 2000. *Community Building on the Web.* Berkeley, CA: Peachpit Press.

12. Howard Rheingold. 1993. *The Virtual Community: Homesteading on the Electronic Frontier.* Reading, MA: Addison-Wesley.

13. Amatai Etzioni. 1993. *The Spirit of Community.* New York: Crown.

14. Roza Tsagarousianou, Damian Tambini, and Cathy Bryan. 1998. *Cyberdemocracy.* London: Routledge.

15. J. M. Ayres. 1999. "From the Streets to the Internet: The Cyber-Diffusion of Contention." *Annals of the American Academy of Political and Social Science* 566: 132–43.

16. Bruce Bimber. 1998. "The Internet and Political Transformation: Populism, Community and Accelerated Pluralism." *Polity* 31 (1): 133–60.

17. Taylor C. Boas. 2000. "The Dictator's Dilemma? The Internet and U.S. Policy Toward Cuba." *The Washington Quarterly* 23(3): 57–67.

18. Robert W. McChesney. 1999. *Rich Media, Poor Democracy: Communication Policy in Dubious Times.* Urbana, IL: University of Illinois Press. P. 121.

19. Internet Software Consortium. *www.isc.org*

20. S. L. Esrock and G. B. Leichty. 1998. "Social Responsibility and Corporate Web Pages: Self-Presentation or Agenda-Setting?" *Public Relations Review* 24(3): 305–19. S. L. Esrock and G. B. Leichty. 1999. "Corporate World Wide Web Pages: Serving the News Media and Other Publics." *Journalism and Mass Communication Quarterly* 76(3): 456–67; For the lack of corporate response by email see Rainier Corporation. July 22, 2000. "Second Annual Rainier Web-Index Study reveals International Internet Communication Breakdown among Public Companies." *www.rainierco.com*

21. Kevin A. Hill and John E. Hughes. 1998. *Cyberpolitics: Citizen Activism in the Age of the Internet.* Lanham, MD: Rowman & Littlefield. Chapter 6.

22. Peter Golding. 2000. "Information and Communications Technologies and the Sociology of the Future." *Sociology* 34(1): 165–84. Anthony G. Wilheim. 2000. *Democracy in the Digital Age: Challenges to Political Life in Cyberspace.* New York: Routledge.

23. Chip Brown. June 1999. "How Is This Different from the Other Stuff Out There?" *American Journalism Review. www.ajr.newslink.org/special/12–4.html*

24. Richard Davis. 1999. *The Web of Politics.* New York: Oxford University Press. P. 45.

25. *www.ajr.newslink.org/news.html*

26. For a comparison see *www.Broadcast.com*

27. Pew Research Center for the People and the Press. 2000. "Internet Sapping Broadcast News Audience." Survey conducted by Princeton Survey Research Associates with fieldwork from April 20–May 13, 2000. *www.people-press.org/media00que.htm* For the analysis of the audience and the trade-off between conventional and online news sources see also D. D. Aikat. "News on the Web: Usage Trends of an On-Line Newspaper." *Convergence: The Journal of Research into New Media Technologies* 4(4): 94–111; Scott L. Althaus and David Tewksbury, 2000. "Patterns of Internet and Traditional News Media Use in a Networked Community." *Political Communication* 17(1): 21–46.

28. MMXI Europe. July 2000. *www.mmxieurope.com/press/releases/20000703.jsp*

29. Pippa Norris. 1999. "The Emergent Internet Age in Europe: A New North-South Divide?" Editorial. *The Harvard International Journal of Press-Politics* 5(1).
30. The AJR Newslink database is updated by regular comparison with dozens of others, such as the databases compiled by state and national press association and news media "jump station" sites. Updates from readers are also solicited via an online submission form. Newslink Associated then manually visits each site suggested or found elsewhere and attempts to categorize it, verify its legitimacy, and locate the best URL for it. Beyond continuous amendments, each section in the database is thoroughly overhauled and checked once or twice a year.
31. Data are drawn from the *UNESCO Statistical Yearbook, 1999*. Paris: UNESCO.
32. The simple correlation between the number of daily newspapers and the number of online newspapers in 174 countries proved strong and significant (R = 0.639 Sig. .001).
33. See Pippa Norris. 2000. A *Virtuous Circle: Political Communications in Post-Industrial Societies*. Cambridge: Cambridge University Press.
34. For a discussion of the conceptual distinctions and theoretical frameworks in the literature, as well as the structure, function, and organization of interest groups and new social movements, see Jeffrey Berry. 1984. *The Interest Group Society*. Boston: Little, Brown; Jack L. Walker. 1991. *Mobilizing Interest Groups in America*: Ann Arbor: University of Michigan Press; Sidney Tarrow. 1994. *Power in Movement*. Cambridge: Cambridge University Press; Charles Tilly. 1978. *From Mobilization to Revolution*. Reading, MA: Addison-Wesley; Doug McAdam, John D. McCarthy, and Mayer N. Zald. Eds. 1996. *Comparative Perspectives on Social Movements*. New York: Cambridge University Press.
35. Howard Frederick. 1992. "Computer Communications in Cross-Border Coalition-Building: North American NGO Networking against NAFTA." *Gazette* 50: 217–42; Margaret E. Keck and Kathryn Sikkink, 1998. *Activists beyond Borders – Advocacy Networks in International Politics*. Ithaca, NY: Cornell University Press; J. Zelwietro. 1998. "The Politicization of Environmental Organizations through the Internet." *Information Society* 14(1): 45–55.

CHAPTER 10. CYBERCULTURE

1. For discussions see, for example, David Holmes. 1997. *Virtual Politics: Identity & Community in Cyberspace*. London: Sage; Tim Jordan. 1999. *Cyberpower. The Culture and Politics of Cyberspace and the Internet*. London: Routledge; Steve Jones. Ed. 1997. *Virtual Culture Identity and Communication in Cybersociety*. Thousand Oaks, CA: Sage; David Porter. 1997. *Internet Culture*. New York: Routledge.
2. Ronald Inglehart. 1977. *The Silent Revolution: Changing Values and Political Styles Among Western Publics*. Princeton, NJ: Princeton University Press; Ronald Inglehart. 1990. *Culture Shift in Advanced Industrial Society*. Princeton, NJ: Princeton University Press; Ronald Inglehart. 1997. *Modernization and Postmodernization: Cultural, Economic and Political Change in 43 Societies*. Princeton, NJ: Princeton University Press; Ronald Inglehart and Wayne E. Baker. 2000. "Modernization, Cultural Change and the Persistence of Traditional Values." *American Sociological Review* 65 February: 19–51; Ronald Inglehart and Pippa Norris. 2000. "The Developmental Theory of the Gender Gap: Women's and Men's Voting Behavior in Global Perspective." *International Political Science Review* 21(4): 441–62.

3. For a discussion of the generational evidence toward globalization see Pippa Norris. "Cosmopolitanism, Citizens and Global Governance." In *Governance in a Globalizing World*. Eds. Joseph Nye and John D. Donahue. Washington, DC: The Brookings Institute Press.

4. Ronald Inglehart. 1997. *Modernization and Postmodernization: Cultural, Economic and Political Change in 43 Societies*. Princeton, NJ: Princeton University Press. P. 79.

5. Pippa Norris. 2000. *A Virtuous Circle: Political Communications in Post-Industrial Societies*. Cambridge: Cambridge University Press. Chapter 4.

6. See, for example, Pippa Norris. 1999. "Who Surfs? New Technology, Old Voters and Virtual Democracy." In *democracy.com?: Governance in a Networked World*. Eds. Elaine Ciulla Kamarck and Joseph S. Nye, Jr. Hollis, NH: Hollis Publishing. Table 6; Pew Research Center for the People and the Press. 1999. "The Internet News Audience Goes Ordinary." January 14. *www.people-press.org*

7. Richard Davis and Diana Owen. 1998. *New Media and American Politics*. New York: Oxford University Press. P. 167.

8. Kevin A. Hill and John E. Hughes. 1998. *Cyberpolitics: Citizen Activism in the Age of the Internet*. Lanham, MD: Rowman & Littlefield.

9. Data for this analysis are drawn from the 1999 Political Typology Survey conducted by the Pew Research Center for the People and the Press. This had three components. The main Typology Survey was conducted among 3,973 adults July 14–Sept. 9, 1999. A subsample of Sept. 28–Oct. 10, 1,411 was re-interviewed from October 7–11, 1999. The Values Update Survey was conducted among 985 adults Sept. 28–Oct. 10, 1999. Full details can be found at *www.people-press. org/typo99que.htm*

10. Data for this analysis are drawn from the spring 1999 Eurobarometer survey conducted in the 15-member states of the EU. Full details can be found at *www.europa.eu*

11. The Pew question (Q19t) was as follows: "Next I'm going to read you some words or phrases and ask you to rate how well each describes you. 10 represents a description that is perfect for you, and 1 represents a description that is totally wrong for you … On this scale of 1 to 10, how well does Internet enthusiast describe you?"

12. The standard item that has been employed in Pew Surveys since the mid-1990s measured the total online population as follows: *"Do you ever go online to access the Internet or World Wide Web or to send and receive email?"*

13. Similar results are reported in Richard Davis and Diana Owen. 1998. *New Media and American Politics*. Oxford: Oxford University Press. P. 169. See also Kevin A. Hill and John E. Hughes. 1998. *Cyberpolitics: Citizen Activism in the Age of the Internet*. Lanham, MD: Rowman & Littlefield.

14. Studies of the 1996 reported that there was a rough partisan balance in the online population between Republicans and Democrats. See Richard Davis and Diana Owen. 1998. *New Media and American Politics*. Oxford: Oxford University Press. P. 170. In the 2000 campaign, however, Media Metrix suggest that registered Republicans comprised 37 percent of the adult online population, whereas registered Democrats represented only 28 percent. In addition, 12 percent had another party affiliation, a relatively high estimate, while 24 percent were unregistered. See Media Metrix. 2000. *Campaign 2000: Party Politics on the World Wide Web*. October. *www.mediametrix.com*

15. See Pippa Norris. 2000. "Cosmopolitanism, Nationalism and Parochialism: Globalization and Cultural Change." In *Governance in a Globalizing World*. Eds. Joseph S. Nye and John D. Donahue. Washington, DC: The Brookings Institute Press.

CHAPTER 11. CIVIC ENGAGEMENT

1. For a more extended discussion of the concept and an analysis of the way that the traditional news media influence civic engagement during an election campaign see Pippa Norris, John Curtice, David Sanders, Margaret Scammell, and Holli A. Semetko. 1999. *On Message: Communicating the Campaign*. London: Sage.
2. Richard Davis and Diane Owen. 1998. *New Media and American Politics*. Oxford: Oxford University Press. P. 185; Michael Margolis and David Resnick. 2000. *Politics as Usual: The Cyberspace "Revolution."* Thousand Oaks, CA: Sage; Pippa Norris 1999. "Who Surfs? New Technology, Old Voters, and Virtual Democracy." In *democracy. com? Governance in a Networked World*. Eds. Elaine Ciulla Kamarck and Joseph S. Nye, Jr. Hollis, NH: Hollis Publishing; Pippa Norris. 1999. "Who Surfs Café Europa?" Paper presented at the Annual Meeting of the American Political Science Association, Atlanta, September.
3. Pippa Norris. 1999. "Who Surfs? New Technology, Old Voters, and Virtual Democracy." In *democracy.com? Governance in a Networked World*. Eds. Elaine Ciulla Kamarck and Joseph S. Nye, Jr. Hollis, NH: Hollis Publishing; Pippa Norris. 1999. "Who Surfs Café Europa?" Paper presented at the Annual Meeting of the American Political Science Association, Atlanta, September.
4. Sidney Verba, Norman Nie, and Jae-on Kim. 1978. *Participation and Political Equality: A Seven-Nation Comparison*. New York: Cambridge University Press.
5. Pippa Norris. 2000. *A Virtuous Circle: Political Communication in Post-Industrial Democracies*. New York: Cambridge University Press.
6. Charles Tilly. 1978. *From Mobilization to Revolution*. Reading, MA: Addison-Wesley; Sidney Tarrow. 1994. *Power in Movement*. Cambridge: Cambridge University Press; Doug McAdam, John D. McCarthy, and Mayer N. Zald. Eds. 1996. *Comparative Perspectives on Social Movements*. New York: Cambridge University Press.
7. Sidney Verba, Norman Nie, and Jae-on Kim. 1978. *Participation and Political Equality: A Seven-Nation Comparison*. New York: Cambridge University Press. Sidney Verba, Kay Schlozman, and Henry E. Brady. 1995. *Voice and Equality*. Cambridge, MA: Harvard University Press.
8. Pippa Norris. 2000. *A Virtuous Circle: Political Communication in Post-Industrial Democracies*. New York: Cambridge University Press.
9. Pippa Norris. 1999. "Who Surfs? New Technology, Old Voters, and Virtual Democracy." In *democracy.com? Governance in a Networked World*. Eds. Elaine Ciulla Kamarck and Joseph S. Nye, Jr. Hollis, NH: Hollis Publishing.
10. Nicholas Negroponte. 1995. *Being Digital*. New York: Knopf.
11. Sidney Verba, Kay Schlozman, and Henry E. Brady. 1995. *Voice and Equality*. Cambridge, MA: Harvard University Press; Steven J. Rosenstone and John Mark Hansen. 1993. *Mobilization, Participation and Democracy in America*. New York: Macmillan.
12. National Telecommunications and Information Administration. 1999. *Falling Through the Net*. Washington, DC: U.S. Department of Commerce. *www. ntia.doc.gov.ntiahome/fttn99*

13. Pippa Norris. 1999. "Who Surfs? New Technology, Old Voters, and Virtual Democracy." In *democracy.com? Governance in a Networked World.* Eds. Elaine Ciulla Kamarck and Joseph S. Nye, Jr. Hollis, NH: Hollis Publishing; Richard Davis and Diana Owen. 1998. *New Media and American Politics.* Oxford: Oxford University Press.
14. Jay G. Blumler and Elihu Katz. Eds. 1974. *The Uses of Mass Communications: Current Perspectives on Gratifications Research.* Beverly Hills, CA: Sage.

CHAPTER 12. CONCLUSIONS: PROMOTING e-DEMOCRACY

1. Richard Coyne. 1999. *Technoromanticism: Digital Narrative, Holism, and the Romance of the Real.* Cambridge, MA: The MIT Press.
2. See, for example, Richard Rhodes. Ed. 1999. *Visions of Technology.* New York: Simon & Schuster; Carroll W. Pursell. 1995. *The Machine in America: A Social History of Technology.* Baltimore: Johns Hopkins University Press; Steven Lubar. 1993. *Infoculture: The Smithsonian Book of Information Age Inventions.* Boston: Houghton Mifflin.
3. See, for example, Andrew L. Shapiro. 1999. *The Control Revolution: How the Internet Is Putting Individuals in Charge and Changing the World We Know.* New York: Public Affairs. See also Christopher Weare. 2000. "Technology and Politics: Linking the Internet to Changes in Democratic Governance." Paper presented at the International Political Science Association World Congress, Quebec, August.
4. Virginia I. Postrel. 1999. *The Future and Its Enemies: The Growing Conflict over Creativity, Enterprise and Progress.* New York: Touchstone Books.
5. See, for example, the cases discussed in Barry Hague and Brian Loader. 1999. *Digital Democracy: Discourse and Decision-Making in the Information Age.* London: Routledge.
6. The reference is to the Hindu fable described in John Godfrey Saxe's poem "The Blind Man and the Elephant."
7. Gabriel Tarde. 1903. *The Laws of Imitation.* New York: Henry Holt.

Select Bibliography

Aldisardottir, L. 2000. "Global Medium – Local Tool? How Readers and Media Companies Use the Web." *European Journal of Communication* 15(2): 241–51.

Abramson, Jeffrey B., Christopher Arterton, and Gary Orren. 1988. *The Electronic Commonwealth: The Impact of New Media Technologies on Democratic Politics.* New York: Basic Books.

Aikat, D. D. "News on the Web: Usage Trends of an On-Line Newspaper." *Convergence: The Journal of Research into New Media Technologies* 4(4): 94–111.

Albarran, Alan B. and David H. Goff. Eds. 2000. *Understanding the Web: Social, Political, and Economic Dimensions of the Internet.* Ames: Iowa State University Press.

Alexander, Janet E. and Marsha Ann Tate. 1999. *Web Wisdom: How to Evaluate and Create Information Quality on the Web.* Mahwah, NJ: Lawrence Erlbaum.

Althaus, Scott L. and David Tewksbury. 2000. "Patterns of Internet and Traditional News Media Use in a Networked Community." *Political Communication* 17(1): 21–46.

Arterton, Christopher F. 1987. *Teledemocracy.* Newbury Park, CA: Sage.

Arunachalam, S. 1999. "Information and Knowledge in the Age of Electronic Communication: A Developing Country Perspective." *Journal of Information Science* 25(6): 465–76.

Atkinson, Rob. 2000. "Creating a Digital Federal Government." *IMP: Information Impacts Magazine.* October. *www.cisp.org/imp*

Auty, Caroline and David Nicholas. 1998. "British Political Parties and Their Web Pages." *Aslib Proceedings* 50(10): 283–96.

Ayres J. M. 1999. "From the Streets to the Internet: The Cyber-Diffusion of Contention." *Annals of the American Academy of Political and Social Science* 566: 132–43.

Barber, Benjamin R. 1984. *Strong Democracy.* Berkeley: University of California Press.

Barber, Benjamin R. 1998. "Three Scenarios for the Future of Technology and Strong Democracy." *Political Science Quarterly* 113(4): 573–90.

Barnes, Samuel and Max Kaase. 1979. *Political Action: Mass Participation in Five Western Democracies.* Beverly Hills, CA: Sage.

Bauer, Christian and Arno Scharl. 2000. "Quantitative Evaluation of Web Site Content and Structure." *Internet Research: Electronic Networking Applications and Policy* 10(1): 31–43.

Bell, Daniel. 1998. "The Internet and the Trajectories of Technologies." *The Tocqueville Review* 19(2): 111–25.

Bellamy, Christine and John A. Taylor. Eds. 1998. *Governing in the Information Age.* Buckingham: Open University.

Bennett, Daniel and Pam Fielding. 1999. *The Net Effect: How Cyberadvocacy Is Changing the Political Landscape.* New York: Capital Advantage.

Bimber, Bruce. 1998. "The Internet and Political Mobilization: Research Note on the 1996 Election Season." *Social Science Computer Review* 16(4): 391–401.

Bimber, Bruce. 1998. "The Internet and Political Transformation: Populism, Community and Accelerated Pluralism." *Polity* 31 (1): 133–60.

Bimber, Bruce. 1999. "The Internet and Citizen Communication with Government: Does the Medium Matter?" *Political Communication* 16: 409–28.

Bimber, Bruce. Forthcoming. "The Gender Gap on the Internet." 2000. *Social Science Quarterly.* 81 (3): 868–876.

Birdsell, David, Douglas Muzio, David Krane, and Amy Cottreau. 1998. "Web Users Are Looking More Like America." *The Public Perspective* 9(3): 33. *www.ropercenter. uconn.edu/pubpr/pp93.htm*

Blumler, Jay G. and Elihu Katz. Eds. 1974. *The Uses of Mass Communications: Current Perspectives on Gratifications Research.* Beverly Hills, CA: Sage.

Boas, Taylor C. 2000. "The Dictator's Dilemma? The Internet and U.S. Policy toward Cuba." *The Washington Quarterly* 23(3): 57–67.

Bolt, David and Ray Crawford. 2000. *Digital Divide: Computers and Our Children's Future.* New York: TV Books.

Bowler, Shaun and David M. Farrell. Eds. 1992. *Electoral Strategies and Political Marketing.* New York: St. Martin's Press.

Braga, Carlos Alberto Primo. 1998. "Inclusion or Exclusion?" *www.unesco.org/ courier/1998 12*

Brophy, P. and E. Halpin. 1999. "Through the Net to Freedom: Information, the Internet and Human Rights." *Journal of Information Science* 25(5): 351–64.

Browning, Graeme. 1996. *Electronic Democracy: Using the Internet to Influence American Politics.* Wilton, CT: Pemberton Press.

Buchanan, Robert W. Jr. and Charles Lukaszewki. 1997. *Measuring the Impact of Your Web Site.* New York: John Wiley. *www.siteimpact.com*

Bucy, Erik P. 2000. "Social Access to the Internet." *The Harvard International Journal of Press-Politics* 5(1): 50–61.

Budge, Ian. 1996. *The New Challenge of Direct Democracy.* Oxford: Polity Press.

Cameron, Maxwell A. Ed. 1998. *To Walk Without Fear: The Global Movement to Ban Landmines.* Oxford: Oxford University Press.

Carlson, Tom and Görab Djupsund. 1999. "Old Wine in New Bottles? Candidates on the Internet in the 1999 Finnish Parliamentary Election Campaign." Paper presented at the XIV Nordic Conference of Mass Communication Research, Kungälv, Sweden.

Case, Steve. 1998. *"Community Update: Election'98". www.aol.com,* keyword Steve Case. October 6, 1998.

Casey, Chris. 1996. *The Hill on the Net: Congress Enters the Information Age.* Boston: AP Professional.

Castells, M. 1996. *The Rise of the Networked Society: The Information Age: Economy, Society and Culture.* Oxford: Blackwell.

Cetron, M. and O. Davies. 1997. *Probable Tomorrows: How Science and Technology Will Transform our Lives in the Next Twenty Years*. New York: St. Martin's Press.

Charles, David and Jeremy Howells. 1992. *Technology Transfer in Europe*. London: Belhaven Press.

Chatterji, Manas. 1990. *Technology Transfer in the Developing Countries*. New York: St. Martin's Press.

Choucri, Nazli. 2000. "Cyberpolitics in International Relations." *International Political Science Review* 21(3): 243–64.

Cisler, Steve. 1999. "Showdown in Seattle: Turtles, Teamsters and Tear Gas." *First Monday* 4(2). *www.firstmonday.dk/issues/issue4 12/cisler/index.html*

Coleman, Stephen, John Taylor, and Wim van de Donk. 1999. *Parliament in the Age of the Internet*. Oxford: Oxford University Press.

Coffman, K. G. and Andrew Odlyzko. 1998. "The Size and Growth Rate of the Internet." *First Monday* 3(10). *www.firstmonday.org/issues/issue3 10/coffman/index.html*

Coombs, W. T. 1998. "The Internet as Potential Equalizer: New Leverage for Confronting Social Irresponsibility." *Public Relations Review* 24(3): 289–303.

Coombs, W. T. and C. W. Cutbirth. 1998. "Mediated Political Communication, the Internet and New Knowledge Elites: Prospects and Portents." *Telematics and Informatics* 15(3): 203–17.

Corrado, Anthony and Charles E. Firestone. 1996. *Elections in Cyberspace: Towards a New Era in American Politics*. Washington, DC: The Aspen Institute.

Corrado, Anthony. 2000. *Campaigns in Cyberspace: Toward a New Regulatory Environment*. Washington, DC: The Aspen Institute.

Coyne, Richard. 1999. *Technoromanticism: Digital Narrative, Holism, and the Romance of the Real*. Cambridge, MA: The MIT Press.

Dahlberg, Lincoln. Spring 1998. "Cyberspace and the Public Sphere: Exploring the Democratic Potential of the Net." *Convergence* 4(1): 71–84.

Dalton, Russell and Martin P. Wattenberg. Forthcoming. *Parties without Partisans: Political Change in Advanced Industrialized Democracies*. Oxford: Oxford University Press.

Darkwa, Osei and Fikile Mazibuko. 2000. "Creating Virtual Communities in Africa: Challenges and Opportunities." *First Monday* 5(5). *www.firstmonday.dk/issues/issue5_5/darkwa/index.html*

Davis, Richard and Diana Owen. 1998. *New Media and American Politics*. New York: Oxford University Press.

Davis, Richard. 1999. *The Web of Politics: The Internet's Impact on the American Political System*. New York: Oxford University Press.

Day, Abby. 1997. "A Model for Monitoring Web Site Effectiveness," *Internet Research: Electronic Networking Applications and Policy* 7(2): 109–15.

De Bens, Els and Gianpietro Mazzolini. 1998. "The Media in the Age of Digital Communication." In *Media Policy: Convergence, Concentration and Commerce*. Ed. Denis McQuail and Karen Siune. London: Sage.

Deloitte Research. 2000. *At the Dawn of e-Government: The Citizen as Customer*. *www.dc.com/deloitte research*

Demchak, Chris C., Christian Friis, and Todd M. La Porte. 1998. "Configuring Public Agencies in Cyberspace: Openness and Effectiveness." *www.cyprg.arizona.edu/Tilburg98F.htm*

De Roy, Olivier Coeur. 1997. "The African Challenge: Internet, Networking and Connectivity Activities in a Developing Environment." *Third World Quarterly* 18: 883–98.

DeConti, Linda. 1998. "Planning and Creating a Government Web Site: Learning from the Experience of U.S. States." *Information Systems for Public Sector Management Working Paper No. 2. www.man.ac.uk/idpm/ispswpf2.htm*

Department of Commerce. 1999. *Falling through the Net. www.ntia.doc.gov/ntia-home/fttn99*

Department of Commerce. 2000. *Falling through the Net. www.ntia.doc.gov/ntia-home/ftn00*

Dertouzos, Michael. 1997. *What Will Be: How the New Information Marketplace Will Change Our Lives.* San Francisco: Harper.

Dogan, Mattei and Domanique Pelassy. 1984. *How to Compare Nations.* Oxford: Blackwell.

Donert, K. 2000. "Virtually Geography: Aspects of the Changing Geography of Information and Communications." *Geography* 85(1): 37–45.

Douglas, Susan J. 1987. *Inventing American Broadcasting 1899–1922.* Baltimore: Johns Hopkins University Press.

Downes, Larry and Chunka Mui. 2000. *Unleashing the Killer App.* Cambridge, MA: Harvard Business School Press. *www.killer-apps.com*

Drake, William J., Shanthi Kalathil, and Taylor C. Boas. 2000. "Dictatorships in the Digital Age: Some Considerations on the Internet in China and Cuba." *IMP: Information Impacts Magazine.* October. *www.cisp.org/imp*

Dulio, David A., Donald L. Goff, and James A. Thurber. 1999. "Untangling Web: Internet Use during the 1998 Election." *PS Online.* March. *www.apsanet.org*

Dutton, William H., Jay Blumler, and Kenneth L. Kraemer. Eds. 1987. *Wired Cities: Shaping the Future of Communications.* Boston: G. K. Hall.

Dutton, William H. Ed. 1996. *Information and Communication Technologies.* Oxford: Oxford University Press.

Dutton, William H. 1999. *Society on the Line: Information Politics in the Digital Age.* Oxford: Oxford University Press.

Dutton, William H. 1999. "The Web of Technology and People: Challenges for Economic and Social Research." *Prometheus* 17(1): 5–20.

Easton, David. 1975. "A Reassessment of the Concept of Political Support." *British Journal of Political Science* 5: 435–57.

Ebo, Bosah. Ed. 1998. *Cyberghetto or Cybertopic? Race, Class and Gender on the Internet.* Westport, CT: Praeger.

Ekre, Huizingh. 2000. "The Content and Design of Web Sites: An Empirical Study." *Information & Management* 37(3): 123–34.

Esrock, S. L. and G. B. Leichty. 1999. "Corporate World Wide Web Pages: Serving the News Media and Other Publics." *Journalism and Mass Communication Quarterly* 76(3): 456–67.

Esrock, S. L. and G. B. Leichty. 1998. "Social Responsibility and Corporate Web Pages: Self-presentation or agenda-setting?" *Public Relations Review* 24(3): 305–19.

Etzioni, Amatai. 1993. *The Spirit of Community.* New York: Crown.

Evans, Philip and Thomas S. Wurster. 1999. *Blown to Bits: How the New Economics of Information Transforms Strategy.* Cambridge, MA: Harvard Business School.

Everard, Jerry. 2000. *Virtual States: The Internet and the Boundaries of the Nation-State.* London: Routledge.

Everett, Margaret. 1998. "Latin America On-Line: The Internet, Development and Democratization." *Human Organization* 57(4): 385–93.

Falk, J. 1998. "The Meaning of the Web." *Information Society* 14(4): 285–93.

Fandy, Mamoun. 1999. "Cyberresistance: Saudi Opposition between Globalization and Localization." *Comparative Studies in Society and History* 41(1): 124–47.

Feather, John. *The Information Society: A Study of Continuity and Change.* London: Library Association.

Fisher, Claude. 1992. *America Calling.* Berkeley: University of California Press.

Frederick, Howard. 1992. "Computer Communications in Cross-Border Coalition-Building: North American NGO Networking against NAFTA." *Gazette* 50: 217–42.

Friedman, Thomas. 1999. *The Lexus and the Olive Tree.* New York: Anchor Books.

Frisk, Alan. 1999. *Virtual Campaigning: The Use of the Internet in the 1998 Elections to the Swedish Parliament.* Independent Research Paper, Part 1 B. *www.algonet.se/~afrisk/internet/index.html*

Fuchs, Dieter and Max Kaase. 2000. "Electronic Democracy." Paper presented at the International Political Science World Congress, Quebec, August.

Hawisher, Gail E. and Cynthia L. Selfe. Eds. 2000. *Global Literacies and the World Wide Web.* London: Routledge.

Galtung, J. and M. Ruge. 1965. "The Structure of Foreign News." *Journal of Peace Research* 1: 64–90.

Garson, G. D. 2000. *Handbook of Public Information Systems.* New York: Marcel Dekker.

Gates, Bill. 1995. *The Road Ahead.* New York: Viking.

Gher, L. A. and H. V. Amin. 1999. "New and Old Media Access and Ownership in the Arab World." *Gazette* 61(1): 59–87.

Gibson, Rachel, Philip E. N. Howard, and Stephen Ward. 2000. "Social Capital, Internet Connectedness and Political Participation: A Four-Country Study." Paper presented at the International Political Science Association World Congress, Quebec, August.

Gibson, Rachel and Stephen J. Ward. 1998. "U.K. Political Parties and the Internet: 'Politics as Usual' in the New Media?" *The Harvard International Journal of Press-Politics* 3(3): 14–38.

Gibson, Rachel and Stephen Ward. 2000. "A Proposed Methodology for Studying the Function and Effectiveness of Party and Candidate Web Sites." *Social Science Computer Review* 18(3): 301–19.

Gibson, Rachel and Stephen J. Ward. Eds. 2000. *Reinvigorating Democracy: British Politics and the Internet.* Aldershot, Hampshire: Ashgate.

Golding, Peter. 1996. "World Wide Wedge: Division and Contradiction in the Global Information Infrastructure." *Monthly Review* 48(3): 70–85.

Golding, Peter. 1998. "Global Village or Cultural Pillage? The Unequal Inheritance of the Communication Revolution." In *Capitalism and the Information Age: The Political Economy of the Global Communication Revolution.* Eds. R. W. McChesney, E. Meiksins Wood, and J. B. Foster. New York: Monthly Review Press.

Golding, Peter. 2000. "Information and Communications Technologies and the Sociology of the Future." *Sociology* 34(1): 165–84.

Grimes, S. 2000. "Rural Areas in the Information Society: Diminishing Distance or Increasing Learning Capacity." *Journal of Rural Studies* 16(1): 13–21.

Grossman, Lawrence. 1995. *The Electronic Commonwealth.* New York: Penguin.

Gurak, Laura. 1997. *Persuasion and Privacy in Cyberspace.* New Haven, CT: Yale University Press.

Hafner, Katie and Matthew Lyon. 1998. *Where Wizards Stay Up Late: The Origins of the Internet.* New York: Touchstone Books.

Hague, Barry and Brian Loader. 1999. *Digital Democracy: Discourse and Decision-Making in the Information Age.* London: Routledge.

Hammond, Allen and Jonathan Lash. 2000. "Cyber-Activism: The Rise of Civil Accountability and Its Consequences for Governance." *IMP: Information Impacts Magazine.* May. *www.cisp.org/imp/may 2000/05 00hammond.htm*

Harcourt, Wendy. Ed. 1999. *Women@ Internet: Creating New Cultures in Cyberspace.* New York: Zed Books.

Hargittai, Eszter. 1999. "Weaving the Western Web: Explaining Differences in Internet Connectivity Among OECD Countries." *Telecommunications Policy* 23(10–11): 701–18.

Harper, Christopher. 1998. *And That's the Way It Will Be.* New York: New York University Press.

Harford, Kathleen. 2000. "Cyberspace with Chinese Characteristics." *Current History.* September: 255–62.

Hauben, Michael and Rhonda Hauben. 1998. *Netizens: On the History and Impact of Usenet and the Internet.* Los Alamitos, CA: IEEE Computer Science Press.

Hayward, Trevol. 1995. *Info-Rich, Info-Poor: Access and Exchange in the Global Information Society.* K. G. Saur.

Hedley, R. A. 1998. "Technological Diffusion or Cultural Imperialism: Measuring the Information Revolution." *International Journal of Comparative Sociology* 39(2): 198–212.

Herron, Erik S. 1999. "Democratization and the Development of Information Regimes: The Internet in Eurasia and the Baltics." *Problems of Post-Communism* 46(4): 56–68.

Hill, Kevin A. and John E. Hughes. 1998. *Cyberpolitics: Citizen Activism in the Age of the Internet.* Lanham, MD: Rowman & Littlefield.

Hoff, Jens, Ivan Horrocks, and Pieter Tops. 2000. *Democratic Governance and New Technology: Technologically Mediated Innovations in Political Practice in Western Europe.* London: Routledge.

Hoffman, Donna L. and Thomas P. Novak. 2000. "The Growing Digital Divide: Implications for an Open Research Agenda." In *Understanding the Digital Economy: Data, Tools and Research.* Ed. B. Kahin and E. Brynjolffson. Cambridge, MA: The MIT Press.

Holmes, David. 1997. *Virtual Politics: Identity & Community in Cyberspace.* London: Sage.

Hurwitz, Roger. 1999. "Who Needs Politics? Who Needs People? The Ironies of Democracy in Cyberspace." *Contemporary Sociology* 28(6): 655–61.

IDEA. *Voter Turnout from 1945 to 1999.* Stockholm: IDEA. *www.int-idea.se*

International Telecommunications Union. 1999. *Challenges to the Network: Internet for Development.* Geneva: ITU. *www.itu.int*

International Telecommunications Union. 1999. *Telecommunications Indicators.* Geneva: ITU. *www.itu.int*

International Telecommunications Union. 1999. *Trends in Telecommunication Reform 1999.* Geneva: ITU. *www.itu.int*

Inter-Parliamentary Union. 2000. *Web Sites of National Parliaments.* Geneva: IPU. *www.ipu.org/english/parlweb.htm*

IriS. 1999. *Consumer Attitudes to the Internet: An 18 Country Study. Executive Summary.* Adligenswill, Switzerland: IriS.

Jellinek, Dan. 2000. "E-government – Reality or Hype?" *IMP: Information Impacts Magazine.* October. *www.cisp.org/imp*

Jeremy, David J. 1992. *The Transfer of International Technology: Europe, Japan and the USA in the Twentieth Century.* Aldershot: Edward Elgar.

Jones, Steve. Ed. 1997. *Virtual Culture: Identity and Communication in Cybersociety.* Thousand Oaks, CA: Sage.

Jones, Steve. Ed. 1998. *Cybersociety 2.0: Revisiting Computer-Mediated Communication and Community.* Thousand Oaks, CA: Sage.

Jones, Steve. Ed. 1999. *Doing Internet Research: Critical Issues and Methods for Examining the Net.* Thousand Oaks, CA: Sage.

Jordan, Tim. 1999. *Cyberpower: The Culture and Politics of Cyberspace and the Internet.* London: Routledge.

Just, Marion, Ann Creigler, and Montague Kern. 1998. "Information, Persuasion and Solidarity: Civic Uses of the Internet in Campaign '96." Paper presented at the Western Political Science Association Annual Meeting, Los Angeles.

Kamarck, Elaine Ciulla. 1999. "Campaigning on the Internet in the Election of 1998." In *democracy.com? Governance in a Networked World.* Eds. Elaine Ciulla Kamarck and Joseph S. Nye, Jr. Hollis, NH: Hollis Publishing.

Kamarck, Elaine Ciulla and Joseph S. Nye, Jr. Eds. 1999. *democracy.com? Governance in a Networked World.* Hollis, NH: Hollis Publishing.

Katz, Raul L. 1988. *The Information Society: An International Perspective.* New York: Praeger.

Katz, Richard and Peter Mair. Eds. 1992. *How Parties Organize.* London: Sage.

Keck, Margaret E. and Kathryn Sikkink. 1998. *Activists beyond Borders – Advocacy Networks in International Politics.* Ithaca, NY: Cornell University Press.

Kedzie, Christopher R. 1997. "Communication and Democracy: Coincident Revolutions and the Emergent Dictator's Dilemma." Washington, DC: RAND. *www.rand.org/publications/RGSD/RGSD127*

Kim, Amy Jo. 2000. *Community Building on the Web.* Berkeley, CA: Peachpit Press. *www.naima.com/community*

Klotz, Robert. 1997. "Positive Spin: Senate Campaigning on the Web." *PS: Political Science and Politics* 30(3): 482–86.

Kofler, Angelika. 1998. "Digital Europe 1998: Policies, Technological Development and Implementation of the Emerging Information Society." *Innovation* 11: 53–71.

Kole, Ellen. S. 1998. "Myths and Realities in Internet Discourse: Using Computer Networks for Data Collection and the Beijing World Conference on Women." *Gazette* 60(4): 343–60.

Kolko, Beth E., Lisa Nakamura, and Gilbert B. Rodman. Eds. 1999. *Race in Cyberspace.* New York: Routledge.

Kominski, Robert and Eric Newburger. 1999. "Access Denied: Changes in Computer Ownership and Use 1984–1997." Paper presented at the annual meeting of the American Sociological Association, Chicago.

Kramarae, Cheris. 1999. "The Language and Nature of the Internet: The Meaning of Global." *New Media and Society* 1(1): 47–53.

Lan, Zhiyong and Santa Falcone. 1997. "Factors Influencing Internet Use: A Policy Model for Electronic Government Information Provision." *Journal of Government Information* 24: 251–57.

La Porte, Todd M., Chris C. Demchak, Martin de Jong, and Christian Friis. 2000. "Democracy and Bureaucracy in the Age of the Web: Empirical Findings and Theoretical Speculations." Paper presented at the International Political Science Association World Congress, Quebec, August.

Lax, S. 1998. "Democracy and Communication Technologies: Superhighway or Blind Alley?" *Convergence: The Journal of Research into New Media Technologies* 4(3): 30–39.

Loader, Brain. Ed. 1998. *Cyberspace Divide: Equality, Agency and Policy in the Information Society.* London: Routledge.

Lubar, Steven. 1993. *Infoculture: The Smithsonian Book of Information Age Inventions.* Boston: Houghton Mifflin.

Lupia, Arthur and Matthew McCubbins. 1998. *The Democratic Dilemma.* Cambridge: Cambridge University Press.

Mansell, R. and Roger Silverstone. 1996. *Communication by Design: The Politics of Information and Communication Technologies.* Oxford: Oxford University Press.

Margolis, Michael and David Resnick. 2000. *Politics as Usual: The Cyberspace "Revolution."* Thousand Oaks, CA: Sage.

Margolis, Michael, David Resnick, and Chin-chang Tu. 1997. "Campaigning on the Internet: Parties and Candidates on the World Wide Web in the 1996 Primary Season." *The Harvard International Journal of Press-Politics* 2(1): 59–78.

Margolis, Michael, David Resnick, and Joel D. Wolfe. 1999. "Party Competition on the Internet in the United States and Britain." *The Harvard International Journal of Press-Politics* 4(4): 24–47.

Martin, W. J. 1995. *The Global Information Society.* London: Ashgate.

Massey B. L. and M. R. Levy. 1999. "Interactivity, Online Journalism and English-Language Web Newspapers in Asia." *Journalism & Mass Communication Quarterly* 76(1): 138–51.

Matthews, Jessica. 1997. "Power Shifts." *Foreign Affairs.* January/February.

McAdam, Doug, John D. McCarthy, and Mayer N. Zald. Eds. 1996. *Comparative Perspectives on Social Movements.* New York: Cambridge University Press.

McChesney, Robert W. 1997. *Capitalism and the New Information Age.* New York: Monthly Review Press.

McChesney, Robert W. 1999. *Rich Media, Poor Democracy: Communication Policy in Dubious Times.* Urbana and Chicago: University of Illinois Press.

McLean, Iain. 1989. *Democracy and New Technology.* Cambridge: Polity Press.

McNight, Lee W. and Joseph P. Bailey. Eds. 1997. *Internet Economics.* Cambridge, MA: The MIT Press.

Media Metrix. 2000. *Campaign 2000: Party Politics on the World Wide Web.* Media Metrix. October. *www.mediametrix.com*

Melody, W. H. 1997. "Identifying Priorities for Building Distinct Information Societies." *Economic & Social Review* 28(3): 177–84.

Meny, J. 1999. *Data Mining Your Website.* Boston, MA: Digital Press.

Miller, James. 2000. "An Unlikely Public Sphere: Constraints on Politics on the Internet." Paper presented at the International Political Science World Congress, Quebec, August.

Mosca, V. "Myth-ing links: Power and Community on the Communication Highway." *Information Society* 14(1): 57–62.

Mowlana, Hamid. 1997. *Global Information and World Communication.* 2nd ed. London: Sage.

Moy, P., M. Pfau, and L. Kahlor. Spring 1999. "Media Use and Public Confidence in Democratic Institutions." *Journal of Broadcasting and Electronic Media* 43(2): 137–58.

Mukerji C. and B. Simon. 1998. "Out of the Limelight: Discredited Communities and Informal Communication on the Internet." *Sociological Inquiry* 68(2): 258–73.

Murdock, Graham and Peter Golding. 1989. "Information Poverty and Political Inequality: Citizenship in the Age of Privatised Communications." *Journal of Communication* 39: 180–95.

Musso, Juliet, Christopher Weare, and Matt Hale. 2000. "Designing Web Technologies for Local Governance Reform: Good Management or Good Democracy?" *Political Communication* 17(1): 1–20.

Negroponte, Nicholas. 1995. *Being Digital.* New York: Knopf.

Neuman, W. Russell. 1998. "The Global Impact of New Technologies." In *The Politics of News: The News of Politics.* Doris Graber, Denis McQuail, and Pippa Norris. Eds. Washington, DC: CQ Press.

Nie, Norman and Lutz Erbring. 2000. *Internet and Society: A Preliminary Report.* Stanford Institute for the Quantative Study of Society, Stanford, CA: Stanford University.

Niece, David C. 1998. "Measuring Participation in the Digital Techno-structure: Internet Access." *ACTS/FAIR Working Paper 44.* Brighton: SPRU. *www.data-bank.it/dbc/fair/WPSERIES.htm*

Nixon, Paul and Hans Johansson. 1999. "Transparency Through Technology: The Internet and Political Parties." In *Digital Democracy: Discourse and Decision Making in the Information Age.* Eds. Barry N. Hague and Brian Loader. London: Routledge.

Norris, Pippa and David Jones. 1998. "Virtual Democracy." *The Harvard International Journal of Press-Politics* 3(2): 1–4.

Norris, Pippa, John Curtice, David Sanders, Margaret Scammell, and Holli Semetko. 1999. *On Message: Communicating the Campaign.* London: Sage.

Norris, Pippa. 1999. "Who Surfs? New Technology, Old Voters, and Virtual Democracy." In *democracy.com? Governance in a Networked World.* Eds. Elaine Ciulla Kamarck and Joseph S. Nye, Jr. Hollis, NH: Hollis Publishing.

Norris, Pippa. 1999. "Who Surfs Café Europa?" Paper presented at the Annual Meeting of the American Political Science Association, Atlanta, September.

Norris, Pippa. 1999. "The Emergent Internet Age in Europe: A New North-South Divide?" *The Harvard International Journal of Press-Politics* 5(1): 1–4.

Norris, Pippa. 2000. "Information Poverty and the Wired World." *The Harvard International Journal of Press-Politics* 5(3): 1–6.

Norris, Pippa. 2000. *A Virtuous Circle: Political Communication in Post-Industrial Democracies.* New York: Cambridge University Press.

Norris, Pippa. Ed. 1999. *Critical Citizens: Global Support for Democratic Governance.* Oxford: Oxford University Press.

Norris, Pippa. For all related papers and books see *www.pippanorris.com*

NTIA. 1999. *Falling through the Net.* Washington, DC: U.S. Department of Commerce. *www.ntia.doc.gov.ntiahome/fttn99*

Nye, David E. 1990. *Electrifying America: The Social Meaning of New Technology.* Cambridge, MA: The MIT Press.

Nye, David E. 1996. *American Technological Sublime.* Cambridge, MA: The MIT Press.

OECD. 1997. *Information Technology Outlook.* Paris: OECD. *www.oecd.org*

OECD. 1999. *Communications Outlook 1999.* Paris: OECD. *www.oecd.org*

OECD. 2000. *Information Technology Outlook.* Paris: OECD. *www.oecd.org*

OECD/PUMA. 1999. *Impact of the Emerging Information Society on the Policy Development Process and Democratic Quality.* Public Management Committee. Paris: OECD PUMA (98) 15. *www.oecd.org/puma/*

Ott, Dana. 1998. "Power to the People: The Role of Electronic Media in Promoting Democracy in Africa." *First Monday* 3(4): April 6. *www.firstmonday.dk/issues/issue3 4/ ott*

Pardo, Theresa A. 2000. "Realizing the Promise of Digital Government." *IMP: Information Impacts Magazine .* October. *www.cisp.org/imp*

Pantic, Drazen. 1997. "Internet in Serbia: From Dark Side of the Moon to the Internet Revolution." *First Monday* 2: April 7.

Papacharissi, Z. and A. M. Rubin. 2000. "Predictors of Internet Use." *Journal of Broadcasting & Electronic Media* 44(2): 175–96.

Patel, Surendra J. General Ed. 1993–5. *Technological Transformation in the Third World.* 5 vols. Aldershot: Avebury.

Peizer, Jonathan. 2000. "Bridging the Digital Divide." *Mediachannel.org* Op-ed. June 21. *www.mediachannel.org/views/oped/peizer.shtml*

Pew Research Center for the People and the Press. 1999. "The Internet News Audience Goes Ordinary." January 14. *www.people-press.org*

Qiu, Jack Linchuan. 1998. "Virtual Censorship in China: Keeping the Gate between the Cyberspaces." *International Journal of Communications Law and Policy* 4(1): 1–25.

Pino, Jose, A. 1998. "Information Access for a Deep Democracy." *Journal of the American Society for Information Science* 35. 542–48.

Pool, Ithiel de Sola. 1983. *Technologies of Freedom: On Free Speech in an Electronic Age.* Cambridge, MA: Belnap/Harvard University Press.

Porter, David. 1997. *Internet Culture.* New York: Routledge.

Poster, Mark. October–December 1999. "National Identities and Communications Technologies." *Information Society* 15(4): 235–40.

Pursell, Carroll W. 1995. *The Machine in America: A Social History of Technology.* Baltimore: Johns Hopkins University Press. WID-LC T14.5.P87 1995

Putnam, Robert. 2000. *Bowling Alone: The Collapse and Revival of American Community.* New York: Free Press. *www.BowlingAlone.com*

Rao, M., S. R. Bhandari, S. M. Iqbal, A. Sinha, and W. U. Siraj. 1999. "Struggling with the Digital Divide: Internet Infrastructure, Policies and Regulations." *Economic and Political Weekly* 34(46–47): 3317–20.

Rash, Wayne, Jr. 1997. *Politics on the Net: Wiring the Political Process.* New York: Freeman.

Rheingold, Howard. 1993. *The Virtual Community: Homesteading on the Electronic Frontier.* Reading, MA: Addison-Wesley.

Rhodes, Richard. Ed. 1999. *Visions of Technology.* New York: Simon & Schuster.

Rich, P. 1999. "American Voluntarism, Social Capital and Political Culture." *Annals of the American Academy of Political & Social Science* 565: 15–34.

Rochlin, G. I. 1997. *Trapped in the Net: The Unanticipated Consequences of Computerization.* Princeton, NJ: Princeton University Press.

Rodan, Garry. 1998. "The Internet and Political Control in Singapore." *Political Science Quarterly* 113(1): 63–89.

Rodriguez, Francisco and Ernest J. Wilson, III. 2000. "Are Poor Countries Losing the Information Revolution?" *The World Bank infoDev Working Paper Series.* May. *www.infoDev.org/library/wilsonrodriguez.doc*

Rood, H. 1999. "A Word about Internet Statistics." *Telecommunication Policy* 23(10–11): 687–88.

Roper, Juliet. 1999. "New Zealand Political Parties Online: The World Wide Web as a Tool for Democratisation or Political Marketing." In *The Politics of Cyberspace.* Eds. Chris Toulouse and Tim Luke. London: Routledge.

Rosenberg, Nathan and Claudio Frischtak. Eds. 1985. *International Technology Transfer: Concepts, Methods and Comparisons.* New York: Praeger.

Rosenstone, Steven J. and John Mark Hansen. 1993. *Mobilization, Participation and Democracy in America.* New York: Macmillan.

Schiller, Dan. 1999. *Digital Capitalism: Networking the Global Market System.* Cambridge, MA: The MIT Press.

Schiller, Herbert I. 1996. *Information Inequality: The Deepening Social Crisis in America.* New York: Routledge.

Schon, Donald A., Bish Sanyal, and William J. Mitchell. Eds. 1999. *High Technology and Low Income Communities: Prospects for the Positive Use of Advanced Information Technology.* Cambridge MA: The MIT Press.

Schultz T. 2000. "Mass Media and the Concept of Interactivity: An Exploratory Study of Online Forums and Reader Email." *Media Culture & Society* 22(2): 205.

Schuman, David W. and Esther Thorson. 1999. *Advertising and the World Wide Web.* Mahwah, NJ: Lawrence Erlbaum.

Schwartz, Edward. 1996. *Netactivism: How Citizens Use the Internet.* Sebastapol, CA: Songline Studios.

Schwartz, Peter and Blair Gibb. 1999. *When Good Companies Do Bad Things.* New York: John Wiley.

Sclove, R. 1995. *Technology and Democracy.* New York: Guilford Press.

Selnow, Gary W. 1998. *Electronic Whistle-Stops: The Impact of the Internet on American Politics.* Westport, CT: Praeger.

Shapiro, Andrew L. 1999. *The Control Revolution: How the Internet is Putting Individuals in Charge and Changing the World We Know.* New York: Public Affairs.

Shenk, David 1997. *Data Smog. Surviving the Information Glut.* New York: HarperCollins.

Shields M. A. 1998. "Equality and Inequality in Information Societies, Part I – Introduction." *Social Science Computer Review* 16(4): 349–52.

Shields, M. A. 1999. "Introduction – Equality and Inequality in Information Societies, Part II." *Social Science Computer Review* 17(1): 74–77.

Spiro, 1994–95. "New Global Communities: Nongovernmental Organizations in International Decision-Making Institutions." *The Washington Quarterly* 18(1): 45–56.

Stowers, G. N. L. 1999. "Becoming Cyberactive: State and Local Governments on the World Wide Web." *Government Information Quarterly* 16(2): 111–27.

Sussman, Leonard R. 2000. "Censor Dot Gov: The Internet and Press Freedom 2000." *Freedom House Press Freedom Survey 2000. www.freedomhouse.org/pfs2000/sussman.html*

Swanson, David and Paolo Mancini. Eds. 1996. *Politics, Media and Modern Democracy.* New York: Praeger.

Tanner, E. "Links to the World: the Internet in Chile, 1983–97." *Gazette* 61(1): 39–58.

Tapscott, Don, David Ticoll, and Alex Lowy. 2000. *Digital Capital: Harnessing the Power of Business Webs.* Cambridge, MA: Harvard Business School.

Tarrow, Sidney. 1994. *Power in Movement.* Cambridge: Cambridge University Press.

Taubman, Geoffrey. 1998. "A not-so World Wide Web: The Internet, China, and the Challenges to Non-Democratic Rule." *Political Communication* 15: 255–72 Ap/Je.

Teich, H. Ed. 1997. *Technology and the Future.* New York: St. Martin's Press.

Thapisa A. P. N. and E. Birabwa. 1998. "Mapping Africa's Initiative at Building an Information and Communications Infrastructure." *Internet Research-Electronic Networking Applications & Policy* 8(1): 49.

Thomas, C. 1998. "Maintaining and Restoring Public Trust in Government Agencies and Their Employees." *Administration and Society* 30: 166–93.

Tilly, Charles. 1978. *From Mobilization to Revolution.* Reading, MA: Addison-Wesley.

Toulouse, Chris and Timothy W. Luke. Eds. 1998. *The Politics of Cyberspace.* London: Routledge.

Tsagarousianou, Roza, Damian Tambini, and Cathy Bryan. 1998. *Cyberdemocracy.* London: Routledge.

UNDP. 1999. *Human Development Report 1999.* New York: UNDP/Oxford University Press.

UNESCO. 1998. *World Communication Report: The Media and Challenges of the New Technologies.* Paris: UNESCO.

Van Audenhove L., J. C. Burgelman, G. Nulens, and B. Cammaerts. 1999. "Information Society Policy in the Developing World: A Critical Assessment." *Third World Quarterly* 20(2): 387–404.

Van Dijk, Jan. 2000. *The Network Society: An Introduction to the Social Aspects of New Media.* London: Sage.

Vedel, Thierry. 2000. "Public Policies for Digital Democracy in the European Union and the U.S." Paper presented at the International Political Science Association World Congress, Quebec, August.

Velzeboer, Maruke. 1996. "Globalization and the Internet: Opening a Window for Grassroots Producers: The Information Age Cuts the Distance from the Grassroots to Markets." *Grassroots Development* 20(2): 12–17.

Verba, Sidney and Norman Nie. 1972. *Participation in America: Political Democracy and Social Equality.* New York: Harper & Row.

Verba, Sidney, Norman Nie, and Jae-on Kim. 1978. *Participation and Political Equality: A Seven-Nation Comparison.* New York: Cambridge University Press.

Verba, Sidney, Kay Schlozman, and Henry E. Brady. 1995. *Voice and Equality.* Cambridge, MA: Harvard University Press.

Voerman, Gerrit. 1998. "Dutch Political Parties on the Internet." *ECPR News* 10(1): 8–9.

Walsh, Ekaterina O. 2000. "The Truth about the Digital Divide." *The Forrester Report.* Forrester Research Inc.

Weare, Christopher, J. Musso, and M. L. Hale. 1999. "Electronic Democracy and the Diffusion of Municipal Web Pages in California." *Administration & Society* 31(1): 3–27.

Webster, Frank. 1995. *Theories of the Information Society.* London: Routledge.

Whillock, Rita Kirk. August 1997. "Cyber-Politics: The Online Strategies of '96" *American Behavioral Scientist* 40(8): 1208–25.

Wilheim, Anthony G. 2000. *Democracy in the Digital Age: Challenges to Political Life in Cyberspace.* New York: Routledge.

Williams, Jason. March 13, 2000. "Arizona: Cradle of Cyberdemocracy – State Makes History as Primary Voters Cast Ballots Online," *Editor & Publisher.* P. 46.

Winston, Brian. 1998. *Media Technology and Society. A History: From the Telegraph to the Internet.* New York: Routledge.

Wittig, M. A. 1996. "Electronic Grassroots Organizing." *Journal of Social Issues* 52(1): 53–69.

World Economic Forum. 2000. *From the Global Digital Divide to the Global Digital Opportunity: Proposals Submitted to the G-8 Kyushu-Okinawa Summit 2000. www.ceip.org*

Wresch, William. 1996. *Disconnected: Haves and Have-Nots in the Information Age.* New Brunswick, NJ: Rutgers University Press.

Wu, Wei and David Weaver. 1997. "On-Line Democracy or On-Line Demagoguery? Public Opinion Polls on the Internet." *The Harvard International Journal of Press-Politics* 2(4): 71–87.

Zelwietro, J. 1998. "The Politicization of Environmental Organizations through the Internet." *Information Society* 14(1): 45–55.

Zittel, Thomas. 2000. "Electronic Democracy – A Blueprint for 21st Century Democracy?" Paper presented at the International Political Science Association World Congress, Quebec, August.

Index